hugo

Chinese
in Three Months

P.C. T'ung
H.D.R. Baker

A DK Publishing Book
www.dk.com

A DK PUBLISHING BOOK

www.dk.com

First American Edition, 1999
10 9 8 7 6 5 4 3 2 1

Published in the United States by
DK Publishing, Inc.
95 Madison Avenue
New York, New York 10016

Copyright © 1999
Ping-cheng T'ung and Hugh D.R. Baker

Library of Congress Cataloging-in-Publication Data
Baker, H.D.R.
Chinese in three months / by H.D.R. Baker and P.C. T'ung. -- 1st
American ed.
       p.   cm. -- (Hugo's simplified system)
       Includes index.
       ISBN 0–7894–4214–0 (alk. paper). -- ISBN 0–7894–4220–5
(w/cassette : alk. paper)
       1. Chinese Language--Conversation and phrase books--
English. I. Title. II. Title: Chinese in 3 months. III. Series.
PL1125.E6B18 1999
495.1'83421 -- dc21   98–31747
                                             CIP

Set in 10/12pt Palatino by
Traverso Design Consultants, London, Great Britain
Printed and bound by LegoPrint, Italy

Preface

There are scores of Chinese dialects, some of them so far removed from each other that they may be thought of as separate languages. All of them are related, but many sound so different that a speaker of one cannot understand the speaker of another. In order to overcome this problem, for most of the 20th century China has been encouraging its people to make use of one standard, universal Chinese language. In the West we usually refer to this language as 'Mandarin': Chinese names for it are **Guanhua** ('officials' language'), **Kuoyu** ('National Language'), and **Putonghua** ('Universal Language' – by which name it is now officially known in mainland China). It is this language, based on the speech of Beijing itself, that we set out to teach here. We shall refer to it quite simply as 'Chinese'.

Our aim is to help you to teach yourself a language which will enable you to communicate in real life, whether your purpose is to do business, to travel, or just to study out of interest. The vocabulary used here is as 'everyday' as we can make it, and we have tried to use it in scenes which are common and natural in China today. This course maintains the Hugo principle of teaching only what is really essential for a firm grasp of practical, up-to-date Chinese.

For your part, you can start your learning of Chinese by throwing away quite a lot of the ideas which you have acquired about other languages: don't look for tenses – there aren't any; don't ask how verbs conjugate – they don't; don't worry about gender; don't think about case – nominative, genitive, accusative and all the rest of their friends don't exist in modern Chinese; say goodbye to irregular verbs, strong and weak nouns, agreements, subjunctives, singulars and plurals, declensions, …

Having emptied your mind by this turn-out, you should be able to find room for some new ideas. There are 'measures', 'particles', and a series of 'word orders' which are really like mathematical formulae into which you fit your vocabulary. Sentences do not necessarily have a subject, conditions are always set out before the main business, and in matters of time and place the larger always comes before the smaller (year before month before day; country before city before street before house number).

None of these is very frightening, and we have tried to present them in as 'user-friendly' a way as we can. In fact, Chinese is simple enough not to need a lot of grammatical jargon, so we cannot claim too much credit if we have succeeded in avoiding technicalities. Sometimes what seems to be a grammatical problem is actually a matter of cultural difference, and you will find that some of our 'grammar notes' seem more like explanations of Chinese culture.

What often seems to alarm the beginner most is the fact that Chinese sings its sounds in four different 'tones'. There isn't any reason to be afraid, it's a problem soon overcome; but tones are important because Chinese has a very restricted sound range (only about 400 different sounds) and having tones increases the number of possible distinct ones. Even so, the limited number means that many words have to share a sound. English, with a much larger sound range, does not escape the problem entirely – think of *to*, *too* and *two*, or *pare*, *pair* and *pear* – but Chinese rarely has the luxury of only three 'homophones'. As an extreme example, an elementary dictionary of Chinese has no fewer than 80 words pronounced **yi**, but by combining them with other sounds to make compound polysyllabic words, misunderstanding is avoided. The book begins with a detailed study of pronunciation and an explanation of the tone system. Using the book together with our audio cassettes is an ideal combination and provides a further dimension to your studies – ask your bookshop for details.

The one area which we have not covered in detail is the written language. To learn Chinese characters is a time-consuming and arduous business because they are not directly connected with speech. English spelling is often ridiculed for being only a poor representation of the sounds of the spoken language ('fish', it is claimed, could be spelled *ghoti*, using the *gh* of *enough*, the *o* of *women*, and the *ti* of *nation*), but the Chinese writing system in some cases does not even pretend to represent the sounds of the language. It uses symbols to represent the *ideas* being spoken as much as the *sounds* by which those ideas are expressed. The snag is that, while English only needs 26 letters to be able to write everything, Chinese needs a different symbol for every idea it has to convey. There are over 50,000 Chinese characters in existence: no one knows them all and somewhere about 4,000 of them are enough for literacy, but to learn even that many would enlarge the scope of this book beyond reason. In Chapter 20 we explain characters more fully and give some common ones which might come in handy in China.

It goes without saying that the long-term student of Chinese will eventually have to get down to learning characters, but meanwhile the *spoken language* can be learned perfectly adequately through the medium of an alphabetised (usually called 'romanised') system. Many ways of romanising Chinese have been invented over the years, but we shall be using the official Beijing government system, called **Hanyu pinyin**. **Hanyu pinyin** spells the sound and adds a mark over the main vowel to represent the tone, so giving all the information needed to pronounce the word correctly. The 'Sounds of Chinese' section which begins the course sets out the system in detail.

Ideally you should spend about an hour a day on the course (maybe a little less if you've not got the cassettes), although there is no hard and fast rule on this. Do as much as you feel capable of doing; it is much better to learn a little at a time, and to learn that thoroughly. At the beginning of each day's session, spend ten minutes recalling what you learned the day before. When you read a conversation, say it out loud if possible; listen to the tape and see how closely you can imitate the native speakers. The exercises will ensure that you remember what you have read and can apply it. You are about to become one of that tiny minority in the world who can converse with that vast majority of people who are Chinese! And so, without further ado, …

Contents

The Sounds of Chinese

There are very few sounds in Chinese which are difficult for a native speaker of English to make. The **Hanyu pinyin** system is on the whole easy to read and sensible in its spellings, but there are some oddities (at least to the eyes of the English speaker) which need to be learned. To help you make sense of the list of sounds, we have given some pronunciation guides; you can use them as a rough model while you listen closely to the tape for the polished version, which you need to copy if you are to acquire a good accent.

The initial consonants

With two exceptions (**-n** and **-ng**) consonants do not appear at the end of syllables, they occur at the beginning; so while Chinese does have words like the English *ban* and *bang* it does not have words ending with other consonants like *of, as, ash, it, up* or *east*. Here is the complete list of initial consonants, with pronunciation guides and an example of each to read while listening to the tape:

b-	much as in *bath*	**bā**
p-	as in *puff*	**pā**
m-	as in *man*	**mā**
f-	as in *fun*	**fā**
d-	much as in *dig*	**dā**
t-	as in *tickle*	**tā**
n-	as in *nasty*	**nā**
l-	as in *large*	**lā**
z-	as in *adze*	**zā**

c-	as in <u>c</u>ats	cā
s-	as in <u>s</u>at	sā
zh-	as in a<u>j</u>ar	zhā
ch-	as in <u>ch</u>ar	chā
sh-	as in <u>sh</u>out	shā
r-	a in <u>r</u>un	rā
j-	as in <u>j</u>eans	jī
q-	as in <u>ch</u>eek	qī
x-	something like kis<u>s y</u>e	xī
g-	much as in <u>g</u>un	gā
k-	as in <u>k</u>ing	kā
h-	as in <u>h</u>uh!	hā

In English some words (like *owe* and *eat*) do not have an initial consonant at all, and the same is true of Chinese. Where such words would begin with an **i**, or a **ü**, **Hanyu pinyin** prefers to use a **y**: so **i** becomes **yi**, **iao** becomes **yao**, **iong** becomes **yong**, **ü** becomes **yu** and **üe** becomes **yue**. Similarly, **w** is used where words might otherwise begin with a **u**: so **u** becomes **wu**, **uang** becomes **wang** and **uo** becomes **wo**.

The vowels and final consonants

a	as in <u>fa</u>ther	mā	chá			
o	as in <u>saw</u>	bō	fó			
e	much as in h<u>er</u>	tē	rè			
er	as "<u>er</u> indoors'	ēr	ěr			
u	much as in sh<u>oe</u>	bū	chù			
ü	as in the French t<u>u</u>	nǚ	jū	qū	xū	yū

This **ü** sound only appears after **n-**, **l-**, **j-**, **q-**, **x-** or on its own. The **u** sound appears after all initial consonants except **j-**, **q-**, **x-**, **y-**. So it is only after **n-** and **l-** that there can be any confusion between them, and it is only after **n-** and **l-** that the *umlaut* **ü** is actually used.

| i | as in b<u>ee</u> | dī | jī | qī | xī |

BUT beware that after **z-**, **c-**, **s-** the **i** is pronounced more like the noise a bee makes (a buzzing behind the teeth) than a full vowel:

| | zī | cī | sī |

AND after **zh-**, **ch-**, **sh-**, **r-** the **i** stands for a buzzing between the curled-back tongue and the roof of the mouth:

		zhī	chī	shī	rī

ai	as in *sky*	pāi	lái
ei	as in *day*	fēi	shéi
ao	as in *now*	cāo	zǎo
ou	as in *owe*	gōu	zǒu
an	much as in *fun*	sān	kàn
en	as in *broken*	cēn	rén
ang	as in *bung*	bāng	máng
eng	try saying *erng*	pēng	zhèng
ong	try saying *oong*	kōng	nóng
ia	as in *yah*	qiā	xià
iao	as in *miaow*	piāo	xiǎo
ie	as in *yes*	diē	liè
iou	as in *yeoman*	jiū	yǒu
ian	as in *yen*	miān	yán

Note how **an** changes sound after **i** or **y**.

in	midway between *sin* and *seen*	qīn	yǐn
iang	much as in *young*	yāng	xiàng
ing	as in *England*	tīng	níng
iong	try saying *yoong*	qióng	yòng
ua	as in *now argue*	guā	zhuā
uo	as in *do or die*	tuō	suǒ
uai	much as in *why*	wāi	huài
uei	midway between *way* and *we*	duī	shuǐ
uan	as in *one*	luàn	kuān
uen	as in *go an' look*	hūn	wén
uang	as in *wonky* (but no *k*)	huāng	wáng
üe	rather as in *you ate*	yuē	xué
üan	between *you enjoy* and *you anger*	juān	yuǎn
ün	much as in *United*	qún	yùn

In Beijing dialect the **er** sound is added to the end of many words, making the language rather like an exaggerated stage version of West Country English. To some extent this is found in standard Chinese too, and here and there in the book you will find an **r** added to a syllable to indicate that this happens. If you listen carefully to the tape at such points, you should be able to hear the effect and to notice that in some cases it changes the pronunciation very markedly.

You will notice from time to time that an apostrophe has crept into a spelling, as with **Xi'an** for example. The purpose of the apostrophe is to separate out the syllables: if we had spelled the word **Xian**, you might have assumed that it was the single syllable **xian** rather than two syllables **xi** and **an**.

The tones

The four tones are:

Tone 1:   A high level tone
Tone 2:   A high rising tone
Tone 3:   A low dipping and rising tone
Tone 4:   A high falling tone

Their patterns can be shown diagrammatically on a scale rising from a low pitch [1] to a high pitch [5]:

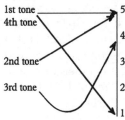

They are represented in **Hanyu pinyin** by marks placed over the main vowel:

Tone 1:	mā	jiā	shēn	xiē	chuāng
Tone 2:	má	jiá	shén	xié	chuáng
Tone 3:	mǎ	jiǎ	shěn	xiě	chuǎng
Tone 4:	mà	jià	shèn	xiè	chuàng

In the text you will see that not all syllables are given a tone mark. This is because (1) grammatical particles do not have a tone, taking their pitch from the words which come before them; (2) in two-syllable words the second syllable may be so little stressed as virtually not to have a tone; or (3) a few single-syllable words, notably **shi** 'to be', **lai** 'to come', and **qu** 'to go', are commonly used without stressed tone in certain contexts. In such cases no tone mark is used. The vast majority of syllables, though, do have tone, and it is necessary to learn the correct tone for every word as it is encountered. The difference between saying 'buy' and 'sell' is the difference between **mǎi** and **mài**, so beware!

Tone can be heard very clearly when a word is pronounced in isolation, though it is to some extent modified when spoken in a sentence. There are cases where tones are very much changed by the tone of the following syllable, the clearest example of which is that where two Third Tone syllables come together the first of them changes into a Second Tone; so **kěkǒu** is pronounced as **kékǒu**, and **wǒ hǎo** is said **wó hǎo**. (But note that you will not find this automatic tone change reflected in the tone-marking.)

Two words of Chinese have their own tone rules. **Yī**, meaning 'one', is pronounced in the First Tone when it is said in isolation, in the Second Tone before a Fourth Tone word, and in the Fourth Tone in front of a First, Second or Third Tone word. **Bù**, meaning 'not', is also pronounced in the Second Tone before a Fourth Tone word and in the Fourth Tone in front of any other tone, and in some contexts it is given no tone at all. You will find that they have been marked accordingly in the text.

Pronunciation practice

1 The four tones

mā	má	mǎ	mà
bā	bá	bǎ	bà
yī	yí	yǐ	yì
wū	wú	wǔ	wù
yū	yú	yǔ	yù
zhōng	huá	yǔ	diào
yīn	yáng	shǎng	qù

2 Two-syllable words

Běijīng	Peking
Shànghǎi	Shanghai
Guǎngzhōu	Canton
Chóngqìng	Chungking
Yúnnán	Yunnan
kòutóu	kowtow
chǎomiàn	chowmein
zásuì	chop-suey
shānbǎn	sampan
táifēng	typhoon

3 Three-syllable words

Máo Zédōng	Mao Tse-tung
Zhōu Ēnlái	Chou En-lai
Dèng Xiǎopíng	Teng Hsiao-ping
Jiāng Zémín	Chiang Tse-min
Cài Rènqióng	Tsai Jen-chiung

4 Neutral tones

zhuō + zǐ	zhuōzi	table
yǐ + zǐ	yǐzi	chair
qián + tóu	qiántou	in front
hòu + tóu	hòutou	behind
tīng + tīng	tīngting	listen
kàn + kàn	kànkan	look
péng + yǒu	péngyou	friend
dōng + xī	dōngxi	thing
huí + lái	huílai	come back
dòu + fǔ	dòufu	bean-curd

Note how a change from full tone to neutral tone can transform the meaning of certain words:

dàyì	= gist	BUT	**dàyi**	= careless
dìdào	= tunnel	BUT	**dìdao**	= genuine
dōngxī	= east & west	BUT	**dōngxi**	= thing

5 Tone changes

Listen carefully to the tape to hear how the tones change when they are used in combination with other tones:

3 + 1	**mǎ + chē**	**mǎchē**	cart
3 + 2	**mǎ + dá**	**mǎdá**	motor
3 + 4	**mǎ + shàng**	**mǎshàng**	at once
3 + 0	**mǎ + hu**	**mǎhu**	casual
3 + 3	**mǎ + biǎo**	**mǎbiǎo**	stopwatch
3 + 3 + 3	**zhǎn + lǎn + guǎn**	**zhǎnlǎnguǎn**	exhibition centre
4 + 4	**zài + jiàn**	**zàijàn**	goodbye

6 The **er** ending

Here are some examples of the **er** ending added to other sounds. Listen carefully to the tape – some of the resulting sounds are not what you might expect from the spellings!

gē + er	= **gēr**
hàomǎ + er	= **hàomǎr**
pái + er	= **páir**
yíkuài + er	= **yíkuàir**
běn + er	= **běnr**
yìdiǎn + er	= **yìdiǎnr**
líng + er	= **língr**
diànyǐng + er	= **diànyǐngr**

Chapter 1
Some essential phrases

- *Greetings and farewells*
- *Thanks and apologies*
- *Using the phone*
- *Polite expressions*

1.1   Hello

Typical greeting between a Chinese and a foreigner at any time:

A: **Nǐ hǎo!** [literally: You well] Hello!
B: **Nǐ hǎo!** Hello to you!

1.2   Morning greeting

A: **Zǎo!** [early] (Good) morning!
B: **Nǐ zǎo!** (Good) morning to you!

1.3   Answering the phone

A: **Wéi, nǐ hǎo!** Hello!
B: **Nǐ hǎo!** Hello!

1.4 A thanks B for his offering

A: **Xièxie, xièxie.**   Thank you.
B: **Búxiè.** [No (need to) thank]   Don't mention it.

1.5 A thanks B for his help

A: **Xièxie.**   Thank you.
B: **Méi guānxi.** [No relevance]   Not at all.
   or **Méi shìr.** [No matter]   It's nothing.

1.6 A apologises to B

A: **Duìbuqǐ.**   (I'm) sorry.
B: **Méi guānxi.** or **Méi shìr.**   It doesn't matter.

1.7 After you

A: **Qǐng.** [Please]   After you.
B: **Nín qǐng.**   After you.
   [You (polite form) please]

1.8 At dinner

At the beginning of a dinner party, host A speaks to guest of
honour B:
A: **Qǐng, qǐng.**   Please help yourself.
B: **Hǎo, hǎo, dàjiā qǐng.**   Yes, everybody
   [OK, everybody please   please start.
   (help himself)]

1.9 A toast

Toasting at a dinner party:
A: **Gānbēi!** [Empty (your) glass]   Bottoms up!/cheers!
B: **Gānbēi!**   Bottoms up!/cheers!

1.10   Welcoming guests

A: **Hūanyíng, hūanyíng!**   Welcome!
B: **Xièxie, xièxie!**   Thank you.

1.11   A knock at the door

A: **Shéi?**   Who (is it)?
B: **Wǒ.**   (It's) me.

1.12   Parting company

A: **Zàijiàn.** [Again see]   See you again./
Goodbye.

B: **Zàijiàn.**   Goodbye.

Chapter 2
Introductions

- *Introducing oneself and others*
- *Formal and informal introductions*

2.1 Pronouns

Singular:

wǒ	I, me
nǐ	you (*singular*)
nín	you (*polite form of address to show respect*)
tā	he, him, she, her

Note that there is no difference between nominative and accusative cases (I and me, she and her) or between the sexes (he and she).

Plural:

wǒmen	we, us
nǐmen	you (*plural*)
tāmen	they, them

It is tempting to conclude from this list of pronouns that **-men** makes plurals, but BEWARE: **-men** only works this way for the pronouns and a few exceptional 'human' nouns when they are used without specific number.

2.2 Names

Chinese people always put their surname before their personal names, so that in the names Mao Zedong and Deng Xiaoping 'Mao' and 'Deng' are surnames.

Of the thousands of surnames in existence, no more than a few dozen are common, and the 20 most common probably account for well over half the population of China. By contrast there is an unlimited number of personal names, some consisting of one Chinese character, some of two.

To ask someone's surname you say **Nín guì xìng?** which literally means 'Your honourable surname?' The answer is **Wǒ xìng ...** 'I am surnamed ...'.

2.3 Nations and nationality

Guó means 'country', and **Zhōngguó** means 'China' (literally: Central country). In some foreign country names, the sound of the foreign word is imitated by the Chinese word:

Yīngguó	Britain (**Yīng** imitates *Eng*land)
Měiguó	USA (**Měi** imitates A*meri*ca)
Fǎguó	France (**Fǎ** imitates *Fra*nce)
Déguó	Germany (**Dé** imitates *Deu*tsch)

In other cases **guó** is not used:

Yìdàlì	Italy
Xībānyá	Spain
Jiānádà	Canada
Rìběn	Japan
Àodàlìyà	Australia

Rén means 'person'. It can be added to the name of a country or place to show that it is where a person comes from:

Zhōngguó rén	a Chinese person
Yīngguó rén	a British person
Běijīng rén	a person from Beijing
Lúndūn rén	a Londoner

Exercise 1

Can you identify the following countries?

1 Hélán   2 Dānmài   3 Yìndù   4 Ài'ěrlán

5 Mòxīgē   6 Mǎláixīyà   7 Sūgélán

[Answers to all exercises are at the end of the book.]

2.4   Verbs

a   Chinese verbs only have one form. So where English has
    lots of forms of the verb 'to be' (am, are, is, was, were, will
    be, would have been, etc.), Chinese only has **shì**. Unless
    stress is required **shi** is pronounced in neutral tone.

> **Wǒ shi Běijīng rén.**
>   I'm from Beijing.
> **Nǐ/Nín shi Běijīng rén.**
>   You're from Beijing.
> **Tā shi Běijīng rén.**
>   He/She's from Beijing.
> **Wǒmen shi Běijīng rén.**
>   We're from Beijing.
> **Nǐmen shi Běijīng rén.**
>   You (*pl*) are from Beijing.
> **Tāmen shi Běijīng rén.**
>   They're from Beijing.

b   The verb **xìng** means 'to be surnamed':

> **Wǒ xìng Wáng.**
>   I am surnamed Wang.

But if the full name is given, **xìng** cannot logically be
used (it would sound silly to say 'I am surnamed John
Henry Smith', too), and then it is **shì** which is used:

Wǒ shi Wáng Hànshēng.
I am Wang Hansheng.

c   The verb **jiào** means 'to call' or 'to be called', so **Wǒ jiào Wáng Hànshēng** could mean either 'I call **Wang Hansheng**' or 'I am called **Wang Hansheng**'. Usually it is obvious which is meant, but to avoid ambiguity it is possible to insert **míngzi** 'name'. **Wǒ míngzi jiào Wáng Hànshēng** can only mean 'I am called **Wang Hansheng**'. The usual way to ask 'What is your full/personal name?' is **Nǐ jiào shénme míngzi?**

Exercise 2

True or false?

1   Máo Zédōng shi Zhōngguó rén.

2   Zhōu Ēnlái shi Shànghǎi rén.

3   Mǎgē Bōluó (*Marco Polo*) shi Yìdàlì rén.

4   Xiāo Bónà (*George Bernard Shaw*) shi Lúndūn rén.

5   Bìjiāsuǒ (*Picasso*) shi Fǎguó rén.

CONVERSATION 2A

Wang Hansheng introduces himself:

Wǒ shi Wáng Hànshēng.
I am Wang Hansheng.
Wǒ xìng Wáng, míngzi jiào Hànshēng.
My surname is Wang. My personal name is Hansheng.
Wǒ shi Zhōngguó rén.
I am a Chinese.
Wǒ shi Běijīng rén.
I'm from Beijing.

And who's this?

Tā shi Lǐ Dàwěi.
He's David Lee.
Tā xìng Lǐ, míngzi jiào Dàwěi.
His surname is Lee, and his personal name is David.
Tā shi Yīngguó rén.
He is British.
Tā shi Lúndūn rén.
He's from London.

2.5 Titles

Chinese people always put their names before their title, so that

Mr Smith would become *Smith Mr*
Mr John Henry Smith becomes *Smith John Henry Mr*
Mr David Lee is **Lǐ Dàwěi xiānsheng**.

Among groups of people who know each other well it is common for older members to be addressed by their surname with **lǎo** 'old' in front. They would address younger and junior people by putting **xiǎo** 'little', 'young' in front of the surname:

| **Lǎo Zhāng** | Old Zhang |
| **Xiǎo Lǐ** | Young Lee |

It is usually better for non-Chinese to stick to the polite forms of address, such as **Wáng xiānsheng** (Mr Wang) and **Wáng xiáojie** (Miss Wang) and **Wáng fūren** (Mrs Wang).

2.6   Nǐ hǎo

Nǐ hǎo is a common greeting, very much like 'hello' in English. Like 'hello', it is also used when answering the phone. **Hǎo** actually means 'good'.

2.7   Particles

Particles are little words that have no meaning on their own, but when added to a sentence they modify its meaning. All particles have neutral tone.

The particle **ma** at the end of a sentence changes a statement into a question.

Tā shi Běijīng rén.
> He's from Beijing.

Tā shi Běijīng rén ma?
> Is he from Beijing?

The particle **ba** at the end of a sentence also asks a question, but it asks it in such a way that it shows that the questioner expects the answer 'Yes', as with the English 'doesn't he?', 'weren't they?' etc.

Nǐ shi Běijīng rén ba?
> You're from Beijing, aren't you?

Of course, the questioner may be contradicted. **Ba** is also used when trying to encourage someone to do something:

Nǐ jiào wǒ Lǎo Lǐ ba.
> Just call me Old Lee.

Exercise 3

Change these statements into questions:

1   Tā shi Běijīng rén.
2   Tā shi Ài'ěrlán rén.
3   Tā xìng Lǐ.
4   Tā jiào Wáng Zhōng.

2.8   Yes and no

Bù is placed in front of verbs to make them negative:

Wǒ bú shi Běijīng rén.
   I am not from Beijing.

There is no need in Chinese to say 'Yes' or 'No' in answering questions. In general, the verb of the question is re-used to give a yes or no answer:

Nǐ shi Yīngguó rén ma?
   Are you British?
Shì.
   Yes.
Bú shi.
   No.

(Remember that **bù** becomes a Second Tone before a Fourth Tone word; see The Sounds of Chinese.)

2.9   This and that

Zhè means 'this'. Its opposite is **nà** 'that':

Nà shi Wáng xiānsheng.
   That's Mr Wang.
Zhè shi Lǐ xiáojie.
   This is Miss Lee.

CONVERSATION 2B

Ms Wang introduces Miss Lee to her colleague Mr Zhang:

W   **Lǎo Zhāng, zhè shi Lǐ xiáojie.**
     Old Zhang, this is Miss Lee.

Z   **Lǐ xiáojie, nǐ hǎo!**
     Hello, Miss Lee.

L   **Nǐ hǎo!**
     Hello.

Z   **Lǐ xiáojie shi Měiguó rén ba?**
     You're from America?

L   **Bú shì, wǒ shi Yīngguó rén. Zhāng xiānsheng
     shi Běijīng rén ma?**
     No, I'm not. I'm British. Are you from Beijing?

Z   **Bú shì, wǒ shi Shànghǎi rén. Xiǎo Wáng shi
     Běijīng rén.**
     No, I'm from Shanghai. Young Wang is from Beijing.

2.10 Possessive

The possessive is formed with the marker **de**, which works
just like the *'s* in English:

Lǐ Dàwěi de míngpiàn
    David Lee's namecard
wǒ de míngpiàn
    my namecard

With close personal relationships the marker **de** is often felt
not to be necessary:

wǒ péngyou
    my friend
nǐ fūren
    your wife

Exercise 4

Say it in Chinese:

1 That is my wife.
2 This is not my name.
3 This is my friend David Lee.
4 That is his namecard.

2.11 Adverbs

Dōu means 'all' or 'both' and comes before a verb:

Tāmen dōu xìng Wáng.
    They're both called Wang.

Yě means 'also' and, like **dōu,** it comes before a verb:

Wǒ yě shi Yīngguó rén.
    I'm British too.

Exercise 5

Read aloud and translate into English:

1 Wǒmen dōu shi péngyou.
2 Tāmen dōu xìng Yáng.
3 Nǐ yě shi Déguó rén ma?
4 Wǒ shi Yīngguó rén, tāmen yě dōu shi Yīngguó rén.

CONVERSATION 2C

British student Mary Stones and her friend John Woods run into Mary's Chinese friend He Ping:

M   **Ēi, Xiǎo Hé, nǐ hǎo!**
    Hey, young He, how are you?
H   **Nǐ hǎo!**
    Hello.
M   **Zhè shi wǒ de péngyou John Woods.**
    This is my friend John Woods.
H   **Nǐ hǎo!**
    Hello.
F   **Nǐ hǎo. Wǒ de Zhōngguó péngyou dōu jiào wǒ Wú Qiáng. Nǐ yě jiào wǒ Wú Qiáng ba.**
    Hello. My Chinese friends all call me Wu Qiang. You can call me Wu Qiang too.
H   **Hǎo. Wú Qiáng. Nǐ yě shi Yīngguó rén ma?**
    Fine, Wu Qiang. Are you from England too?
F   **Wǒ bú shi Yīngguó rén, wǒ shi Sūgélán rén.**
    No, I'm from Scotland.

2.12 Names can be confusing

There are different ways of romanising the sounds of Chinese and different ways of writing Chinese names. The name of the Chinese leader **Dèng Xiǎopíng** might appear as **Teng Hsiao-p'ing**, or **Teng Hsiao P'ing**, or even **Hsiao-p'ing Teng**. In this book we shall use the standard form adopted by Beijing, writing the surname first and putting the personal name (whether of one or two characters) as one word after it. You will find only **Dèng Xiǎopíng** here, not a trace of a **Hsiao-p'ing Teng**.

Beijing has also adopted a standard way of writing foreigners' names in Chinese, using syllables which more or less give the sound of the names, and dividing Christian names from surnames with a dot. For example:

| Alistair Cook | **Alisitaier • Kuke** |
| John Masefield | **Yuehan • Maisifeierde** |

But sometimes foreigners are given Chinese names which still sound something like the original foreign name (with the surname first):

Bāo Nǐgǔ	for Nicholas Bodman
Wěi Mùtíng	for Martin Wilber
Wú Qiáng	for John Woods

CONVERSATION 2D

David Lee and his wife meet a Chinese official at a formal reception:

D **Nín hǎo!**
Hello. How do you do?

O **Nǐmen hǎo! Nín guì xìng?**
How do you do? May I ask your (sur)name?

D **Wǒ xìng Lǐ. Wǒ jiào Lǐ Dàwěi. Zhè shi wǒ fūren.**
My name is Lee, David Lee. This is my wife.

O **Lǐ fūren hǎo!**
How do you do, Mrs Lee?

W **Nín hǎo!**
How do you do?

O **Wǒ xìng Wáng. Zhè shi wǒ de míngpiàn.**
My (sur)name is Wang. This is my card.

D **Xièxie.** *[Reads the card]* **Wáng xiānsheng de míngzi jiào Wáng Jiàn ma?**
Thank you … Is your name Wang Jian?

O **Bú jiào Wáng Jiàn. Wǒ jiào Wáng Jí'ān.**
No, I'm not called Wang Jian. I'm called Wang Ji'an.

D **Duìbuqǐ! Duìbuqǐ!**
I'm sorry.

O **Méi guānxi.**
That's all right.

Exercise 6: Pronunciation practice

Practise saying these sentences. If you have the cassettes, listen to them and repeat:

Wǒ xìng Wáng, bú xìng Wāng.
Tā xìng Liú, bú xìng Liǔ.
Tā jiào Wáng Guāng, bú jiào Wáng Guǎng.
Tā jiào Lí Tiānzhòng, bú jiào Lǐ Tiánzhōng.

Exercise 7

Translate into Chinese:

1 My name is Lee. I'm from England.

2 Are you from Beijing?

3 We all call him Old Wang.

4 His wife is from America too.

5 This is not my namecard.

6 All his friends are from Hong Kong (**Xiānggǎng**).

Chapter 3
Other people

- *Name and nationality*
- *Address and phone number*

3.1   Question words (1)

shéi?	who?
shéi de?	whose?
shénme?	what? what kind of?
něi?	which?

All these words are used in the same part of the sentence as their answer words come. So

'Who is he?' is	**Tā shi <u>shéi</u>?**
because the answer is	**Tā shi <u>Wáng xiānsheng</u>.**
and	
'Whose passport?' is	**<u>Shéi de</u> hùzhào?**
because the answer is	**<u>Wǒ de</u> hùzhào.**
and	
'What nationality is he?' is	**Tā shi <u>něi</u> guó rén?**
because the answer is	**Tā shi <u>Yīngguó</u> rén.**

Exercise 8

Using a question word to replace the underlined words, make up questions for the following answers:

1 Tā xìng <u>Wáng</u>.

2 Tā jiào <u>Wáng Píng</u>.

3 Tā shi <u>Zhōngguó</u> rén.

4 Nà shi <u>wǒ de hùzhào</u>.

5 Tā shi <u>wǒ péngyou de</u> péngyou.

3.2   Leaving out the subject

Once the subject under discussion has been established, or when it is very obvious, there is no need to mention it. In Conversation 3A, **Jiào shénme míngzi?** ('What's your first name?') and **Něi guó rén?** ('What nationality?') may not seem 'grammatical', but they are perfectly all right in the context.

CONVERSATION 3A

David Lee loses his passport in the departure lounge of Beijing Airport. Suddenly he hears a Chinese official, with a foreign passport in his hand, shouting:

O **Zhè shi shéi de hùzhào?**
   Whose passport is this?

L **Wǒ de.**
   (It's) mine.

O **Nǐ xìng shénme?**
   What's your surname?

L **Wǒ xìng Lǐ.**
   My surname is Lee.

→

O	**Jiào shénme míngzi?**
	What's your first name?
L	**David, David Lee.**
	David, David Lee.
O	**Něi guó rén?**
	What nationality?
L	**Yīngguó rén.**
	British.
O	**Zhè shi nǐ de hùzhào ma?**
	Is this your passport?
L	**Shì, shì. Xièxie, xièxie.**
	Yes it is. Thank you very much.

3.3   Particles

Like the particles **ma** and **ba** (2.7), the particle **a** appears at the end of a sentence. It does not make a question out of a statement, but it does help to reinforce a question word such as **shéi** which has been used earlier in the sentence, and it makes the question sound less abrupt.

Tā xìng shénme a?
   What's his surname?

3.4   Negative questions

Chinese has negative questions in the same way as English does. It forms these questions, logically enough, by using the negative form of the verb with the particle **ma** added at the end of the sentence, so:

Isn't she British?   **Tā bú shi Yīngguó rén ma?**

3.5 The Overseas Chinese

People who are ethnically Chinese but who live outside China are usually known as 'Overseas Chinese' in English, and as **Huáqiáo** in Chinese.

Other words using **qiáo** (to live abroad) are:

Yingqiáo	British expatriates
Měiqiáo	American expatriates
wàiqiáo	aliens

3.6 The adverb 'jiù'

Jiù has a number of different meanings, one of which is 'just'. So **Jiù shi tā** means 'That's exactly who he is', 'That's the chap'.

Exercise 9

Fill in the blanks with appropriate adverbs:

1 Tā … shi Lúndūn rén. (*She is also a Londoner.*)

2 Wǒ fūren … xìng Zhāng. (*My wife's name is Zhang too.*)

3 Tāmen … shi Yīngguó Huáqiáo. (*They are all British Overseas Chinese.*)

4 Tā … shi Lǐ Huá. (*She is the person called Li Hua.*)

5 Nǐmen … … shi Wáng xiānsheng de péngyou ma? (*Are you all Mr Wang's friends too?*)

3.7 The verb 'rènshi'

Rènshi means 'to recognise', 'to know', 'to get to know'. It is mostly used with people ('I know her') or Chinese characters ('I don't recognise that character').

Wǒ rènshi tā, kěshi bú rènshi tā fūren.
I know him, but I don't know his wife. (**kěshi** = but)

CONVERSATION 3B

Wang loves tennis and has a poster of a tennis star on his wall. His friend Jones, a student of Chinese, looks at this poster:

F **Zhè shi shéi a?**
Who is this?

W **Zhāng Dépéi.**
Zhang Depei.

F **Zhāng Dépéi? Zhè bú shì Michael Chang ma?**
Zhang Depei? Isn't this Michael Chang?

W **Shì, jiù shi tā.**
Yes, it's him.

F **Tā shi Zhōngguó rén ma?**
Is he Chinese?

W **Tā shi Huáqiáo.**
He's an Overseas Chinese.

F **Něi guó Huáqiáo?**
From which country?

W **Měiguó Huáqiáo.**
America.

F **Nǐ rènshi tā ma?**
Do you know him?

W **Wǒ rènshi tā, kěshi tā bú rènshi wǒ.**
Yes, I do, but he doesn't know me.

3.8 The numbers 0 to 10

0 líng	1 yī	2 èr	3 sān
4 sì	5 wǔ	6 liù	7 qī
8 bā	9 jiǔ	10 shí	

On the telephone and in other circumstances where it is necessary to be clearly understood (such as with bus numbers, room numbers, etc.) the word for 'one' is usually pronounced **yāo** instead of **yī**. Telephone numbers are given just as in English, so '5601' is **wǔ-liù-líng-yāo**.

Exercise 10

Read these telephone numbers aloud in Chinese:

1 104   2 999   3 01328-756261

4 0171-234 5689   5 0181-533 6472

3.9   Age

Suì means 'year of age', and in Conversation 3C **shí suì** means 'ten years old'.

3.10   Question words (2)

Jǐ means 'how many?'. **Duōshao** can mean either 'how many?' or 'how much?'. Generally, **jǐ** expects a small number as its answer, perhaps no more than ten or so; if a larger number is expected, **duōshao** is used.

Some new words

fùqin	father
mǔqin	mother
jiā	home, family
hàomǎ	number
diànhuà hàomǎ	phone number
hùzhào hàomǎ	passport number
wéi	hello! (on the phone)

CONVERSATION 3C

Billy Wood, a ten-year-old British boy, loses his way in the suburbs of Beijing and is led to the police station:

P **Nǐ jiào shénme míngzi?**
What's your name?

B **Wǒ jiào Billy Wood.**
My name is Billy Wood.

P **Jǐ suì?**
How old are you?

B **Shí suì.**
Ten years old.

P **Nǐ shi něi guó rén?**
Where are you from?

B **Wǒ shi Yīngguó rén.**
I'm British.

P **Nǐ fùqin jiào shénme míngzi?**
What's your father's name?

B **Jiào Ted Wood.**
Ted Wood.

P **Nǐ jiā de diànhuà hàomǎ shi duōshao?**
What's your home ('s) phone number?

B **Wǔ-líng-èr liù-yāo-bā-jiǔ.**
502-6189.

P [*Rings the number*] **Wéi, nǐ hǎo. Shì Wood xiānsheng ma?**
Hello, is that Mr Wood?

3.11 The verb 'zhīdao'

While **rènshi**, as we have seen, means 'to know a person', **zhīdao** means 'to know a fact':

Nǐ zhīdao <u>tā de diànhuà hàomǎ</u> ma?
    Do you know his phone number?
Nǐ zhīdao <u>tā shi něi guó rén</u> ma?
    Do you know what nationality he is?

Notice that the Chinese of the second example shows very clearly how there are really two questions here, one embedded within the other:

(1) **Nǐ zhīdao ma?**
Do you know?
(2) **Tā shi něi guó rén?**
What nationality is he?

Some new words

fàndiàn	hotel
gōngsī	company
fángjiān	room
qǐng	please, will you please
jiē	to connect
jīnglǐ	manager (can be used as a title)

CONVERSATION 3D

Mr Laker asks his Chinese assistant for a telephone number:

L **Wáng xiáojie, nǐ zhīdao Běijīng Fàndiàn de diànhuà ma?**
Miss Wang, do you know the phone (number) for the Beijing Hotel?

W **Zhīdao. Èr-sān-sì yāo-qī-bā-liù.**
Yes, I do. (It's) 234-1786.

L **Dàxīn Gōngsī de fángjiān hàomǎ shi duōshao?**
What's the room number for the Daxin Company?

W **Yāo-èr-wǔ-jiǔ.**
1259.

[Laker dials]

O **Nǐ hǎo. Běijīng Fàndiàn.**
Hello. Beijing Hotel.

→

L   **Qǐng jiē yāo-èr-wǔ-jiǔ.**
Connect me to 1259, please.

Z   **Nǐ hǎo. Dàxīn Gōngsī.**
Hello. Daxin Company.

L   **Wéi, shì Zhāng jīnglǐ ma? Wǒ shi Léikè.**
Is that Manager Zhang? I'm Laker.

Z   **Òu, Léikè xiānsheng, nǐ hǎo?**
Oh, Mr Laker, how are you?

Exercise 11: Pronunciation practice

Yī èr sān.
Sān èr yī.
Yī èr sān sì wǔ liù qī.
Qī liù wǔ sì sān èr yī.

Exercise 12

Translate into Chinese:

1 *A:* What's his surname?
    B: His name is Wang.

2 *A:* What's your phone number?
    B: 0121-486 5739.

3 *A:* Whose passport is this?
    B: It's my friend's.

4 *A:* Do you know what nationality she is?
    B: Yes, I do. She's French.

5 *A:* Is Manager Lin from Shanghai?
    B: No, he is an Overseas Chinese from Japan.

6 *A:* Hello, is that Mr Zhang?
    B: Yes, speaking. You're …?

Chapter 4
Requests

- *In the hotel reception*
- *In the hotel café*
- *On an outing*

4.1 The verb 'yǒu' (1)

Yǒu means 'to have'. It has one distinctive feature in that, unlike all other verbs, its negative can only be formed with **méi**, not **bù**. So:

I have no namecard. **Wǒ méi you míngpiàn.**

Some new words

yào	to want
dānrénfáng	single room
shuāngrénfáng	double room
chá	tea
wèishēngjiān	bathroom
tián biǎo	to fill in a form

4.2   Choice-type questions (1)

Chinese can ask questions simply by offering a choice
of answers:

Nǐ shi Yīngguó rén shi Měiguó rén?
　　Are you British or American?
Nín yào dānrénfáng, yào shuāngrénfáng?
　　Do you want a single room or a double room?

4.3   Measure words (1)

Whenever Chinese counts nouns, it counts them with special
measure words. 'Three cups of tea' is **sān bēi chá**, and here it
is clear that **bēi** (cup) is measuring the amount of tea, just as
the word 'cups' is in the English version. The same principle
applies, though, even when there is no obvious appropriate
measure: 'three men', 'five namecards', 'ten bicycles' have
no measures in English, but in Chinese they do.

The most common measure word is **gè**. It is used (generally
with neutral tone) for people and for many other things.

sì ge rén　　　　four people

Other measures are:

wèi	for people to whom you wish to be polite
jiān	for rooms
píng	'a bottle of'

Suì (year of age), **nián** (year), and **tiān** (day) are unusual in
that they are nouns which carry with them their own
measuring function. So it is correct to say **shí suì** (ten years
old), **liù nián** (six years) and **wǔ tiān** (five days).

Note that when the number 'two' appears before a measure
word, Chinese uses not **èr**, as might be expected, but **liǎng**:

liǎng nián	two years
liǎng ge rén	two people

Exercise 13

Fill in the blanks where necessary:

1   yí … rén (*one person*)
2   liǎng … chá (*two cups of tea*)
3   sān … dānrénfáng (*three single rooms*)
4   sì … suì (*four years old*)
5   wǔ … Zhōngguó péngyou (*five Chinese friends*)

4.4   Making a contrast

Yǒu shuāngrénfáng says quite simply 'We have a double room', but changing the order to **Shuāngrénfáng yǒu** points to a contrast and conveys the meaning 'As to a *double room*, that we have (but if you'd asked for a *single room*, now …)'.

4.5   The verb 'dài'

Dài basically means 'to bring with', 'to lead', or 'to carry'. In Conversation 4A it is translated as 'with', but that should be understood as a short way of saying 'come with':

Dài wèishēngjiān ma?
Does it come with bathroom?

4.6   The verb 'zhù'

Zhù means 'to live' or 'to dwell', but it also translates 'to stay' in the sense of 'to stay overnight'.

4.7   The adverb 'xiān'

Xiān means 'first'. Like **yě, dōu** and **jiù** (2.11 and 3.6), it comes right in front of the verb:

Xiān tián biǎo.
First fill in the form.

CONVERSATION 4A

A tourist and his friend talk to the hotel receptionist:

R **Nǐ hǎo!**
   Hello.

T **Nǐ hǎo! Yǒu fángjiān ma?**
   Hello. Do you have any rooms?

R **Nín yào dānrénfáng, yào shuāngrénfáng?**
   Do you want single rooms or a double room?

T **Wǒmen yào yì jiān shuāngrénfáng.**
   We want a double room.

R **Shuāngrénfáng yǒu.**
   We have a double room.

T **Dài wèishēngjiān ma?**
   With bathroom?

R **Dài. Nǐmen zhù jǐ tiān?**
   Yes. How many days will you be staying?

T **Sān tiān.**
   Three.

R **Hǎo. Qǐng xiān tián biǎo.**
   Fine. Please fill in the form first.

4.8 Here and there

Nàr means 'there' and **zhèr** means 'here'. If you think of them as meaning 'that place' and 'this place', you will probably be reminded of another pair of words, **nà** and **zhè**, which we met in 2.9. Clearly they are connected.

4.9 Is that OK?

Kěyǐ means 'may', 'can' or 'it is possible that'. It is often tagged onto the end of a sentence with the particle **ma** to give the meaning 'Is that OK?' 'Do you agree?'. Another 'question tag' meaning 'Is that OK?' is **hǎo ma?** (**hǎo** = good, fine, nice).

4.10 The verb 'xiǎng'

Xiǎng literally means 'to think', but when it appears in front of other verbs it means 'would like to':

Wǒ xiǎng zhù wǔ tiān.
   I'd like to stay for five days.

Exercise 14

Change the following into negatives:

1   Wǒ xiǎng zhù Běijīng Fàndiàn.

2   Tāmen dōu yǒu hùzhào.

3   Nǐmen yào shuāngrénfáng ma?

4   Nín yǒu míngpiàn ma?

5   Wǒmen de fángjiān dōu dài wèishēngjiān.

4.11 The colour of tea

In Chinese, tea (**chá**) is classified as 'red' (**hóng**) for fermented varieties and 'green' for unfermented. **Hóng** is translated as 'black' in Conversation 4B, because in English the two types are normally known as 'black' and 'green' rather than 'red' and 'green'.

4.12 The adverb 'zhǐ'

Zhǐ 'only' is another adverb like **yě, dōu, jiù** and **xiān**, and like them it must come immediately in front of a verb.

Some new words

zuò	to sit	**Kěkǒu Kělè**	Coca-Cola
hē	to drink	**táng**	sugar
kāfēi	coffee	**niúnǎi**	(cow's) milk
jiǔ	alcoholic drink	**chī**	to eat
píjiǔ	beer	**diǎnxin**	pastries, snacks

CONVERSATION 4B

A tourist and three friends in a hotel café. A waitress meets them at the door.

W   **Nǐ hǎo! Jǐ wèi?**
      Hello. How many?

T   **Wǒmen sì ge rén. Zuò nàr kěyǐ ma?**
      Four of us. Can we sit over there?

W   **Kěyǐ ... Nǐmen xiǎng hē shénme?**
      Yes ... What would you like to drink?

T   **Yǒu hóngchá ma?**
      Do you have black tea?

W   **Méi you. Yǒu kāfēi.**
      No. We have got coffee.

T   **Yǒu píjiǔ ma?**
      Do you have any beer?

W   **Yǒu.**
      Yes.

T   **Hǎo. Wǒmen yào liǎng bēi kāfēi, yì píng píjiǔ, yíge Kěkǒu Kělè.**
      Good. We want two cups of coffee, a bottle of beer and a Coca-Cola.

W   **Kāfēi yào táng ma?**
      Do you need sugar for the coffee?

T   **Zhǐ yào niúnǎi, bú yào táng.**
      Just milk, no sugar.

W   **Chī diǎnxin ma?**
      Do you want some pastries?

T   **Bú yào, xièxie.**
      No, thank you.

4.13 To be or not to be?

Chǎo means 'noisy' or 'to be noisy'; **rè** means 'hot' or 'to be hot'. And so it is with all adjectives (big, beautiful, difficult, etc.), so that normally there is no question of translating the verb 'to be' when it comes before an adjective:

Niúnǎi bú rè.
> The milk is not hot.

Wǒ hěn hǎo.
> I'm very well. (**hěn** = very)

But just occasionally you may wish to give particularly strong emphasis to an adjective, and then Chinese does make use of the verb 'to be' (**shì**):

Yìdàlì kāfēi shì hěn hǎo.
> Italian coffee *is* very good.

and in Conversation 4C there is another example:

Èr lóu shì hěn chǎo.
> The second floor is indeed very noisy.

4.14 Too much!

'To be too noisy' is **tài chǎo le**. **Tài** means 'too much', and **le** is a particle which shows that something is excessive or 'over the top'. So:

Tài rè le!
> It's too hot!

Tài hǎo le!
> Great! Fantastic!

4.15 Floors

Lóu means 'a building' or 'a floor'. The Chinese count their storeys in the same way as the Americans; that is, the ground floor is counted as the first floor. **Èr lóu** is the floor

45

above the ground floor, the one which the British call 'the first floor', **sān lóu** is the British 'second floor', and so on. But in this book we will translate **èr lóu** as 'second floor', **sān lóu** 'third floor', etc.

4.16 The verb 'yǒu' (2)

As we saw in 4.1, **yǒu** means 'to have':

Nǐ yǒu diànhuà ma?
Have you got a phone?

But after place words ('here', 'on the table', etc.) **yǒu** is used like 'there is' and 'there are' in English:

Èr lóu yǒu wèishēngjiān ma?
Is there a bathroom on the second floor?

4.17 Number

Hàomǎ is a noun meaning 'number', as we have seen. **Hào** is a measure word also meaning 'number', but it is used where in English we might abbreviate to 'no.'. Compare the following examples:

nǐ de diànhuà hàomǎ
your telephone number
sān hào fáng(jiān)
room no. 3

Exercise 15

What do they mean?

1 Wǒ de fángjiān méi you diànhuà.

2 Sān lóu yǒu liǎng ge wèishēngjiān.

3 Lúndūn yǒu Zhōngguó gōngsī ma?

4 Tāmen nàr yǒu chá, yě yǒu kāfēi.

Some new words

shì   business, matter, affair
huàn   to change, exchange
bǐjiào   rather, quite, comparatively
pà   to fear, be afraid of
diàntī   a lift

CONVERSATION 4C

A tourist complains to the hotel receptionist about his room:

R   **Nín yǒu shénme shì?**
     Can I help you?

T   **Wǒ de fángjiān tài chǎo le. Kěyǐ huàn yì jiān ma?**
     My room is too noisy. Can I change it?

R   **Nín zhù jǐ hào fáng?**
     What's your room number?

T   **Èr lóu, èr-yāo-bā.**
     Second floor, 218.

R   **Èr lóu shì hěn chǎo. Liù lóu kěyǐ ma?**
     The second floor is indeed very noisy. Will the sixth floor do?

T   **Kěyǐ.**
     Yes.

R   **Kěshi liù lóu bǐjiào rè.**
     But it's rather hot on the sixth floor.

T   **Wǒ bú pà rè.**
     I'm not afraid of heat.

R   **Wǒmen zhèr méi you diàntī.**
     There isn't a lift here.

T   **Méi guānxi.**
     That doesn't matter.

4.18 Doubling up

It is quite common for Chinese to double words for emphasis:

Kěyǐ, kěyǐ!
Of course that's OK!

With some verbs, such as **xiūxi** 'to rest', doubling up gives a sense of 'having a little go at':

Xiūxi xiūxi ba!
Have a little rest!

4.19 Measure words (2)

When the object of a verb is in the singular, it is quite common to omit the word **yī** 'one', but the measure word is still used as if **yī** were there:

Hē (yì) bēi kāfēi ba!
Have a cup of coffee!

4.20 Choice-type questions (2)

As we have seen, one way of asking straightforward questions is to add **ma** to a statement:

Kāfēi rè ma?
Is the coffee hot?

Another way of making questions is by using the positive and negative forms of a verb or an adjective together, effectively giving a choice of two answers from which to pick:

Kāfēi rè bu rè?
Is the coffee hot?
Nǐ hē bu hē chá?
Will you have some tea?
Nǐ xiǎng bu xiǎng xiūxi?
Do you want to rest?

Wǒ kě(yǐ) bu kěyǐ chōu-yān?
    May I smoke? (**chōu-yān** = to smoke; **chōu** = to drag;
    yān = smoke, cigarette)
Nǐ zhī(dao) bu zhīdao …?
    Do you know that …?

Exercise 16

Make choice-type questions out of the following:

1   Tā shi Běijīng rén.

2   Tā yǒu Zhōngguó péngyou.

3   Tā xiǎng hē hóngchá.

4   Tā bú rènshi Zhāng Dépéi.

5   Nàr bú rè.

4.21 Particles

The particle **a** (3.3) has an additional use, which is to make
mild rhetorical questions of the 'Oh, so that's how it is,
is it?' type:

Òu, tā shi Zhōngguó rén a?
    Oh really, he's Chinese?
Bù kěyǐ chōu-yān a?
    So we can't smoke?

Ba, you will remember (2.7), expresses encouragement:

Nǐ hē ba!   Go ahead and drink!

4.22 Don't!

Bié is short for **bú yào**, and either of them can be used to
give negative commands: 'Don't!' So both **Bié zuò nàr!** and
Bú yào zuò nàr! mean 'Don't sit there!'

Bié chǎo!   Quiet!

Some new words

fēngjǐng	scenery
piàoliang	(to be) beautiful
zhī	(measure for stick-like things)
yān	smoke, cigarette
zhǔn	to permit, be permitted
shuǐ	water
kuàngquánshuǐ	mineral water
zhào xiàng	to take a photograph

CONVERSATION 4D

A British student and his Chinese companion enter a pavilion at the top of a scenic mountain:

S   **Zhèr fēngjǐng tài piàoliang le!**
     The scenery here is fantastic!

C   **Zuò zhèr xiūxi xiūxi ba!**
     Sit here and take a rest!

S   **Hǎo. Chōu zhī yān ba!**
     Good. Have a cigarette!

C   **Duìbuqǐ. Zhèr bù zhǔn chōu-yān.**
     Sorry. No smoking allowed here.

S   **Òu, bù zhǔn chōu-yān a?**
     Oh, so there's no smoking?

C   **Hē bu hē shuǐ? Wǒ zhèr yǒu kělè, yě yǒu kuàngquánshuǐ.**
     Do you want a drink? There's some cola here, and some mineral water.

S   **Tào hǎo le. Wǒ hē kuàngquánshuǐ. Zhèr zhǔn bu zhǔn zhào xiàng?**
     Great! I'll have mineral water. Is it all right to take photos here?

C   **Zhǔn. Nǐ zhào ba! Kěshi bié zhào wǒ!**
     Yes. Go ahead and take! But don't go taking me!

Exercise 17: Pronunciation practice

Yān, jiǔ, wǒ dōu yǒu.

Nǐ yào chōu-yān, qǐng chōu-yān.

Nǐ yào hē-jiǔ, qǐng hē-jiǔ.

Exercise 18

Translate into Chinese:

1 *A*:   Have you got two single rooms?

  B: No, we only have one double room.

2 *A*:   How many days will you be staying?

  B: Five.

3 *A*:   What would you like to drink?

  B: Two teas and one coffee.

4 *A*:   Our room is too hot!

  B: Do you want to change it?

5 *A*:   Is drinking allowed here?

  B: No, I'm sorry. Neither drinking nor smoking is allowed.

6 *A*:   Is the scenery there beautiful?

  B: Yes, and the people there are also beautiful.

Chapter 5

Locations

- *Asking for someone at a hotel*
- *Asking where something is*
- *Asking about places of interest*

5.1 Politeness

Qǐng wèn literally means 'Please may I ask … ' (**wèn** is 'to ask (a question)') and it is used as a polite lead-in to asking questions, especially of strangers:

Qǐng wèn nín guì xìng?
  May I ask your name?

5.2 Location (1)

Zài means 'to be there, to be in':

Wáng xiānsheng zài ma?
  Is Mr Wang there?
Tā bú zài.
  He's not in.

In front of place words, **zài** means 'to be at/in/on' and is used to show the location of things:

zài jiā	at home
zài èr lóu	on the second floor
zài zhèr	here, at this place
zài nàr	there, at that place
zài nǎr?	where? at which place?
Wáng jīnglǐ zài nǎr?	Where is Manager Wang?
Tā zài Xiānggǎng.	He's in Hong Kong.

5.3   Full sets

Note that we now have two parallel sets of similar words:

zhè (this)	**zhèr** (this place, here)
nà (that)	**nàr** (that place, there)
něi? (which?)	**nǎr?** (which place? where?)

5.4   Doubling up

We saw in 4.18 that doubling the verb **xiūxi** gave it the meaning 'have a little rest'. When single-syllable verbs are doubled, they can appear either as *verb-verb* or as *verb* **yi** *verb* (**yī** = one):

wèn (to ask):	**wèn yi wèn** or **wènwen** to make an enquiry
kàn (to look at):	**kàn yi kàn** or **kànkan** to have a look at

Qǐng nǐ wènwen Lǎo Wáng zài bu zài.
    Please ask if Old Wang is in.
Qǐng nǐ kàn yi kàn zhè shi shénme.
    Please see what this is.

5.5   The verb 'yǒu'

The negative of **yǒu**, remember, is **méi you** (4.1). When **méi you** is followed by an object, it is often shortened just to **méi**:

Wǒ méi hùzhào.
    I haven't got a passport.

Méi rén jiē.
   No one's answering the phone.
Tā jiā méi (you) diànhuà.
   There's no phone in his house.

Some new words

yàoshì	key
yīnggāi	ought to, should
kěnéng	maybe
kāfēitīng	café
qù	to go

CONVERSATION 5A

A visitor goes to the hotel to look for Miss Laker:

V **Qǐng wèn Léikè xiáojie zài ma?**
   Excuse me, is Miss Laker in?
R **Tā zhù jǐ hào fáng?**
   What's her room number?
V **Sān-líng-jiǔ-yāo.**
   3091.
R **Wǒ kànkan.** *[Checks keys]* **Yàoshì bú zài, rén yīnggāi zài.**
   Let me see. The key isn't here; she should be in.

[Rings 3091, but there is no answer]

   Méi rén jiē. Kěnéng zài kāfēitīng.
   No answer. Maybe she's in the café.
V **Kāfēitīng zài nǎr?**
   Where's the café?
R **Zài èir lóu. Nín qu kànkan ba.**
   On the second floor. You can go and have a look.
V **Hǎo. Xièxie nǐ.**
   OK. Thank you.
R **Méi shìr.**
   Not at all.

5.6   Location (2)

Some common place words which go with **zài** are:

zài qiántou	in front
zài hòutou	behind
zài shàngtou	on top, over, above
zài xiàtou	below, under
zài yòubianr	on the right
zài zuǒbianr	on the left
zài lǐtou	inside
zài wàitou	outside

Wáng xiáojie zài wàitou.
> Miss Wang is outside.

Kāfēitīng zài yòubianr.
> The café is on the right.

Remember that when the Beijing dialect **-er** ending is added to words ending in **-n**, the **n** sound is lost, so that **biānr** is pronounced as if it were spelled **biār**.

Exercise 19

Say it in Chinese:

1   Is Mr Lee in?

2   Is anybody at home?

3   The bathroom is on the first floor.

4   She is inside.

5   The café is on the left.

6   Beijing Hotel is just up ahead.

5.7   Money

Qián 'money' is measured in units of currency. In China the basic units are called **kuài** or **yuán**, and they are divided into ten **máo** (i.e. a **máo** is ten cents, 'a dime'), which in turn are divided into ten **fēn**:

Duōshao qián?
  How much?
shí kuài (qián)
  10 yuan
jiǔ kuài sān (máo qián)
  9 yuan 30 cents
bā kuài qī máo wǔ
  8 yuan 75 cents

Just as in English we say 'two pounds ten' rather than 'two pounds ten pence', so Chinese leaves off obvious units, as in **jiǔ kuài sān** above.

Some new words

cèsuǒ	the toilet
fùjìn	nearby
jiē	street
yuǎn	far, distant
jìn	near, close
jiǎo fèi	to pay fees, pay charges

CONVERSATION 5B

After a meal, a tourist asks the waiter for the toilet:

T   **Qǐng wèn, cèsuǒ zài nǎr?**
    Excuse me, where's the toilet?
W   **Duìbuqǐ, wǒmen zhèr méi cèsuǒ.**
    Sorry, we don't have one here.
T   **Méi cèsuǒ?! Fùjìn yǒu ma?**
    No toilet? Is there one nearby?
W   **Dōnghuá Jiē yǒu yí ge.**
    There's one on Donghua Street.

T	**Yuǎn ma?**
	Is it far?
W	**Hěn jìn. Jiù zài qiántou.**
	Very close. Just up ahead.

[Tourist finds the place but is stopped by attendant]

A	**Èi, xiān jiǎo fèi!**
	Hey, pay up first!
T	**Shénme? Yào qián? Duōshao?**
	What? There's a charge? How much?
A	**Yì máo.**
	Ten cents.

5.8 Buying and selling

Be very careful! The only difference in Chinese between buying and selling is in the tones:

mǎi   to buy   **mài**   to sell

5.9 Measure words

We saw in 4.3 that, whenever a noun is counted, the appropriate measure word must be used. Measure words are also used when a noun is specified with 'this', 'that' or 'which?':

Něi ge rén?   Which person?

In front of numbers and measure words, **zhè** is often pronounced **zhèi** and **nà** is often pronounced **nèi**;

Nèi ge rén
  that person
zhèi píng píjiǔ
  this bottle of beer
nèi sān bēi kāfēi
  those three cups of coffee

When it is clear which noun is referred to, it is possible to leave it out, but still the measure word is used:

Něi wèi xiáojie?
 Which young lady?
Zhèi wèi.
 This one.

5.10 Place words as adjectives

Place words like **qiántou** and **yòubianr** can be used as adjectives:

qiántou (de) nèige rén	the person in front
yòubianr (de) nèige	the one on the right

5.11 The numbers 11–99

In 3.8 we counted only as far as ten. Eleven is 'ten and one', twelve is 'ten and two', and so on up to nineteen. Twenty is 'two tens', twenty-one is 'two tens and one' … up to ninety-nine:

11	shíyī	20	èrshí	30	sānshí
12	shí'èr	21	èrshiyī	40	sìshí
13	shísān	22	èrshi'èr	50	wǔshí
14	shísì	23	èrshisān	60	liùshí
15	shíwǔ	24	èrshisì	70	qīshí
16	shíliù	25	èrshiwǔ	80	bāshí
17	shíqī	26	èrshiliù	90	jiǔshí
18	shíbā	27	èrshiqī	91	jiǔshiyī
19	shíjiǔ	28	èrshibā	95	jiǔshiwǔ
		29	èrshijiǔ	99	jiǔshijiǔ

Exercise 20

Say the prices:

1	¥0.50	2	¥1.20	3	¥18.00
4	¥45.50	5	¥67.30	6	¥99.99

5.12 Particles

Ne added to the end of a phrase or sentence has the effect of asking a question with the minimum number of words. Often it will translate as 'And how about … ?' Note the economy of effort in the following:

Nǐ hǎo ma?
    How are you?
Wǒ hǎo. Nǐ ne?
    I'm fine. How about you?

Exercise 21

Fill in the blanks with question words:

1   Qǐng wèn nèi ge rén shi … ?

2   Qǐng wèn Lǐ xiānsheng zhù … hào fáng?

3   Qǐng wèn kāfēitīng zài … ?

4   Qǐng wèn nèi wèi xiáojie xìng … ?

5   Qǐng wèn zhèi ge … qián?

6   Qǐng wèn … yǒu cèsuǒ?

Some new words

bíyānhú	snuff bottle
guì	expensive
dōngxi	a thing

CONVERSATION 5C

A tourist wants to buy snuff bottles at a department store:

T **Nǐmen zhèr mài bíyānhú ma?**
Do you sell snuff bottles?
S **Mài. Zài sì lóu.**
Yes. On the fourth floor.

[On the fourth floor]

T **Xiáojie, wǒ kànkan zhèi ge bíyānhú kěyǐ ma?**
Miss, can I have a look at this snuff bottle?
S **Něi ge? Zhèi ge ma?**
Which one? This one?
T **Bú shi. Shì hòutou nèi ge. Duōshao qián?**
No, the one behind. How much?
S **Bāshi kuài.**
80 yuan.
T **Nèi ge ne? Zuǒbianr nèi ge?**
How about that one? The one on the left?
S **Liùshiwǔ kuài.**
65 yuan.
T **Dōu tài guì le.**
Both are too expensive.
S **Kěshi dōngxi hǎo.**
But they are good quality.

5.13 Shīfu

Shīfu is a term of respect for master craftsmen, such as chefs or jade-carvers, but it is now commonly used as a polite colloquial form of address to anyone (male or female) who is serving you.

5.14 More on 'de'

We met the little word **de** in 2.10 in its role as the possessive
marker (**wǒ de míngpiàn**: my card). It has another important
role as the link word joining adjectives to nouns. Simple
single-syllable adjectives like **hǎo** 'good' go straight in front
of nouns just as in English:

hǎo rén	a good chap
rè chá	hot tea

but when an adjective has more than one syllable or is
modified by an adverb, it is normally linked to the noun
it refers to by **de**:

piàoliang de xiáojie	a beautiful girl
hěn rè de chá	very hot tea

5.15 Compass points

The four compass directions are:

dōng	east	**nán**	south
xī	west	**běi**	north

and they are generally given in that order. To make place
words out of them, it is only necessary to add **biānr**, to
give **dōngbianr** 'the east', **nánbianr** 'the south', etc. The
intermediate directions. NE, SE, SW and NW are always
expressed in reverse order from English, so SE actually
becomes ES (**dōngnán**), NE becomes EN (**dōngběi**), and so on.

61

5.16 Rhetorical questions

Questions showing great surprise or assuming the agreement of the listener in advance are expressed with **Bú shi … ma!?**

Nà bú shi Lǐ xiānsheng ma?
Isn't that Mr Lee?

5.17 Location (3)

The little word **zài** introduces place words, as we have seen with such phrases as **zài nàr** 'over there', **zài lǐtou** 'inside' and **zài Běijīng** 'in Beijing'. We can extend its use now to deal with phrases like 'behind Mr Wang' (**zài Wáng xiānsheng (de) hòutou**) and 'on the right of that person' (**zài nèi ge rén (de) yòubianr**). So the pattern is:

zài *noun* (**de**) *place word*
zài wǒ (de) hòutou   behind me
zài Běijīng Fàndiàn   on the right of Beijing Hotel
  (de) yòubianr

Exercise 22

Give their relative locations:

1 Ài'ěrlán zài Yīngguó (de) …

2 Rìběn zài Zhōngguó (de) …

3 Xībānyá zài Fǎguó (de) …

4 Jiānádà zài Měiguó (de) …

5 Shànghǎi zài Běijīng (de) …

5.18 The City God

In traditional times **Chénghuáng**, the City God, had a temple (**miào**) in every administrative city of the Chinese empire. When a new chief official was posted to the city, his first duty was to report his arrival to **Chénghuáng** by worshipping him and seeking his spiritual help in the work of ruling. Some City God temples still survive in China, where they have become tourist attractions for Chinese and foreigners alike.

5.19 Particles

We have seen (3.3) that **a** reinforces a question word coming earlier in the sentence. It also can be used to stress the obviousness of a fact. So if you were to ask 'Why is his English so fluent?', the answer might be:

Tā shi Yīngguó rén a.
(Because) he's English (of course)!

Some new words

fènr	(measure for newspapers)
wǎnbào	evening paper
hǎowánr	enjoyable, amusing, 'fun'
dìfang	place, location
gōngyuán	park
shìchǎng	market
zíyóu shìchǎng	free market
bǎihuò dàlóu/gōngsī	department store

CONVERSATION 5D

A tourist asks an old newspaper seller about local places of interest:

T   **Shīfu, mǎi fènr wǎnbào.**
    Evening paper, please, squire.
S   **Yì máo èr.**
    12 cents.
T   **Shīfu, zhèr fùjìn yǒu hǎowánr de dìfang ma?**
    Are there any interesting places nearby?   →

S   **Yǒu. Nǐ kàn, dōngbianr jiù shi gōngyuán.**
       Xībianr yǒu ge zìyóu shìchǎng.
       Yes. Look, the park's there to the east, and to the west
       there's a free market.

T   **Chénghuáng Miào zài běibianr ma?**
       Is the City God Temple north of here?

S   **Bù, zài nánbianr.**
       No, it's south.

T   **Yuǎn ma?**
       Is it far?

S   **Bù yuǎn. Nǐ kàn, nà bú shi bǎihuò dàlóu ma?**
       Jiù zài bǎihuò dàlóu hòutou.
       No. Look, isn't that the department store? It's just
       behind that.

T   **Chénghuáng Miào lǐtou yǒu shénme?**
       What's inside the temple?

S   **Yǒu shénme? Yǒu Chénghuáng a!**
       Inside? The City God!

Exercise 23: Pronunciation practice

1   chǎng, shìchǎng, zìyóu shìchǎng

2   lóu, dàlóu, bǎihuò dàlóu

3   diàn, fàndiàn, Běijīng Fàndiàn

4   yuán, gōngyuán, Tiāntán Gōngyuán

Exercise 24

Translate into Chinese:

1   *A:*   Hello, is Mr Wang there?

      B: Sorry, he's not in.

2   *A:*   Where are they?

      B: They're all in the café.

3   *A:*   Excuse me, where is the toilet?

      B: On the 2nd floor.

4   *A:*   How much is this teapot (**cháhú**)?

      B: ¥16.50.

5   *A:*   Where's his house?

      B: It's to the east of the park.

6   *A:*   Can I have a look at your evening paper?

      B: Yes, go ahead.

Chapter 6
Directions

- *Asking for directions*
- *Taking a bus*
- *Taking a taxi*

6.1 How do I get there?

Zěnme? means 'how?'. **Zǒu** basically means 'to walk' but it also has many of the same meanings as the English word 'go', as for instance when we say that a watch 'goes' or a car 'goes'.

Zěnme zǒu?   asks in which direction to go in order to get somewhere.

Zěnme qù?   asks by what means to get somewhere; that is, whether by bus, by train, on foot, etc.

6.2 Travel by ...

Zuò means 'to sit' or 'to sit on'. It also means 'to travel by'. **Chē** means 'a wheeled vehicle' and can refer to a car, a bus, a train or whatever according to context:

zuò-chē	to travel by vehicle
zuò-diàntī	to ride in a lift

6.3 For preference

Háishi means 'or would it be?' and is used in questions where the answer requires a choice, such as 'Are you British or Chinese?': **Nǐ shi Yīngguó rén háishi Zhōngguó rén?** The answer simply requires the choosing of one of the alternatives **Wǒ shi Yīngguó rén** or **Wǒ shi Zhōngguó rén**.

6.4 Go west, young man

Wǎng means 'towards' and **guǎi** 'to turn'. **Wǎng xī guǎi** literally means 'towards the west turn', so 'turn to the west'.

Exercise 25

Give directions in Chinese:

1   Go forward.

2   Turn east.

3   Turn left.

4   No right turn ahead.

5   Go to the park.

6.5 The particle 'le'

Le is a sentence particle which is used in many different ways. It indicates that something has happened and that a new state of affairs has come about:

Tā zhīdao le.
    He knows now.
Tā zǒu le.
    She has left.
Tā dào le.
    He has arrived. (**dào** = to arrive at, to reach)

Exercise 26: A taste of 'le'

Translate:

1 Tā qù Shànghǎi le.
2 Lǐ xiáojie dào Běijīng le.
3 Tāmen dōu zhīdao le.
4 Tā qù gōngyuán le.
5 Nǐ kàn wǎnbào le ma?

Some new words

tóngzhì	comrade
Tiān'ānmén	Tiananmen
zǒu-lù	to walk
xǐhuan	to like, be fond of
tiáo	(measure word for long flexible things)
dà	big
dàlù	main road
yìzhí	direct(ly), straight
cóng … dào …	from … to …
kèqi	polite
bú kèqi	impolite; don't be polite = don't mention it

CONVERSATION 6A

A tourist asks a policeman the way:

T **Tóngzhì, qǐng wèn qù Tiān'ānmén zěnme zǒu?**
   Comrade, how do I get to Tiananmen, please?
P **Zuò-chē háishi zǒu-lù?**
   By bus or on foot?
T **Wǒ xǐhuan zǒu-lù.**
   I prefer to walk.

> *P* **Hǎo, dào qiántou nèi tiáo dà lù wǎng xī guǎi, yìzhí zǒu, jiù dào le.**
> *OK, turn west when you get to the main road ahead, then just keep going and you'll get there.*
>
> *T* **Wǎng xī guǎi? Něi biānr shi xī a?**
> *Turn west? Which way is west?*
>
> *P* **Cóng nán wǎng běi, wǎng xī guǎi jiùshi wǎng zuǒ guǎi.**
> *You are going from south to north, and turning west means turning to the left.*
>
> *T* **À, zhīdao le. Xièxie.**
> *Oh, got it! Thank you.*
>
> *P* **Bú kèqi.**
> *Not at all.*

6.6 All change!

Dǎo-chē means 'to change buses or trains'. You may also hear people say **huàn-chē** with the same meaning.

6.7 Bus routes

Lù literally means 'a road', 'a way', but is also used for 'a bus route', **so jiǔ lù** is 'a number 9 bus'. Up to a number 99, the routes are counted in a straightforward manner (**èrshi'èr lù**, **bāshiliù lù**, etc.), but three-figure bus numbers are generally 'spelled out' as **sān-sān-yāo** (331), **yāo-liù-bā** (168), and so on.

6.8 Measure words

The correct measure word for a bus ticket and other objects of flat, sheet-like appearance is **zhāng**, but when asking for 'two tickets' on a bus it is usual to ask for **liǎng ge** and not **liǎng zhāng**, perhaps indicating that the speaker is thinking of the number of persons travelling rather than the number of tickets for them.

Exercise 27

Practise with measure words:

1 yí ... tóngzhì (*one comrade*)
2 liǎng ... cèsuǒ (*two toilets*)
3 èrshiwǔ ... (*no. 25*)
4 sì ... (*no. 4 bus*)
5 wǔ ... wǎnbào (*5 copies of the evening paper*)
6 liùshíbā ... wǔ (*¥68.50*)

6.9   Giving change

When giving change, the verb **zhǎo** (which literally means 'to look for') is used:

Zhǎo nǐ bāmáo.
   80 cents change for you.

6.10 The adverb 'hái'

Hái means 'in addition', 'still' or 'yet'. It comes, like other adverbs, before the verb:

Nǐ hái yǒu qián ma?
   Do you still have some money?

Some new words

shāngdiàn	shop, store
Yǒuyì Shāngdiàn	Friendship Store
bǎihuò shāngdiàn	department store
Qiánmén	Qianmen (place name)
děi	must, should, have to
zhàn	stop, station, stand

CONVERSATION 6B

Two tourists take a bus to the Friendship Store:

T   **Tóngzhì, zhèi chē dào Yǒuyì Shāngdiàn ma?**
    Comrade, does this bus go to the Friendship Store?
C   **Bú dào. Nǐ děi zài Qiánmén dǎo-chē.**
    No, you'll have to change at Qianmen.
T   **Dǎo jǐ lù?**
    To what number?
C   **Jiǔ lù.**
    A number 9.

[On the number 9 bus]

T   **Yǒuyì Shāngdiàn, liǎng ge.**
    Two to the Friendship Store.
C   **Sān máo.**
    30 cents.
T   **Zhè shi yí kuài.**
    Here's one yuan.
C   **Zhǎo nǐ qī máo.**
    … and 70 cents change.
T   **Hái yǒu jǐ zhàn?**
    How many more stops?
C   **Sān zhàn.**
    Three.

6.11   Nǐ nǎr?

Nǐ nǎr? is used over the telephone to mean 'Where are you calling from?', 'Who's calling?' It is really asking which place of work the caller is from.

6.12 Abbreviations

Dàxué 'big learning' is the word for university. (**Xiǎoxué** 'little learning' is a junior school, and **zhōngxué** 'middle learning' is a secondary school.) The full name of Beijing Normal University is **Běijīng Shīfàn Dàxué**, but people often shorten that to **Běishīdà**, using only the first syllables of the three words. Similarly Beijing University is called **Běidà** as an abbreviation of **Běijīng Dàxué**. But be warned, not all abbreviations work on the first syllables, so it is not wise to make up your own shortcuts.

Exercise 28: Revision of 'like' and 'would like to'

Select appropriate words from A and B and put them into the pattern **Wǒ xǐhuan ... , wǒ xiǎng qù ...** *to make four meaningful sentences:*

A		B	
1	mǎi dōngxi	1	Xībānyá
2	hē chá	2	Guìlín
3	rè de dìfang	3	kāfēitīng
4	kàn fēngjǐng	4	bǎihuò dàlóu

6.13 To drive

Kāi-chē means 'to drive a car/bus, etc.' 'To drive to' is **kāidào**, using the verb 'to arrive at' for 'to'. So:

Kāidào nǎr?
   Drive to where?
Kāidào Yǒuyì Shāngdiàn.
   Drive to the Friendship Store.

6.14 The adverbs 'jiù' and 'mǎshang'

Jiù we met before (3.6) meaning 'just', 'exactly'. It has another meaning: 'immediately', 'at once'.

Mǎshang literally means 'on horseback', but it also means 'immediately', 'at once'. Sometimes it combines with **jiù** as **mǎshang jiù**, but the meaning of the two together is still the same.

Like other adverbs we have met, both of these come just before the verb:

Wǒ mǎshang jiù kàn.
I'll look at it immediately.

6.15 Build-up words

Chinese is very clever at piling up words to make new ones. Here are three sets of build-ups, with the literal meaning in brackets:

1 **chē**	vehicle
huǒchē	railway train (fire vehicle)
huǒchēzhàn	railway station (fire vehicle stop)

2 **chē**	vehicle
qìchē	motor vehicle (steam vehicle)
chūzūqìchē	taxi (out rent steam vehicle)
chūzūqìchēzhàn	taxi-rank, taxi-office (out rent steam vehicle stop)

3 **xué**	study
xuésheng	student (study person)
liúxuéshēng	student studying abroad (stay study person)
liúxuéshēng lóu	Foreign Students' Building (stay study person building)

Exercise 29: Guesswork

Use the vocabulary you know to make new words to translate the following into Chinese:

1 hot water   4 car key

2 West Station   5 The Gate of Friendship

3 Far East Company 6 no market for snuff bottles

CONVERSATION 6C

A British student, David Young, phones for a taxi:

R **Nǐ hǎo, chūzūqìchēzhàn.**
   Hello, Taxis.
D **Wéi, nǐ hǎo, yǒu chē ma?**
   Oh, hello, are there any cabs?
R **Qù nǎr?**
   Where to?
D **Huǒchēzhàn.**
   The railway station.
R **Nǐ nǎr?**
   Where are you calling from?
D **Běishīdà.**
   Beijing Normal University.
R **Shénme míngzi?**
   The name?
D **Wǒ jiào Yáng Dàwěi. Yīngguó liúxuéshēng.**
   David Young. I'm a British student.
R **Chē kāidào nǎr?**
   Where should the car come to?
D **Běishīdà liúxuéshēng lóu.**
   The Foreign Students' building at Beijing Normal.
R **Hǎo, mǎshang jiù qù.**
   OK, we're on our way.

6.16 Compound verbs (1)

Lái 'come' and **qù** 'go' are used with other verbs to show direction towards or away from the speaker. So **kāilai** means 'to drive towards me' and **kāiqu** means 'to drive away from me'. The driver of the taxi in Conversation 6D tells Miss A to **shànglai** 'get in' because he is already in the car, so **lái** shows that she is moving towards him.

The verb **shàng** means 'to embark on', 'to mount', 'to ascend', and its opposite is **xià** 'to disembark', 'to descend':

shànglai	come up	**xiàlai**	come down
shàngqu	go up	**xiàqu**	go down

6.17 Purpose in coming or going

In English, 'come to' and 'go to' often convey a sense of purpose (like 'in order to'); think, for example, of 'He's come to read the gas meter'. **Lái** and **qù** (often in neutral tone) work much the same way in Chinese:

Wǒ yào qu kàn péngyou.
   I will go to see friends.

Exercise 30

Practise saying the sentences and translate into English:

1   Wǒ yào qù Yǒuyì Shāngdiàn mǎi dōngxi.

2   Tā xiǎng lái Yīngguó liúxué.

3   Wǒ xiǎng qù běibianr kàn péngyou.

4   Nǐ xiǎng bu xiǎng qù gōngyuán wánr?

5   Wǒ xiǎng qù zìyóu shìchǎng kànkan.

Some new words

shǒudū	capital city
jùchǎng	theatre
(fēi)jīchǎng	airport
fēijī	aircraft
duì	correct
huàjù	a play

CONVERSATION 6D

Miss A is going to the Capital Theatre to see a play. She stops a cab:

D **Qù nǎr, xiáojie?**
Where to, miss?

A **Shǒudū Jùchǎng, qù ma?**
Capital Theatre, OK?

D **Shànglai ba!**
Get in.

[On the way]

A **Shīfu, zhè lù bú duì ba?**
Driver, surely this isn't the right way, is it?

D **Nín bú shi yào qù Shǒudū Jīchǎng ma?**
Didn't you want the Capital Airport?

A **Bú shi, bú shi. Wǒ yào qù Shǒudū Jùchǎng.**
No, no, I want the Capital Theatre.

D **Shénme? Shǒudū Jùchǎng?!**
What? The Capital Theatre?

A **Shì a. Wǒ yào qu kàn huàjù, bú shi yào qu zuò fēijī.**
Yes, I'm going to see a play, not to catch a plane.

Exercise 31: Pronunciation practice

Qìchē, qìchē, wǒ yào zuò chūzūqìchē.

Kělè, kělè, wǒ yào hē Kěkǒu Kělè.

Zuò qìchē, hē kělè.

Wǒ, wǒ, wǒ … nǎr yǒu cèsuǒ?

Exercise 32

Translate into Chinese:

1 *A*: Excuse me, where's the Friendship Store?

   B: Look, it's over there. Just behind that big hotel.

2 *A*: Comrade, how do I get to Peking University, please?

   B: It's a long way. I don't know how to get there either.

3 *A*: Excuse me, does this bus go to Tiananmen?

   B: Yes, it does. Two more stops.

4 *A*: Have they all gone to China?

   B: Yes, they have.

Chapter 7

Time

- *Checking in at a hotel*
- *Asking about train times*
- *Asking about meal times*

7.1 The days go by

qiántiān	the day before yesterday
zuótiān	yesterday
jīntiān	today
míngtiān	tomorrow
hòutiān	the day after tomorrow

7.2 Dates

Chinese generally prefers to list the general before the particular, and with dates this means that the year (**nián**) is given before the month (**yuè**) and the month before the day (**hào** or **rì**).

The year   1984 is **yī-jiǔ-bā-sì nián**, and
2005 is **èr-líng-líng-wǔ nián**.

The months are simply numbered from one to twelve:

January	**yí yuè**
February	**èr yuè**
March	**sān yuè**
December	**shí'èr yuè**

The days are also simply numbered from one to thirty-one:

the first	**yí hào** or **yí rì**
the second	**èr hào** or **èr rì**
the thirty-first	**sānshiyī hào** or **sānshiyī rì**

Remembering the year-month-day order, we can now translate:

| 7th July | **qī yuè qī hào/rì** |
| 1st October 1949 | **yī-jiǔ-sì-jiǔ nián shí yuè yí hào/rì** |

Exercise 33

Say it in Chinese:

1   28th August 1842

2   10th October 1911

3   4th June 1989

4   15th November 1990

5   31st January 2010

7.3   The particle 'le' again

With **yǐjing** 'already', the particle **le** (see also 6.5) shows that
a state of affairs has already come into being:

Tā yǐjing yǒu le.
   He's already got it.
Wǒmen yǐjing méi you le.
   We've run out already.

Exercise 34

Put into English:

1 Tā yǐjing qù Zhōngguó le.

2 Nèi ge dōngxi wǒ yǐjing mǎi le.

3 Wǒmen yǐjing rènshi le.

4 Huǒchē yǐjing dào le.

5 Jīntiān yǐjing wǔ hào le.

7.4 'Nà': in that case

We have already met **nà** with the meaning 'that'. It is also used to mean 'Oh, in that case …'.

7.5 Question words

We saw in 3.1 that **shénme** means 'what' or 'what kind of'. It regularly combines with **shíhou** (time), **dìfang** (place), **rén** (person) and **shì** (matter) to make other questions:

shénme shíhou?
    what time? when?
shénme dìfang?
    what place? where?
shénme rén?
    what person? who?
shénme shì?
    what matter? what's up?

Some new words

dǎsuan	to intend to, plan to
dàoqī	to expire, reach time limit
qùnián	last year
jīnnián	this year
míngnián	next year
wèntí	question, problem

80

CONVERSATION 7A

A tourist checks in at hotel reception:

R **Nín hǎo!**
   Hello?
T **Yǒu fángjiān ma?**
   Have you a room?
R **Yǒu. Qǐng xiān tián biǎo.**
   Yes. Please fill in the form first.

[Receptionist checks the form]

R **Nín dǎsuan zhù jǐ tiān?**
   How long are you planning to stay?
T **Sì tiān. Jīntiān shi qī yuè bā hào ba?**
   Four days. Today is 8th July, isn't it?
R **Bù, jīntiān shi qī yuè jiǔ hào.**
   No, it's the 9th.
T **Òu, yǐjing jiǔ hào le. Nà wǒ zhǐ néng zhù sān
   tiān le. Shí'èr hào wǒ děi qù Shànghǎi.**
   *Oh, it's the 9th already. In that case I can only stay
   three days. On the 12th I have to go to Shanghai.*
R **Nín de hùzhào shénme shíhou dàoqī?**
   When does your passport expire?
T **Míngnián liù yuè shíbā rì.**
   18th June next year.
R **Hǎo, nà méi wèntí.**
   Good, then there's no problem.

7.6 The marker 'de' again

In 5.14 we met **de** used to join adjectives to nouns, as in
piàoliang de xiáojie 'a beautiful girl'. **De** will also join
adjectival clauses to nouns in the same way:

hǎowánr de dìfang
   a place where it is good fun
zuò huǒchē de rén
   people who travel by train

Note that English puts the relative clauses after the noun, but Chinese is consistent in putting both adjectives and adjectival clauses in front of the noun. Here are some more examples:

mǎi kāfēi de qián
   money for buying coffee
lái Yīngguó de liúxuéshēng
   foreign students coming to Britain
qù Shànghǎi de piào
   tickets for Shanghai

Exercise 35

Translate into Chinese:

1   people who drink tea

2   shops which sell snuff bottles

3   a train ticket to Tianjin

4   buses which go to Tiananmen

5   people who travel by air

7.7   The express

A fast train is called a **kuàichē**. (**Kuài** means 'fast'.) **Tèkuài** is an express and is short for **tèbié kuàichē** 'especially fast train'.

7.8   The question word 'něi?'

Něi? 'which?' is normally followed by a measure word, as we saw in 5.9, so that 'which bottle of beer?' is **něi píng píjiǔ?** Note that **nián** 'year', **tiān** 'day' and **suì** 'year of age'

act as measure words, so that **něi tiān?** means 'which day?'
and **něi nián?** means 'which year?'. Unlike these words, **yuè**
can occur with or without the measure word **ge**: either **něi
yuè?** or **něi ge yuè?** means 'which month?'.

7.9   Days of the week

Xīngqī (literally: 'star period') means 'week'. 'One week' is
either **yì xīngqī** or **yí ge xīngqī**.

'Sunday' is **xīngqītiān** or **xīngqīrì**, and the other days of the
week are simply counted starting from Monday:

xīngqīyī	Monday
xīngqī'èr	Tuesday
xīngqīliù	Saturday

To ask 'Which day of the week?' the question word **jǐ?** 'how
many?' is used:

Jīntiān (shi) xīngqī jǐ?
    What day of the week is it today?

Exercise 36

Give a quick answer:

1   Jīntiān wǔ hào, míngtiān jǐ hào?

2   Zuótiān xīngqīsān, jīntiān xīngqī jǐ?

3   Jīntiān èrshiyī hào, hòutiān èrshijǐ hào?

4   Qiántiān jiǔ yuè sānshi hào, jīntiān jǐ yuè jǐ hào?

7.10   Yet more on 'de'

We have seen that **de** either makes the possessive (2.10) or
links adjectives and adjectival clauses to nouns. Quite often
the noun can be omitted if it is clear what is meant:

Kàn wǎnbào ma? Zhè shi jīntiān de.
 Do you want to read the evening paper? This is today's.
Zhèi bēi kāfēi shi wǒ de, nèi bēi shi nǐ de.
 This cup of coffee is mine, that one is yours.
Qù Běijīng de piào yǒu, qù Shànghǎi de méi you.
 I've got the ticket for Beijing, but not the one for
 Shanghai.

Some new words

chēcì	train number
wǎn	late

CONVERSATION 7B

A tourist at the Beijing Railway Station ticket office:

T   **Tóngzhì, mǎi zhāng qù Tiānjin de tèkuài.**
    Comrade, I'd like a ticket for the express to Tianjin.
C   **Něi tiān zǒu?**
    Which day will you be travelling?
T   **Hòutiān, xīngqīliù.**
    The day after tomorrow, Saturday.
C   **Shì sì yuè yí hào ma? Něi ge chēcì?**
    Is that 1st April? Which number train?
T   **71 cì tèkuài.**
    Express no. 71.
C   **71 cì de piào méi you le. 73 cì kěyǐ ma?**
    There are no tickets for no. 71 left. Is no. 73 OK?
T   **73 cì dào Tiānjin tài wǎn le. Xīngqītiān de 71 cì
    hái yǒu piào ma?**
    *No. 73 gets into Tianjin too late. Are there still any
    tickets for no. 71 on Sunday?*
C   **Sì yuè èr hào de hái yǒu.**
    Yes, there are for 2nd April.
T   **Nà wǒ mǎi zhāng sì yuè èr hào de.**
    Then I'll buy one for 2nd April.
C   **Hǎo, qī kuài.**
    Fine, that's 7 yuan.

7.11 Clock time

To cope with clock time you need the following words:

zhōng	a clock
diǎn	a dot (used for 'an hour')
fēn	a minute
bàn	half
kè	a notch (used for 'a quarter')

'One o'clock' is **yì diǎn zhōng** (literally: one dot on the clock).
'Six o'clock' is **liù diǎn zhōng** (six dots on the clock).

When it is clearly understood that you are talking about time,
you can leave out the **zhōng**, so 'six o'clock' can also be **liù
diǎn**, and when the minutes are mentioned **zhōng** is almost
never used. Time is told quite logically:

6 o'clock	**liù diǎn (zhōng)**
6.15	**liù diǎn yí kè** (six dots and one notch)
6.30	**liù diǎn bàn**
6.45	**liù diǎn sān kè** (six dots and three notches)
6.25	**liù diǎn èrshiwǔ**
6.37	**liù diǎn sānshiqī**
6.05	**liù diǎn líng wǔ (fēn)**

Remember that **líng** means 'zero'.

Exercise 37

Tell the time in Chinese:

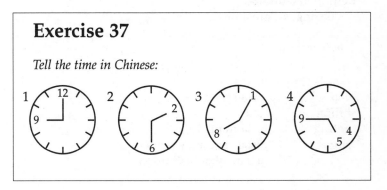

7.12 Hi, ho, hi, ho!

'To go to work' is **shàng bān**. As we saw in 6.16, **shàng** means 'to go up to' or 'to climb', and its opposite is **xià** 'to go down to', 'to climb down'. It is not illogical, then, that 'to finish work' is **xià bān**. This same pair **shàng/xià** will occur again. **Bān** means 'shift'.

7.13 Open and shut

Kāi mén means 'to open the door'. Its opposite is **guān mén** 'to shut the door'. But when **kāi mén** is used of shops being 'open for business' its opposite is **xiūxi** 'resting' rather than **guān mén**.

7.14 Sentences without verbs

Where there can be no ambiguity about the connection between two nouns, Chinese is sometimes content to do without the verb **shì**:

Jīntiān xīngqī jǐ?
    What day of the week is it today? (See 7.9)
Tā Měiguó rén.
    He's American.
Běijīng hǎo dìfang.
    Beijing is a great place.

Some new words

xiànzài	now
biǎo	a watch
shíjiān	time
cāntīng	restaurant
fànguǎnr	restaurant (independent of a hotel or institution)

CONVERSATION 7C

A tourist asks the hotel receptionist about eating:

T **Qǐng wèn xiànzài jǐ diǎn le? Wǒ de biǎo hái shi Lúndūn shíjiān.**
Excuse me, what's the time? My watch is still on London time.

R **Jiǔ diǎn shí fēn.**
Ten past nine.

T **Cāntīng hái kāi ma?**
Is the restaurant still open?

R **Duìbuqǐ, cāntīng yǐjing xià bān le.**
Sorry, it's closed already.

T **Fùjìn yǒu fànguǎnr ma?**
Are there any restaurants nearby?

R **Yǒu, kěshi yě dōu xià bān le.**
Yes, but they'll all be shut too.

T **Míngtiān xīngqītiān. Shāngdiàn kāi mén ma?**
Tomorrow is Sunday. Will the shops be open?

R **Kāi. Xīngqītiān shāngdiàn bù xiūxi.**
Yes. They don't close on Sundays.

T **Jǐ diǎn kāi mén?**
What time do they open?

R **Bā diǎn bàn.**
Half past eight.

7.15 What's it like?

We saw in 6.1 that **zěnme?** means 'how?' **Zěnme?** also
combines with **yàng** ('kind', 'type', 'sort') to make the
word **zěnmeyàng?** meaning 'What's it like?', 'What was
it like?', 'How was it?', 'How's it going?', 'What do you
think?' and so on.

Nèi ge huàjù zěnmeyàng?
  How was that play?
Jiǔ zěnmeyàng?
  What's the wine like?

7.16 Morning, noon and …

Morning or a.m. is 'above noon':   **shàngwǔ**
Afternoon or p.m. is 'below noon':   **xiàwǔ**
Midday is 'mid-noon':   **zhōngwǔ**

(Note the appearance of **shàng** and **xià** again.) Another way
of saying 'morning' or 'in the morning' is **zǎoshang**, and
'evening' or 'in the evening' is **wǎnshang**. Here you can see
the reappearance of the words **zǎo** 'early' and **wǎn** 'late'.

7.17 Exceedingly so

Jíle can be tacked on to adjectives to give great emphasis
to them:

hǎo jíle   superb, wonderful, fantastic
rè jíle   extremely hot, sweltering

7.18 To invite

Qǐng has cropped up before, first of all in Chapter 1 in a
number of polite expressions, and then in 5.1 as part of the
expression **Qǐng wèn** 'Please may I ask … ?'. As well as
'please', **qǐng** also means 'to invite' or 'to stand treat':

Tā yào qǐng wǒ hē píjiǔ.
He's inviting me to have a beer.

7.19 Two-faced constructions

The example sentence in 7.18 is interesting because **wǒ** has two jobs to do. Looked at one way it is the object of the verb **qǐng** (**Tā yào qǐng wǒ**: He's inviting me), but you can also see that it is subject of the verb **hē** (**Wǒ hē píjiǔ**: I have a beer). The Chinese construction is straightforward, though the English disguises this two-faced role by using the infinitive 'to have'. In the following example English uses 'who is surnamed', but the Chinese remains simple, with **yí ge péngyou** acting as both object and subject at the same time:

Wǒ yǒu yí ge péngyou xìng Wáng.
I've got a friend [who is] surnamed Wang.

Exercise 38

Translate into English and note how the structures of the two languages differ:

1 Wǒ yǒu yí ge péngyou shi Xiānggǎng rén.

2 Tā yào qǐng wǒ qu hē-jiǔ.

3 Tā wèn wǒ yǒu duōshao qián.

4 Wǒ rènshi yí ge huáqiáo yǒu shí ge Zhōngguó fànguǎnr.

7.20 See you!

We met the word **jiàn** ('to see') in the expression **zàijiàn** 'goodbye' in 1.12. **Jiàn** is often used with other words as well when saying goodbye.

Míngtiān jiàn. See you tomorrow.
Liù diǎn jiàn. See you at six o'clock.
Běijīng jiàn.   See you in Beijing.

máng	busy
ānpái	to arrange; arrangements
huì	meeting
kāi huì	to hold/attend a meeting or conference
kǎoyā	Peking duck
jiē	to meet, pick up (lit: to receive)

CONVERSATION 7D

Old Wang invites Peter to eat Peking duck:

W   **Wéi, shì Peter ma? Wǒ Lǎo Wáng a.**
Hello, is that Peter? It's Old Wang here.

P   **Èi, Lǎo Wáng, nǐ hǎo!**
Hey, Old Wang, how are you?

W   **Zhèi liǎng tiān zěnmeyàng? Máng ma?**
How's it been these last couple of days? Busy?

P   **Zuótiān hěn máng, jīntiān bú tài máng.**
Very busy yesterday, not too busy today.

W   **Jīntiān yǒu shénme ānpái?**
What arrangements have you got for today?

P   **Shàngwǔ shí diǎn zhōng yǒu ge huì, zhōngwǔ shí'èr diǎn Huáyuǎn Gōngsī qǐng chī-fàn.**
I've got a meeting at 10 o'clock this morning, then at midday the Huayuan Company is giving a lunch.

W   **Wǎnshang ne?**
What about the evening?

P   **Wǎngshang méi shì.**
Nothing this evening.

W   **Hǎo jíle. Wǒ qǐng nǐ chī kǎoyā. Liù diǎn yí kè wǒ lái fàndiàn jiē nǐ.**
Splendid. I'll invite you to have Peking duck. I'll come to the hotel at 6.15 to pick you up.

P   **Hǎo, tài xièxie le. Liù diǎn yí kè jiàn.**
Fine, thank you very much indeed. See you at 6.15.

Exercise 39: Pronunciation practice

Jǐ yuè jǐ hào jǐ diǎn jǐ fēn lái?

Sì yuè sì hào sì diǎn sìshisì fēn lái.

Jǐ yuè jǐ hào jǐ diǎn jǐ fēn qù?

Qī yuè qī hào qī diǎn qī fēn qù.

Exercise 40

Translate into Chinese:

1   A: When will you go to Japan?

    B: The fifth of September.

2   A: Is she coming on Saturday?

    B: No, she's coming on Sunday.

3   A: Have you got the time, please?

    B: Ten past ten.

4   A: What time do you get off work on Saturday?

    B: Twelve-thirty.

5   A: Do you know Manager Lee of the Huayuan Company?

    B: No, I don't, but I have a good friend who knows him.

6   A: What time does the train get in?

    B: It's already in.

Chapter 8
Describing things

- *Discussing an outing*
- *Discussing the weather*
- *Describing people*
- *Clothes colours and sizes*

8.1 Adverbs of degree

Adjectives can be modified with other words just as in English. **Hěn** 'very', **zhēn** 'truly' and **tài** 'too' all work as in English, though you will remember from 4.14 that **tài** usually has the particle **le** to help it out:

hěn hǎowánr	very good fun
zhēn piàoliang	really beautiful
tài rè le	too hot

Two other words which can modify adjectives are **zhème** and **nàme**. They both mean 'so', but you will probably have realised that they are versions of our old friends **zhè** and **nà**, so that there is a slight difference. **Zhème** really means 'so much as this', and **nàme** means 'so much as that':

zhème rè	so hot as this
nàme chǎo	so noisy as that

8.2 Comparison

To make straightforward comparisons between things, you use the formula:

XXX bǐ YYY *adjective*

Zhèi ge bǐ nèi ge hǎo.
This one is better than that one.
Xiǎo Wáng bǐ xiǎo Lǐ piàoliang.
Wang is prettier than Lee.
Jīntiān bǐ zuótiān lěng.
Today is colder than yesterday. (**lěng** = cold)

If you want to say 'even more … than', you simply insert **gèng** into the pattern:

XXX bǐ YYY gèng *adjective*

Jīntiān bǐ zuótiān gèng lěng.
Today is even colder than yesterday.
Zhèi ge bǐ nèi ge gèng guì.
This is even dearer than that.

8.3 The measure word 'dù'

Dù means 'a degree', as used in measuring heat or angles: **sānshiwǔ dù** '35°C'. In China temperature is measured in degrees Celsius.

8.4 Location

Here are four place words which use **shàng** and **xià**:

shānshang	on the mountain, up the hill
shānxia	at the foot of the mountain/hill
lóushang	upstairs
lóuxia	downstairs

Exercise 41

Make sentences showing simple comparison, as in the following example:

Běijīng líng dù, Lúndūn wǔ dù.
Běijīng bǐ Lúndūn lěng.

1 Shǒudū Fàndiàn yǒu jiǔshi ge fángjiān, Huáyuán Fàndiàn yǒu qīshi ge fǎngjiān.

2 Píjiǔ ¥1.50, kuàngquánshuǐ ¥1.20.

3 Shānshang 20°C, shānxia 28°C.

4 Lóushang de zhōng 10.55, lóuxia de zhōng 10.50.

[*Tip: The Chinese word for 'fast' was in the expression 'fast train' in 7.7.*]

8.5   You'd better ...

'You'd better ...' or 'It would be better if ...' is translated by **háishi ... ba**:

Zhèi ge dà, háishi mǎi zhèi ge ba.
This one's bigger, it'd be better to buy this one.
Jīntiān tài wǎn le, nǐ háishi míngtiān qù ba.
It's too late today, you'd better go tomorrow.
Háishi qǐng tā lái ba, wǒ bú rènshi lù.
It'd be better to ask him to come here, I don't know the way.

8.6   To straddle

The verb **qí** 'to straddle' is used for riding horses, and it has been adopted for riding bicycles too:

Tā xǐhuan qí mǎ (horse).
She likes riding horses.
Wǒ qí zìxíngchē (bicycle) **qù.**
I am going by bike.

94

8.7 Duration of time

Yì nián 'for one year', **yí (ge) xiǎoshí** 'for an hour', **wǔ fēn zhōng** 'for five minutes' are time expressions which show duration, the time over which something goes on. Chinese puts such expressions after the verb:

zuò liǎng tiān (de) huǒchē
   travel by train for two days
qí sìshi fēn zhōng (de) chē
   ride a bike for 40 minutes
hē yì wǎnshang de jiǔ
   to be drinking all evening

The marker **de** is often inserted between the time expression and the object of the verb.

8.8 How come?

We met **zěnme?** meaning 'how?' in 6.1. It also means 'how come?' or 'how could it not be?':

Nǐ zěnme bú rènshi wǒ le?
   How come you don't recognise me?
Jīntiān zěnme zhème rè?
   How come it's so hot today?

Exercise 42

Translate into English:

1   zhù sān ge xīngqī

2   chī liǎng nián de Zhōngguó fàn

3   shàng bā (ge) xiǎoshí de bān

4   zuò shíwǔ ge xiǎoshí de fēijī

5   qí èrshi fēn zhōng de chē

Some new words

tiānqi	weather
wánr	to play, amuse oneself
liángkuai	cool
gōnggòngqìchē	bus (lit: 'public motor car')
jǐ	crowded

CONVERSATION 8A

A tourist discusses an outing with a Chinese friend:

T **Jīntiān zhēn rè!**
It's really hot today!

F **Shì a! Bǐ zuótiān gèng rè le. Wàitou yǐjing sānshiwǔ dù le.**
You're right. It's even hotter than yesterday. It's already 35° outside.

T **Tiānqi zhème rè, dào nǎr qu wánr ne?**
The weather's so hot, where can we go to amuse ourselves?

F **Qù Xiāngshān ba. Shānshang liángkuai.**
Let's go to the Fragrant Hills. It's cool in the mountains.

T **Zěnme qù ne?**
How do we get there?

F **Zuò gōnggòngqìchē ba. Zuò chē bǐ qí chē kuài.**
How about taking the bus? It's quicker than going by bike.

T **Gōnggòngqìchē tài jǐ le, háishi qí chē qù ba.**
The bus is too crowded. It'd be better to go by bike.

F **Lù nàme yuǎn, děi qí liǎng ge xiǎoshí; nǐ bú pà rè ma?**
It's such a long way, it'd take two hours by bike; aren't you afraid of the heat?

T **Zěnme bú pà? Kěshi wǒ gèng pà jǐ.**
How couldn't I be? But I mind the crowding even more.

F **Hǎo, zǒu ba!**
OK, let's go!

8.9 To go or not to go

Zǒu and **qù** can both be translated as 'to go', but they are not really the same. **Zǒu** often means 'to leave', while **qù** means 'to go somewhere'. Compare the following two sentences:

Tā míngtiān zǒu.
> He's going [i.e. leaving] tomorrow.

Tā míngtiān qù.
> He's going (there) tomorrow.

8.10 'Shàng' and 'xià' again

Used with 'week' and 'month', yet another function of this pair is to indicate 'last' and 'next':

shàng (ge) xīngqī	last week
xià (ge) xīngqī	next week
shàng (ge) yuè	last month
xià (ge) yuè	next month
shàng (ge) xīngqīliù	last Saturday
xià (ge) yuè bā hào	the 8th of next month

8.11 Really?

Zhēn de ma? is the idiomatic way to say 'Really!?', 'Is that true!?'. As with many other idiomatic expressions, it is not very helpful to try to analyse why it has that meaning.

8.12 More on 'le'

The sentence particle **le**, which we met in 6.5, shows that a new state of affairs has come about. When it is used with a negative (**bù** or **méi**) the English translation is usually 'no longer' or 'no more':

Xièxie nín, wǒ bù hē le.
   Thank you, I can't drink any more.
Tā bù lái le.
   He's not coming any more [though he said he would].

Exercise 43

Complete the following, showing change of state, as in the example:

Zuótiān hěn lěng, jīntiān …
Zuótiān hěn lěng, jīntiān bù lěng le.

1   Zuótiān tā yǒu qián, jīntiān …

2   Qiántiān tā xiǎng chī kǎoyā, jīntiān …

3   Shàngwǔ hěn máng, xiànzài …

4   Zuótiān chē hěn jǐ, jīntiān …

8.13 It's raining

The Chinese for 'to rain' is **xià-yǔ**, literally 'comes down rain'. Similarly, 'to snow' is **xià-xuě** 'comes down snow'. Note that 'it's raining now' is **xià-yǔ le**, the **le** showing that, while it wasn't raining before, things have changed. (There is no equivalent for the 'it' of the English 'it's raining'.)

Some new words

zhàng	account
zhàngdān	the bill
jié zhàng	to settle the bill
nuǎnhuo	warm
dōngtiān	winter
cháng	often
tiānqi yùbào	weather forecast

CONVERSATION 8B

A tourist in search of good weather wants to check out of his hotel:

T **Wǒ míngtiān zǎoshang qù Guǎngzhōu, xiànzài jié zhàng hǎo ma?**
I'm going to Guangzhou tomorrow morning; can I settle the bill now?

R **Hǎo, zhè shi nín de zhàngdān. Nín bú shi xià xīngqīyī zǒu ma?**
Fine, here is your bill. Weren't you leaving next Monday?

T **Běijīng tài lěng le, wǒ xiǎng zhǎo ge nuǎnhuo de dìfang.**
Beijing is too cold. I want to find somewhere warm.

R **Guǎngzhōu shì bǐ Běijīng nuǎnhuo, kěshi dōngtiān cháng xià-yǔ.**
Guangzhou is indeed warmer than Beijing, but it frequently rains in winter.

T **Shì ma?**
Is that so?

R **Wǒ kànkan tiānqi yùbào.**
I'll have a look at the forecast.

T **Zěnmeyàng?**
What's it like?

R **Guǎngzhōu míngtiān yǒu yǔ.**
Guangzhou will have rain tomorrow.

T **Běijīng ne?**
And what about Beijing?

R **Běijīng kěnéng xià-xuě.**
Beijing may have snow.

T **Zhēn de ma? Tài hǎo le! Wǒ bù zǒu le. Wǒ jiù xǐhuan kàn xià-xuě.**
Really? Terrific! I won't leave. I just love to watch it snowing.

8.14 Male and female

Although the words **nánrén** 'a male person' and **nǚrén** 'a female person' do exist, they are best avoided as general words for 'man' and 'woman'. It is more colloquial to say **nán de** and **nǚ de**.

8.15 The topic of conversation

Quite often Chinese states at the beginning of a sentence or speech the topic under discussion. It is rather like the English 'As for X'. To translate it formally each time as 'As for X' would be tedious and unnatural, but it is helpful to understand that the stating of this topic allows a full sentence to be used as a comment upon it. We could analyse the statement **Tā rén hěn hǎo** 'He is a very nice person' as:

Tā (topic)	As for him
rén (subject)	the person
hěn hǎo	is very nice.

Exercise 44

Translate into English:

1 Nèi ge dìfang, tiānqi bù hǎo, dōngxi yě guì.

2 Shānshang, fēngjǐng piàoliang, tiānqi liángkuai.

3 Shǒudū Fàndiàn, dìfang hǎo, fángjiān dà.

4 Dàhuá Cāntīng, lù yuǎn, kěshi kǎoyā hǎo.

8.16 Sure to

It is strange that sometimes we use the word 'certainly' when the fact is that we cannot be certain at all. The Chinese word **yídìng** works just like 'certainly':

Míngtiān yídìng xià-yǔ.
　　It will certainly rain tomorrow.
Wǒ yídìng lái kàn nǐ.
　　I will surely come to see you.

8.17　A little while

Yíhuìr works either as a time word showing when
something happens ('in a little while', 'in a moment') or
as a duration of time showing how long something goes
on for ('for a moment', 'for a while'). In the first case it
comes before the verb:

Tā yíhuìr jiù lái.
　　He will be here in a moment.

But 'duration of time' words come after the verb (see 8.7), so:

Tā xiǎng qu wánr yíhuìr.
　　He wants to go to play for a while.
Wǒmen xiūxi yíhuìr ba.
　　Let's rest for a bit.

Some new words

tóufa	hair (on the head)
cháng	long
pàng	fat (of people)
shòu	thin, slim, skinny
dài	to wear (accessories)
yǎnjìngr	spectacles, glasses
děng	to wait, wait for

CONVERSATION 8C

Describing Ms Wang over the phone:

A   **Wéi, qǐng wèn Xiǎo Wáng zài ma?**
      Hello, is Little Wang there, please?

B   **Něi ge Xiǎo Wáng? Wǒmen zhèr yǒu liǎng ge Xiǎo Wáng.**
      Which Little Wang? We have two Little Wangs here.

A   **Duìbuqǐ, wǒ bù zhīdao tā de míngzi, shì wèi nǚ tóngzhì.**
      I'm sorry, I don't know the name, but it's a woman.

B   **Liǎng ge Xiǎo Wáng dōu shi nǚ de.**
      Both the Little Wangs are women.

A   **Tā tóufa hěn cháng.**
      She has long hair.

B   **Rén pàng bu pàng?**
      Is she on the large side?

A   **Hěn shòu.**
      No, slim.

B   **Dài yǎnjìngr ma?**
      Does she wear glasses?

A   **Bú dài.**
      No.

B   **Nà yídìng shi Wáng Huá. Qǐng děng yíhuìr, wǒ qu jiào tā.**
      That's bound to be Wang Hua. Please wait a moment, I'll go and call her.

8.18 Colours

Some common colour words are:

hóng	red
huáng	yellow
lǜ	green
lán	blue
bái	white
hēi	black

The word for 'colour' is **yánsè**, and it often combines with the basic colour words to make the colour adjectives. **Hóng yánsè de chē** is 'a red car'. **Hóng sè de** is a shorter version of this, so **hóng sè de chē** also means 'a red car'.

Sometimes a colour word does not need these props, but attaches directly to a noun. **Hēi yǎnjìngr** is a word for 'sunglasses', and **hóng tóufa** is 'ginger hair'.

8.19 Size

We have met **hào** before in the sense of 'number'. It is also used in the terms for sizes:

xiǎo hào	small size
zhōng hào	medium size
dà hào	large size
tè-dà hào	extra-large size
liù hào	size six

8.20 Enough

Gòu means 'enough'. As an adverb it goes in front of adjectives:

gòu dà	big enough
bú gòu dà	not big enough

but unlike most Chinese adjectives, **gòu** cannot occur in front of a noun, it can only follow the noun:

rén gòu   enough people
rén bú gòu   not enough people
Wǒ de qián bú gòu.   I haven't got enough money.

Exercise 45

Add a bit of colour:

1   Yīngguó rén xǐhuan hē ... chá.

2   Fǎguó rén xǐhuan hē ... jiǔ.

3   Zhōngguó rén de tóufa shi ... yánsè de.

4   Tiānqi hěn hǎo, tiān shi ... yánsè de.

   *[Tip: **tiān** means 'heaven' or 'sky' as well as 'day'.]*

Exercise 46: Pronunciation practice

Wǒ xǐhuan qí chē; tiān rè qí, tiān bú rè yě qí.

Tā xǐhuan kàn huàjù; xià-yǔ qù, bú xià-yǔ yě qù.

Some new words

jiàn	(measure words for some items of clothing)
dàbèixīnr	T-shirt
zì	a Chinese character
chuān	to wear, put on (clothes)

CONVERSATION 8D

A tourist is buying a T-shirt:

T   **Xiáojie, kànkan nèi jiàn dàbèixīnr kěyǐ ma?**
    May I have a look at that T-shirt, miss, please?

S   **Něi jiàn? Shì zhèi jiàn lǜ de ma?**
    Which one? Is it this green one?

T   **Bú shi. Shì nèi jiàn huáng de, shàngtou yǒu hēi zì de.**
    No, it's that yellow one, the one with black writing on it.

S   **Nà shi zhōng hào de. Nín chuān dà hào de ba?**
    That's a medium. You take a large, surely?

T   **Dà hào de hái shi bú gòu dà.**
    Large is still not big enough.

S   **Wǒmen yǒu tè-dà hào de.**
    We have extra-large.

T   **Kànkan kěyǐ ma?**
    May I see it?

S   **Méi you huáng de le. Hóng de kěyǐ ma?**
    There are no yellow ones left. Will a red one be OK?

T   **Wǒ bù xǐhuan hóng yánsè. Yǒu lán de ma?**
    I don't like red. Have you got it in blue?

S   **Lán de yě méi you tè-dà hào de le. Bái de zěnmeyàng?**
    We've got no more extra-large in blue either. How about white?

T   **Hǎo ba, wǒ mǎi jiàn bái de.**
    All right, I'll buy a white one.

Exercise 47

Translate into Chinese:

1   *A*:   What is winter like in Canada?

    B: It's extremely cold.

2   *A*:   Is it very warm in Hong Kong in March?

    B: Yes, it's warmer than Shanghai.

3   *A*:   Does your friend wear glasses?

    B: No, she doesn't.

4   *A*:   What size do you take?

    B: I don't know. It could be size 42.

5   *A*:   What colour would you prefer?

    B: I like the yellow one.

Chapter 9
Likes and dislikes

- *Buying a present*
- *In a vegetarian restaurant*
- *Exercising in the park*
- *Declining an invitation*

9.1 Prepositional phrases before the verb

There are a number of phrases (introduced by prepositions in English) which in Chinese are introduced by verbs (often called coverbs) and placed before the main verb of the sentence. Here are some of them:

zuò huǒchē qù Zhōngguó
    to go to China <u>by train</u>
    [sit train go China]
zài Shànghǎi kāi huì
    to attend/hold a meeting <u>in Shanghai</u>
    [be at Shanghai attend/hold meeting]
gěi péngyou mǎi dōngxi
    to buy something <u>for a friend</u>
    [provide friend buy thing]
tì tā wèn yi wèn
    to ask <u>on his behalf</u>
    [substitute him ask]

9.2 More titles

Tàitai is another word for 'Mrs' or 'wife'. It is widely used among Chinese people outside Mainland China. Elderly women are respectfully addressed and referred to everywhere as **Lǎo tàitai**.

9.3 Correct!

Duì bu duì? 'Is that correct?', 'Do you agree?' gets the answer **Bú duì** 'No' or **Duì le** 'Yes'. **Duì le** is often used to show agreement with something someone has just said: 'You're quite right!'.

Exercise 48

Add the information in brackets to the sentences:

1 Tā yào qù Zhōngguó. (*by air*)

2 Qǐng nǐ bié chōu-yān. (*here*)

3 Qǐng nǐ mǎi fènr wǎnbào. (*for me*)

4 Nǐ kěyǐ qǐng Wáng Xiānsheng lái ma? (*on our behalf*)

9.4 More about comparison

To say something is 'a bit more ...' than something else, the expression **yìdiǎnr** is added to the comparative pattern which we met in 8.2:

XXX bǐ YYY *adjective* **yìdiǎnr**

Kāfēi bǐ chá guì yìdiǎnr.
Coffee is a bit more expensive than tea.
Shànghǎi bǐ Xiānggǎng lěng yìdiǎnr.
Shanghai's a little colder than Hong Kong.
Tā de tóufa bǐ wǒ (de (tóufa)) cháng yìdiǎnr.
Her hair is a bit longer than mine.

9.5   Creative opposition

A number of Chinese words are created by putting together two words with opposite meanings:

pàng + shòu (fat + thin)   = **pàngshòu** build
dà + xiǎo (big + small)   = **dàxiǎo** size
mǎi + mài (buy + sell)   = **mǎimai** business, trade
duō + shǎo (many/much   = **duōshao** quantity, how
+ few/little)   many?, how much?

9.6   Almost the same

'Almost', 'nearly', can be translated by **chàbuduō** (literally: 'differs not much').

Zhèi liǎng jiàn chàbuduō (dà).
These two items are almost the same size.
Jīntiān chàbuduō yǒu èrshíbā dù.
It's about 28° today.

Exercise 49

Make a comparison between A and B, as in the example:

A   Kāfēi ¥1.80.

B   Píjiǔ ¥2.00.

Píjiǔ bǐ kāfēi guì yì diǎnr.

1   A   Běijīng shí dù.

     B   Shànghǎi shí'èr dù.

2   A   Qù Tiān'ānmén sān zhàn.

     B   Qù Yǒuyì Shāngdiàn wǔ zhàn.

3   A   Lǎo Lǐ de biǎo 7:32.

     B   Huǒchēzhàn de zhōng 7:30.

4   A   Zuò gōnggòngqìchē qù yì xiǎoshí.

     B   Qí chē qù yì xiǎoshí shí fēn zhōng.

xiǎomián'ǎo	quilted jacket
píngcháng	usually, normally
qīngchu	clear
gāo	tall, high
xuǎn	to choose, pick

CONVERSATION 9A

A tourist buys a present for his wife in a department store:

T **Xiáojie, wǒ xiǎng mǎi jiàn xiǎomián'ǎo.**
Miss, I'd like to buy a quilted jacket.

S **Shi gěi nín fūren mǎi ma?**
Are you buying it for your wife?

T **Duì le, gěi wǒ tàitai.**
Right, it's for my wife.

S **Tā píngcháng chuān jǐ hào de?**
What size does she normally wear?

T **Wǒ bú tài qīngchu. Tā bǐ nǐ gāo yìdiǎnr.**
I'm not too sure. She's a little taller than you are.

S **Pàngshòu ne?**
And her build?

T **Chàbuduō. Kěnéng bǐ nǐ pàng yìdiǎnr.**
Much the same. Perhaps she's a bit fatter than you.

S **Wǒ chuān 36 de; wǒ xiǎng 38 de yīnggāi kěyǐ.**
Tā xǐhuan shénme yánsè?
I take a 36; I think a 38 should be all right. What colour does she like?

T **Òu, zhè wǒ yě bú tài qīngchu. Nǐ tì wǒ xuǎn yí jiàn ba.**
Oh, I'm not too sure about that either. Will you choose one for me?

S **Zhèi jiàn hóng de zěnmeyàng?**
How about this red one?

T **Hǎo jíle! Jiù mǎi zhèi jiàn. Wǒ tàitai yídìng xǐhuan.**
Terrific! I'll take this one. My wife is sure to like it.

9.7 Vegetarian

Sùcài is 'a vegetable dish' or 'vegetarian food', and
sùcàiguǎnr is 'a vegetarian restaurant'. 'A vegetarian' is
chī-sù de (rén): 'a person who eats vegetables'.

9.8 What's it made of?

To say what something is made of or from, the formula is
XXX shi yòng YYY zuò de (lit: X is made using Y). **Yòng**
means 'to use', and **zuò** is 'to make':

Zhè shi yòng niúnǎi zuò de.
   This is made from milk.

9.9 Similarity

To show similarity, the pattern is **XXX gēn YYY yíyàng**
adjective (lit: X with Y the same …). **Gēn** means 'with' and
yíyàng 'the same' (lit: 'of one kind'):

Tā gēn wǒ yíyàng gāo.
   He is as tall as I am.
Lóushang gēn lóuxia yíyàng rè.
   Upstairs and downstairs are equally hot.

Exercise 50

*Use the 'similarity' pattern to make new sentences, as in the
following example:*

A   Jīntiān Lúndūn èr dù.

B   Běijīng yě shi èr dù.

Lúndūn gēn Běijīng yíyàng lěng.

1   A   Bíyānhú ¥95.

     B   Xiǎomián'ǎo yě shi ¥95.

                                   →

2 A Qù Tiān'ānmén sì zhàn.

   B Qù Bǎihuò Dàlóu yě shi sì zhàn.

3 A Zuò chē qù bàn xiǎoshí.

   B Qí chē qù yě shi bàn xiǎoshí.

4 A Xiǎo Wáng chuān 44 hào de.

   B Xiǎo Lǐ yě chuān 44 hào de.

9.10 Even more so

We met in 8.2 the pattern **XXX bǐ YYY gèng** *adjective* for 'X is even more … than Y'. A very similar pattern is:

XXX bǐ YYY hái *adjective*

Zhèi jiàn bǐ tè-dà hào de hái dà.
   This one is even bigger than extra-large.

This pattern is stronger than the one using **gèng**, and gives the impression that something is almost 'better than the best'.

Some new words

càidān	menu
jī	chicken
yā	duck
yú	fish
ròu	meat (usually pork)
dòufu	bean-curd
tǔdòur	potato
yàngzi	appearance
wèidao	taste, flavour
cháng	to taste
bú cuò	'not bad' (= very good)

CONVERSATION 9B

A vegetarian in a vegetarian restaurant:

V   **Shīfu, nǐmen zhèr bú shi sùcàiguǎnr ma?**
    Waiter, isn't this a vegetarian restaurant?
W   **Shì a. Wǒmen zuò de dōu shi sùcài.**
    Yes, it is. Everything we cook is vegetarian.
V   **Kěshi càidān shang zěnme jī, yā, yú, ròu dōu yǒu
    a? Wǒ shi chī-sù de.**
    *But how come there are chicken, duck, fish and meat all
    on the menu? I'm a vegetarian.*
W   **Nà dōu bú shi zhēn de.**
    None of those are the real thing.
V   **Bú shi zhēn de jī, yā, yú, ròu?**
    Not real chicken, duck, fish and meat?
W   **Bú shi. Jī, yā shi yòng dòufu zuò de; yú shi yòng
    tǔdòur zuò de.**
    *Not real. The chicken and duck are made of bean-curd,
    the fish from potato.*

[The food arrives]

V   **Zhè yú de yàngzi gēn zhēn de yíyàng; wèidao yě
    yíyàng hǎo ma?**
    *This fish looks exactly like the real thing. Is the flavour
    as good?*
W   **Nín chángchang, wèidao bǐ zhēn de hái hǎo.**
    Try it; the flavour is even better than the real thing.
V   **Ǹg, shì bú cuò.**
    Mm, it's really not bad.

9.11 Coming and going

We have up to now used **lái Lúndūn** for 'to come to
London', and **qù Běijīng** for 'to go to Beijing'. There is an
alternative pattern:

dào Lúndūn lái
> to come to London

dào Běijīng qù
> to go to Beijing

The two patterns are equally acceptable – you may take your pick.

9.12 In the process of happening

To show that something is going on at a particular time, Chinese uses **zài** before the verb, often adding **ne** at the end of the sentence too:

Tāmen zài kāi huì.
> They are in a meeting.

Lǎo Wáng zài chī-fàn ne.
> Old Wang is eating.

The negative ('something is *not* going on') is formed by putting **méi (you)** before the **zài**.

Tāmen méi zài kāi huì.
> They are not in a meeting.

9.13 Measure words

The measure word **xiē** is very useful for indicating an unspecified plural number of things. It can be used with any noun, regardless of which measure word that noun usually takes:

liǎng tiáo lù	two roads
zhèi tiáo lù	this road
něi xiē lù?	which roads?

Xiē also acts as a measure for uncountable things like 'water', which do not have a 'singular' measure word:

nèi xiē niúnǎi that milk

Xiē (or **yìxiē**) can also be used to mean 'a few', 'some', 'a certain amount of ':

yìxiē rén   some people, a few people

9.14 Seems like

Hǎoxiàng means 'seems like', 'seems as if', 'seems to be':

Tā hǎoxiàng shi Rìběn rén.
　　She seems to be Japanese.
Hǎoxiàng yào xià-yǔ.
　　It seems as if it will rain.

9.15 Some action verbs

liàn qìgōng
　　to practise qigong [deep-breathing exercises]
dǎ tàijíquán
　　to do taichi [shadow-boxing exercises]
tiào-wǔ
　　to dance

Exercise 51: What are they doing now?

Say it in Chinese:

1　They are resting.

2　They are dancing.

3　They are drinking downstairs.

4　They are reading the weather forecast.

5　They are not smoking.

9.16 Once, twice, three times

The measure word for 'occasion', 'occurrence', 'time' is **cì**:

zhèi cì	this time
yí cì	once
liǎng cì	twice
shàng cì	last time
xià cì	next time

Some new words

zǎochen	morning, in the morning
kōngqì	air
ài	to love, love to
duànliàn	to exercise, train
gànmá	doing what? up to what?
hǎokàn	'nice to look at', good-looking
xué	to learn
lǎoshī	a teacher
xíng	OK, all right, will do
tèbié	special; specially

CONVERSATION 9C

The park in the morning:

T **Gōngyuán li rén zhēn bù shǎo.**
  What a lot of people in the park!

C **Zǎochen kōngqì hǎo. Dàjiā dōu ài dào zhèr lai duànliàn.**
  In the morning the air is good. Everyone likes to come here to exercise.

T **Éi, nèi xiē rén zài gànmá ne?**
  Eh, what are those people up to?

C **Wǒ yě bù qīngchu, hǎoxiàng shi zài liàn qìgōng.**
  I'm not sure either, they seem to be practising qigong.

T **Zhè jǐ wèi lǎo tàitai tiào de shi shénme wǔ a?**
  What dance is it that these old ladies are doing?

116

C	**Zhè bú shi tiào-wǔ, tāmen zài dǎ tàijíquán ne.**
	That isn't dancing, they are doing taijiquan.
T	**Tàijíquán a? Zhēn hǎokàn; wǒ yě xiǎng xuéxue.**
	Taijiquan? It's really attractive; I'd like to learn it too.
C	**Hǎo a. Míngtiān bié zǒu le, wǒ gěi nǐ zhǎo wèi lǎoshī.**
	Great. Don't leave tomorrow, and I'll find a teacher for you.
T	**Zhèi cì bù xíng. Míngnián wǒ tèbié lái xué.**
	It's no good this time. Next year I'll come here specially to learn it.

9.17 Cuisines

As well as 'vegetable', **cài** means 'a cuisine', 'a style of cooking'. Here are three well-known cuisines:

Sìchuān cài   Sichuan (or Szechwan) food [hot and spicy]
Guǎngdōng cài Cantonese food [sophisticated, great variety]
Fǎguó cài   French food

9.18 Later, after a while

We saw in 8.17 that **yíhuìr** means 'a little while'. A fuller form **děng (yí) huìr** can also be used when referring to a future occurrence. **Děng** you will recognise as the verb 'to wait'.

Děng huìr jiàn.
   See you in a while.
Děng huìr qǐng nǐ qu kànkan Lǎo Lǐ.
   Please go to see Old Lee in a bit.

9.19 Both ... and ...

Where 'both ... and ...' are used to make two comments about the same subject, Chinese uses **yòu ... yòu ...** Usually the comments are very short, uncomplicated ones:

Nèi xiē chē yòu guì yòu bù hǎo.
    Those cars are both expensive and no good.
yòu gāo yòu dà
    both high and large

9.20 Although

'Although' is **suīrán**, and it is usually followed in the second
half of the sentence by **kěshi** (but):

Tā suīrán shi Zhōngguó rén, kěshi bú ài chī Zhōngguó cài.
    Although he's Chinese, he doesn't like Chinese food.

9.21 Is it the case that?

Shì bu shi can be inserted into a sentence to highlight a
question about what follows it:

Tā shì bu shi ài tiào-wǔ?
    Does she like dancing? (Is it the case that she
    likes dancing?)
Míngtiān shì bu shi yào xià-yǔ?
    Will it rain tomorrow?

9.22 Most

The superlative is simply formed by putting **zuì** in front of
the adjective or verb:

zuì gāo de shān
    the highest mountain
zuì guì de cài
    the most expensive dishes
Tā zuì xǐhuan tiào-wǔ.
    He likes dancing best.
Tā shuō chī-sù zuì hǎo.
    She says eating vegetarian food is best.

Exercise 52: Revision

Who are they? Say it in Chinese:

1 those who smoke

2 those who do not eat meat

3 those who love to drink tea

4 those who want to go to China

5 those who do taichi in the morning

Some new words

wèikǒu	appetite
wǎn	bowl (measure word/noun)
miàn	noodles
gānjìng	clean
wèishén me?	why?
tǎoyàn?	to dislike, loathe
wèir	taste, flavour, smell
yānwèir	the smell of smoke

CONVERSATION 9D

Declining an invitation:

A **Wǎnshang xiǎng chī shénme? Wǒ qǐng nǐ chī Sìchuān cài, hǎo bu hǎo?**
What would you like to eat this evening? Supposing I invite you to have Sichuan food?

B **Xièxie nǐ, kěshi wǒ jīntiān wèikǒu bú tài hǎo; děng huìr qù lóuxia chī wǎn miàn jiù xíng le.**
Thank you, but I don't have much appetite today. It'll be quite enough to go downstairs for a bowl of noodles in a little while.

→

A	**Zhèr cāntīng yòu guì yòu bù hǎo, háishi dào wàitou qu chī ba.**
	The restaurant here is expensive and not good either. It'd be better to go outside to eat.
B	**Wàitou de cài suīrán bǐ zhèr hǎo, kěshi ...**
	Although the food outside is better, still ...
A	**Kěshi shénme? Shì bu shi pà bù gānjìng?**
	But what? Are you afraid it's not clean?
A	**Bú shi, bú shi.**
	Not at all.
A	**Nà shi wèishénme?**
	In that case why?
B	**Fànguǎnr li chōu-yān de rén tài duō, wǒ zuì tǎoyàn yānwèir.**
	There are too many smokers in the restaurants, and I hate the smell of smoke.

Exercise 53: Pronunciation practice

yā
kǎoyā
Běijīng kǎoyā
chī Běijīng kǎoyā
xǐhuan chī Běijīng kǎoyā
dōu xǐhuan chī Běijīng kǎoyā
shí ge rén dōu xǐhuan chī Běijīng kǎoyā
Wǒmen shí ge rén dōu xǐhuan chī Běijīng kǎoyā

yú
mǎi yú
tiāntiān mǎi yú
rén tiāntiān mǎi yú
sān ge rén tiāntiān mǎi yú
nèi sān ge rén tiāntiān mǎi yú
chī yú de nèi sān ge rén tiāntiān mǎi yú
Ài chī yú de nèi sān ge rén tiāntiān mǎi yú

Exercise 54

Translate into Chinese:

1   *A*:   Will you choose one for me, please?

    B: OK. I think the red one is the best.

2   *A*:   Are you two the same height?

    B: No, he is slightly taller than I am.

3   *A*:   Shall we invite her to have roast duck?

    B: That won't do. She is a vegetarian.

4   *A*:   What is he doing now?

    B: He's just resting.

5   *A*:   I would like to learn taichi; can you find me a teacher?

    B: No problem.

Chapter 10
Actions

- *Phoning a big company*
- *At an international conference*
- *Describing what happened*
- *Seeing the doctor*

10.1 Sentence particle 'le'

We saw in 6.5 that **le** at the end of a sentence indicates that a new state of affairs has come about. A further use of this particle is to show that some event has taken place:

Nǐ hē-jiǔ le ma?
Did you have a drink/Have you had a drink?
Tā qù Zhōngguó le.
He's gone to China/He went to China.

In the negative, **méi** ('not', as in **méi you**) is used, but **le** is not:

Tāmen zuótiān méi kāi huì.
They didn't have a meeting yesterday.

There are various question forms which can be used; all the following mean 'Did he take photos?':

Tā zhào xiàng le ma?
Tā zhào xiàng le méi you?
Tā zhào xiàng le méi zhào?

Exercise 55: Where is he?

Translate into English:

1 Tā bú zài zhèr, tā qù gōngyuán le.

2 Tā bú zài jiā, tā dào gōngsī qù le.

3 Tā méi lai shàng bān, tā mǎi dōngxi qù le.

4 Tā yě qu hē-jiǔ le ma?

10.2 Abroad and back again

'To go abroad' is **chū guó** (literally: to exit the country). 'To return from abroad' is **huí guó** (lit: to return to the country).

10.3 Along with

Gēn means 'the heel' and it is also a verb which means 'to follow'. From this come the meanings 'along with', 'with' and 'and':

Lǎo Wáng gēn Lǎo Lǐ
   Old Wang and Old Lee
Wǒ gēn Wáng lǎoshī xué.
   I study with Teacher Wang.

Gēn is another verb of the kind which we met in 9.1 (coverbs).

10.4 Àiren

Àiren means 'loved person' and is used for either 'husband' or 'wife'. It has become common usage in Mainland China but has not caught on elsewhere.

Some new words

shuō-huà	to speak (lit: to speak speech)
yīyuàn	hospital
bìng	illness, disease
bìng le	to become ill
shēng háizi	to give birth to a child

CONVERSATION 10A

A customer phones a big company:

R **Nǐ hǎo. Dàhuá Gōngsī.**
Hello, Dahua Company.

C **Wéi, qǐng wèn Wáng jīnglǐ zài ma?**
Hello, is Manager Wang there, please?

R **Wáng jīnglǐ bú zài, tā chū guó le.**
No, he's gone abroad.

C **Chū guó le?! Tā dào nǎr qù le?**
Out of the country? Where's he gone?

R **Dào Rìběn qù le.**
He's gone to Japan.

C **Lǐ jīnglǐ yě qù le ma?**
Has Manager Lee gone too?

R **Lǐ jīnglǐ méi qù.**
No.

C **Wǒ kěyǐ gēn Lǐ jīnglǐ shuō-huà ma?**
May I speak with him?

R **Duìbuqǐ, Lǐ jīnglǐ jīntiān méi lái. Tā dào yīyuàn qù le.**
I'm sorry, Manager Lee hasn't come in today. He's gone to the hospital.

C **Òu, tā bìng le.**
Oh, he's ill.

R **Méi you. Tā àiren zài yīyuàn shēng háizi ne.**
No, his wife is having a baby in there.

10.5 Still and yet

Hái means 'still' or 'yet' (as we saw in 6.10) and is very often accompanied by the sentence particle **ne**:

Tā hái bù zhīdao ne.
    She still doesn't know.
Tā hái méi chī ne.
    She has not yet eaten.

Exercise 56: 'Already' and 'not yet'

Give both affirmative and negative answers to the questions, as in the example:

Tā qù Rìběn le ma?   A Yǐjing qù le.

                             B Hái méi qù ne.

1   Nǐ chī-fàn le ma?

2   Wáng jīnglǐ lái le ma?

3   Nǐmen jié zhàng le méi you?

4   Dōngxi dōu mǎi le ma?

10.6 It says in the newspaper

Bào is 'a newspaper'. 'It says in the newspaper' is **bào shang shuō**:

Bào shang shuō míngtiān yào xià-yǔ.
    It says in the newspaper that it will rain tomorrow.

10.7 News and news

There are two different words in Chinese for two different meanings of 'news'. **Xīnwén** is news which is in the newspapers or in a broadcast, news in the public domain; **xiāoxi** is 'tidings', information about certain people or events:

Bào shang yǒu shénme xīnwén?
What news is there in the paper?
Nǐ yǒu méi you Lǎo Wáng de xiāoxi?
Any news of Old Wang?

10.8 Active or passive?

Many Chinese verbs work either actively or passively
depending on context:

Zuótiān méi zhào xiàng a?
(We) weren't photographed yesterday, surely?/
(We) didn't take any photos yesterday, did we?
Yú chī le.
The fish has eaten./The fish has been eaten.

Some new words

zǎofàn	breakfast
kàn bào	to read a newspaper
zhàopiàn	a photograph
jìzhě	reporter
shuì-jiào	to sleep

CONVERSATION 10B

Delegates chatting at an international conference:

A **Chī zǎofàn le ma?**
    Have you had breakfast?
B **Hái méi ne, xiànzài qu chī. Nǐ ne?**
    Not yet, I'm going to have it now. What about you?
A **Wǒ yǐjing chī le. Kàn bào le ma?**
    I've already eaten. Have you read the newspaper?
B **Hái méi ne. Yǒu shénme xīnwén?**
    Not yet. What's the news?
A **Bào shang yǒu wǒmen kāi huì de xiāoxi.**
    There's some news about our conference.

126

> B　**Shì ma? Zài nǎr? Gěi wǒ kànkan.**
> *Is there? Where? Show me.*
>
> A　**Jiù zài zhèr. Nǐ kàn, hái yǒu wǒmen de zhàopiàn.**
> *Just here. Look, there are our photographs as well.*
>
> B　**Zuótiān méi zhào xiàng a?**
> *We weren't photographed yesterday, surely?*
>
> A　**Zhào le. Yǒu hěn duō jìzhě zài nàr zhào xiàng.**
> *Yes, we were. There were lots of reporters there taking photos.*
>
> B　**Wǒ zěnme bù zhīdao a?**
> *How come I didn't know?*
>
> A　**Nǐ kàn, zhè bú shi nǐ ma? Zài nàr shuì-jiào ne!**
> *Look, isn't this you? You were sleeping!*

10.9　The verb suffix 'le'

The sentence particle **le**, as we have seen (6.5 and 10.1), shows that the general state of affairs has changed or that a certain event has taken place. When attention is focused on the *detail* of how that action was carried out, and especially when that detail takes the form of a numbered or quantified object, **-le** is attached to the verb in order to emphasise the completion of the action. So while 'sentence particle **le**' is used where the completion of *the whole process* is covered by **le**:

Tā zuótiān qu mǎi dōngxi le ma?
　　Did she go shopping yesterday?

'verb suffix **-le**' is used to emphasise the completion of *the action*:

Tā zuótiān mǎi-le shenme?
　　What did she buy yesterday?

Here are two more examples using verb suffix **le**:

Tā zuótiān mǎi-le liǎng jiàn xiǎomián'ǎo.
　　She bought two quilted jackets yesterday.

127

Tā jīnnián lái-le sān cì Lúndūn.
She has been to London three times this year.

Exercise 57: Shift of emphasis – particle 'le' versus suffix '-le'

Translate into English:

1   A: Nǐ zuótiān hē jiǔ le ma?

     B: Hē le.

     A: Nǐ hē-le jǐ píng (jiǔ)?

2   A: Nǐ qu kàn péngyou le ma?

     B: Qù le.

     A: Nǐ kàn-le jǐ ge (péngyou)?

3   A: Nǐ qù Rìběn le ma?

     B: Qù le.

     A: Nǐ zài Rìběn zhù-le jǐ tiān?

4   A: Nǐ mǎi xiǎomián'ǎo le ma?

     B: Mǎi le.

     A: Nǐ mài-le jǐ jiàn (xiǎomián'ǎo)?

5   A: Nǐ dǎ tàijíquán le ma?

     B: Dǎ le.

     A: Nǐ dǎ-le duōshao fēn zhōng (de tàijíquán)?

10.10 Hit the phone, Jack!

The verb **dǎ** means 'to hit', so **dǎ rén** means 'to hit someone'. But **dǎ** has additional uses beyond 'to hit':

dǎ diànhuà
   to make a phone call
dǎ yú
   to catch fish
dǎ zhēn
   to have/give an injection (**zhēn** = a needle)

10.11 Verbal measure words

In 9.16 we met the word **cì** (time). It is helpful to think of **cì** as a 'verbal measure word' which counts the number of times the verb takes effect:

qù liǎng cì Zhōngguó
   to go to China twice

There are a number of other verbal measure words. Here are two of them:

zhēn: dǎ èrshí zhēn
   to have/give twenty injections
tàng: qù yí tàng
   to go once (**tàng** 'a trip' and **cì** 'a time' are interchangeable here)

10.12 Yet again!

We met the adverb **yòu** in the 'both … and …' pattern (9.19). Its basic meaning is 'again', 'yet again', 'furthermore':

Tā zuótiān yòu lái le.
   He turned up yet again yesterday.

10.13 Finishing off

Wán means 'to end', 'to finish'. It can be attached to other verbs to show that the action has finished:

shuōwán
   to finish speaking
chīwán
   to finish eating

Hǎo, as we know, means 'good'. It too can be attached to certain verbs to show that the action has been completed:

zuòhǎo
> to finish doing

Fàn zuòhǎo le.
> The food is cooked (and ready to eat).

Later we shall be meeting several more verb endings similar to **wán** and **hǎo**, all of which show the result of the action initiated by the verb.

Exercise 58: Action sequences

Practise repeating these sequences, which show three stages of action:

Planning	Carrying out	Result
xiǎng chī →	zài chī →	chīwán le
(want to eat)	*(eating)*	*(finished eating)*
xiǎng kàn (bào)	zài kàn (bào)	kànwán le
xiǎng zhào (xiàng)	zài zhào (xiàng)	zhàowán le
dǎsuan kāi (huì)	zài kāi (huì)	kāiwán le

Some new words

Chángchéng	the Great Wall
zhàoxiàngjī	camera
jiāojuǎnr	film
yígòng	altogether
bǎi	a hundred
néng	can, be able
xíngli	baggage, luggage
shōushi	to pack, to put in order
zhǔnbèi	to prepare, get ready
shàng	to go to (lit: to go up to)

CONVERSATION 10C

Describing what went on before:

A   **Nǐ zuótiān dào nǎr qù le? Wǒ dǎ-le sān cì diànhuà, nǐ dōu bú zài.**
Where did you go yesterday? I phoned three times but each time you weren't there.

B   **Duìbuqǐ, wǒ qù-le yí tàng Chángchéng.**
I'm sorry, I took a trip to the Great Wall.

A   **Zěnme yòu qù Chángchéng le?**
How come you went there again?

B   **Shàng cì qù, wàng-le dài zhàoxiàngjī, méi zhào xiàng.**
Last time I went I forgot to take my camera, so I didn't get any photos.

A   **Zuótiān zhào-le hěn duō zhāng ba?**
You took lots yesterday, did you?

B   **Jiāojuǎnr dōu zhàowán le; yígòng zhào-le yìbǎi duō zhāng.**
I finished all my film; more than a hundred shots altogether.

A   **Nǐ zhēn ài zhào xiàng!**
You really like photography!

B   **Nàme hǎo de fēngjǐng, zěnme néng bú zhào?**
It's such wonderful scenery; how could I not take it?

A   **Xíngli dōu shōushihǎo le ma?**
Is your luggage all packed?

B   **Chàbuduō le. Chīwán fàn jiù zhǔnbèi shàng jīchǎng.**
More or less. When the meal is over I'll get ready to go to the airport.

10.14 Bù shūfu

Shūfu means 'comfortable' and **bù shūfu** should therefore mean 'uncomfortable'. And so it does, but **bù shūfu** has another meaning too: 'unwell', 'off colour'.

10.15 All by oneself

Yí ge rén literally means 'one person' but it is often used to mean 'all by oneself', 'all alone', 'alone and unaided':

Yí ge rén chī-le yì zhī kǎoyā.
He ate a whole roast duck himself.
Tā yí ge rén qù.
He's going alone.
Wǒ yí ge rén zuò.
I'll do it all on my own.

10.16 Three times a day

Yì tiān sān cì (one day three times) is the way to say 'three times a day'. Notice that the number of occurrences *follows* the time during which they happen. When a verb is involved, it splits the number of occurrences from the specified time:

yì tiān chī sān cì
eat three times a day
yí ge xīngqī qù liǎng tàng
go twice a week

Exercise 59

Say it in Chinese:

1 once a week

2 twice a month

3 three trips a year

4 four injections a day

10.17 Insignificant

Yàojǐn means 'important'. The negative **bú yàojǐn** 'unimportant' is often used to mean 'that doesn't matter', both in the sense of 'that's insignificant' and in the polite sense as a response to someone's apology.

Some new words

dùzi	stomach, belly
téng	to ache, hurt
tù	to vomit
zhī	(measure word for most animals)
tāng	soup
fā shāo	to have a fever/a temperature
dàifu	doctor
chī yào	to take medicine
yàopiànr	(medicinal) tablet
měi	each, every (usually followed by a measure word)
piànr	(measure word for tablets)

CONVERSATION 10D

A tourist sees the doctor:

D **Shénme dìfang bù shūfu?**
What's the problem?

T **Dùzi téng, xiǎng tù.**
My stomach aches and I feel sick.

D **Zhōngwǔ chī shénme le?**
What did you have for lunch?

T **Péngyou qǐng chī-fàn, chī-le yì zhī kǎoyā?**
A friend invited me: a whole roast duck.

D **Shénme?! Nǐ yí ge rén chī-le yì zhī kǎoyā?**
What!? You had a whole roast duck to yourself?

T **Bú shi, wǒmen sì ge rén.**
No, there were four of us.

→

D	**Hē-jiǔ le ma?**
	Did you have any alcohol?
T	**Tāmen sān ge rén hē-le liù píng píjiǔ. Wǒ zhǐ hē-le yì wǎn tāng.**
	The three of them drank six bottles of beer. I only had a bowl of soup.
D	**Nǐ méi fā shāo, bú yàojǐn, dǎ yì zhēn jiù hǎo le.**
	You aren't running a temperature, so it isn't serious. One injection and you'll be better.
T	**Éi, dàifu, wǒ zuì pà dǎ zhēn, chī yào kěyǐ ma?**
	Oh, doctor, I hate injections; could I take some medicine (instead)?
D	**Zěnme wàiguó rén dōu pà dǎ zhēn? Hǎo ba, gěi nǐ diǎnr yàopiànr, yì tiān sān cì, měi cì liǎng piànr.**
	Why is it that foreigners are all scared of injections? All right then, I'll give you some tablets; three times a day, two tablets each time.

Exercise 60: Pronunciation practice

Shéi yào qù yīyuàn, gōngyuán gēn fànguǎnr?

Wǒ yào mǎi yǎnjìngr, bèixīnr gēn jiāojuǎnr.

Exercise 61

Translate into Chinese:

1   *A*:   Hello, can I speak to Mr Lee, please?

      B: I'm sorry, he has already gone back to his country.

2   *A*:   How many phone calls did you make yesterday?

      B: One hundred and twenty-three altogether.

3   *A*:   What's the news in the paper?

      B: It says there are a lot of people going abroad this year.

4   *A*:   Have you finished eating?

      B: Not yet, I'll come when I finish my soup.

5   *A*:   Has he got a fever?

      B: 38.6°C. Shall we send for a doctor?

6   *A*:   Do you often have Chinese food?

      B: Yes, about twice a month.

Chapter 11
Arriving in China

- *At the immigration desk*
- *The customs check*
- *Being met at the airport*

11.1 To know how to

Huì means 'to know how to', 'to be able to (because of knowing how)':

Tā huì zuò kǎoyā.
> She can cook (lit: make) roast duck.

Wǒ bú huì chōu-yān, yě bú huì hē-jiǔ.
> I don't smoke or drink.

(This is a polite formula for declining a cigarette or a drink.)

11.2 Languages

In Chapter 10 we met **shuō-huà** 'to speak' (lit: to speak speech). From this root it is easy to form the names of languages:

shuō Rìběn huà
> to speak Japanese

Pǔtōnghuà is 'Universal language' (Mandarin), **Guǎngdōng huà** is 'Guangdong language' (Cantonese), and there are many other dialects in China, all of whose names are formed with **huà** in the same way.

Yǔ also means 'language' and it too can be combined with country names, though it is done in an abbreviated form:

Yīngyǔ	English
Déyǔ	German
Fǎyǔ	French
wàiyǔ	foreign language

In this style 'Chinese' is **Hànyǔ**, the language of the **Hànrén**, the majority (Chinese) people of China. **Hànyǔ** therefore does not include the languages of the many minority peoples of China. Note that **Zhōngguó huà** also refers to the language of the **Hànrén**, but it is used when thinking of that language in contrast with the languages of other countries.

11.3 A few

Apart from its function as the question word 'how many?', **jǐ** can be used without stress to mean 'a few', 'several':

Tā zhǐ yǒu ji ge Zhōngguó péngyou.
  He has only a few Chinese friends.

11.4 Before and after

Yǐqián means 'before' and **yǐhòu** 'after'. Both of them come after the words they refer to (sometimes dropping the **yǐ**):

shuì-jiào yǐqián	before going to bed
chī-fàn yǐhòu	after eating
sān tiān (yǐ)qián	three days ago/before
sān tiān (yǐ)hòu	three days afterwards/later

Yǐqián and **yǐhòu** can also stand alone as time-words
meaning 'formerly' and 'afterwards':

Tā yǐqián zài zhèr mài bào.
   He sold newspapers here formerly.

11.5 The verb suffix 'guo'

Guò means 'to go through', and as a verb suffix it means 'to
have gone through the experience of', 'to have experienced':

Tā qù-guo Zhōngguó.
   She has been to China.
Wǒ xué-guo Yīngyǔ.
   I have learned English.

The negative is formed by adding **méi** before the verb, but
note that, unlike the verb suffix **-le**, the **-guo** does not drop
off in the negative form:

Wǒ méi chī-guo Sìchuān cài.
   I've never had Szechuanese food.

The question forms are **qù-guo ma?** or **qù-guo méi you?**
'have you ever been (there)?'.

Exercise 62

Answer the questions using Chinese:

1 Yīngguó nǚwáng (*the Queen*) qù-guo
   Zhōngguó ma?

2 Bùshí (*George Bush*) zài Běijīng zhù-guo ma?

3 Dèng Xiǎopíng lái-guo Yīngguó ma?

4 Nǐ gēn Máo Zédōng shuō-guo huà ma?

11.6 Or is it …?

To ask someone to decide between two alternatives, the pattern used is **shi … háishi …**:

Tā shi Yìdàlì rén háishi Xībānyá rén?
> Is he Italian or Spanish?

Nǐ (shi) ài hē chá háishi ài hē kāfēi?
> Do you prefer tea or coffee?

Some new words

jù	(measure for speech) phrase, sentence
rùjìngkǎ	immigration card, entry card
tián	to fill in
tiánhǎo	to finish filling in
lǚyóu	to go travelling, go touring
cānjiā	to take part in, participate in
jiāoyìhuì	trade fair
yāoqǐng	to invite
yāoqǐngxìn	letter of invitation

CONVERSATION 11A

A tourist arrives at the Immigration desk and speaks to the immigration officer.

T **Nǐ hǎo! Zhè shi wǒ de hùzhào.**
> *Hello. This is my passport.*

O **Òu, nín huì shuō Zhōngguó huà a.**
> *Oh, you can speak Chinese.*

T **Zhǐ huì shuō jǐ jù.**
> *Only a few phrases.*

O **Nín de rùjìngkǎ ne? Tiánhǎo le ma?**
> *Your immigration card? Has it been filled in?*

T **Tiánhǎo le. Zài zhèr.**
> *Yes, here it is.*

O **Yǐqián lái-guo Zhōngguó ma?**
> *Have you been to China before?*

→

T	**Shí nián qián lái-guo yí cì. Zhè shi dì'èr cì.**
	I came once ten years ago. This is my second time.
O	**Zhèi cì shi lái lǚyóu háishi lái …?**
	Have you come as a tourist this time, or …?
T	**Shi lái cānjiā jiāoyìhuì.**
	I've come to take part in a trade fair.
O	**Něi ge jiāoyìhuì?**
	Which one?
T	**Tiānjin Jiāoyìhuì. Zhè shi yāoqǐngxìn.**
	The Tianjin Trade Fair. This is the invitation letter.
O	**Hǎo, xíng le.**
	OK, that's fine.
T	**Xièxie, zàijiàn.**
	Thank you. Goodbye.

11.7 The 'shi … de' construction

This useful construction allows you to pick out one
circumstance surrounding an action (the part immediately
following **shi**) for special stress. In response to the statement

Tā mǎi-le yí ge zhàoxiàngjī.
> He (has) bought a camera.

the following questions might be asked:

Tā shi zài nǎr mǎi de?
> Where did he buy it?

Tā shi shénme shíhou mǎi de?
> When did he buy it?

Tā shi gēn shéi qu mǎi de?
> With whom did he go to buy it?

Naturally enough, this pattern only operates for actions
which have already taken place.

Exercise 63

Answer the following using the information provided:

1 Yīngguó nǚwáng shi shénme shíhou dào
   Zhōngguó qù de? (*October 1986*)

2 Zhèi píng jiǔ shi zài nǎr mǎi de? (*Hong Kong*)

3 Tā shi zěnme lái de? (*by air*)

4 Tā shi qùnián jǐ yuè zǒu de? (*July*)

11.8   Verb + result

In 10.13 we met **wán** and **hǎo** as verb endings which give the
result of the verb's action. **Kāi**, 'to open', is another such
ending, used to show that as a result of the verb's action
something has been opened:

dǎkāi mén
  to open the door
Qǐng nǐ dǎkāi xíngli.
  Please open your bags.

Exercise 64

Fill in the blanks with 'results':

1 Wǒ yǐjing mǎi ... dōngxi le. (*to have done the
   shopping*)

2 Hóng de yǐjing mài ... le. (*to be sold out*)

3 Biǎo yǐjing tián ... le. (*to have completed*)

4 Zhèi píng jiǔ méi you dǎ ... . (*to be open*)

11.9 Of course

Dāngrán is an adverb meaning 'of course'. Unlike other adverbs we have met, it does not have to be placed immediately before the verb:

Tā dāngrán zhīdao wǒ shi shéi.
Of course he knows who I am.
Dāngrán wǒmen yīnggāi wènwen tā.
Of course we should ask him (about it).

11.10 That old pal of mine

When a possessive is used with specifying words like **nèi** or **zhèi** it goes at the front of the phrase, not behind as in English:

wǒ nèi wèi péngyou
that friend of mine
tā zhèi píng jiǔ
this bottle of wine of his

11.11 To be 'into'

The verb **gǎo** means 'to be engaged in', 'to get up to', 'to work as', 'to be in':

gǎo dìzhì
to do geology
gǎo xīnwén de
(lit: one who does journalism) journalist

Some new words

jiǎnchá	to inspect, examine
tiáo	(measure for cartons of cigarettes)
wēishìjì	whisky
bāor	parcel, package
lǐwù	present, gift
kuài	(measure) 'lump of'
shítou	stone, rock, pebble

142

CONVERSATION 11B

A tourist has his luggage inspected by a customs officer.

T **Shi zài zhèr jiǎnchá xíngli ma?**
Is this where the luggage is examined?

O **Shì. Éi, nǐ de Zhōngguó huà bú cuò a. Shi zài nǎr xué de?**
Yes. Hey, your Chinese is pretty good. Where did you learn it?

T **Zài Yīngguó xué de.**
In Britain.

O **Dài yān, jiǔ le ma?**
Have you brought any tobacco or alcohol?

T **Dài-le liǎng tiáo yān, yì píng wēishìjì.**
I've got two cartons of cigarettes and a bottle of whisky.

O **Shi zài nǎr mǎi de?**
Where were they bought?

T **Fēijī shang.**
On the plane.

O **Zhè bāor li shi shénme dōngxi?**
What's in this parcel?

T **Gěi péngyou de lǐwù, yí kuài shítou.**
A present for a friend. A rock.

O **Shítou? Dǎkāi kànkan kěyǐ ma?**
A rock? Will you open it (for me) to have a look?

T **Dāngrán kěyǐ. Wǒ zhèi wèi péngyou shi gǎo dìzhì de, jiù xǐhuan shítou.**
Of course. This friend of mine is in geology. He just loves rocks.

11.12 Multi-functional words

Dàibiǎo can be a verb meaning 'to represent', or a noun meaning 'a representative':

Tā shi Yīngguó dàibiǎo.
>   She is the British representative.

Tā dàibiǎo Yīngguó dào Rìběn qu kāi huì.
>   He is going to Japan to represent Britain at a conference.

Many other Chinese words have more than one function like this.

11.13 Transport delayed

When a scheduled train, bus or flight is delayed it is said to be **wǎn-diǎn** 'behind (scheduled) time'.

11.14 For a long time

Jiǔ means 'a long while', 'for a long while':

Tā zài Shànghǎi zhù-le hěn jiǔ.
>   He lived in Shanghai for a long while.

11.15 This many so far

The sentence **Tā zài Zhōngguó zhù-le sān nián** means 'He lived in China for three years'. With another **le** added to the end of the same sentence the meaning changes:

Tā zài Zhōngguó zhù-le sān nián le.
>   He has been living in China for three years.

The use of both verb suffix **-le** and particle **le** with a numbered object shows that the action of the verb has continued up to a certain time. That time might be past, present or future, so there are two other possible translations of the double **le** sentence: 'He had been living …' and 'He will have been living …'.

... chōu-le wǔ zhī yān le.
    ... has smoked five cigarettes (so far).
... wèn-le bā ge rén le.
    ... had asked eight people (up to then).

Exercise 65: So far

Translate into English:

1   Tā zài Shànghǎi zhù-le sān nián le.

2   Wǒmen xué-le liǎng nián Hànyǔ le.

3   Tā yǐjing mǎi-le shí jiàn dàbèixīnr le.

4   Tā yǐjing shuō-le wǔ ge xiǎoshí le.

5   Wǒ yǐjing zhào-le liǎng bǎi zhāng le.

11.16 This having been done

To show that one action was completed before another began or begins, **-le** is used as a suffix attached to the first verb:

Wǒ <u>chī-le</u> fàn jiù qù.
    I will go when I've eaten. [<u>Having eaten</u> I will go.]
Wǒ <u>chī-le</u> fàn jiù qù le.
    I went when I'd eaten. [<u>Having eaten</u> I then went.]

11.17 Just so long as you've ...

Jiù hǎo le tacked on to the end of a remark gives the idea of 'that's all that matters', 'then everything's OK':

Dào-le jiù hǎo le.
    Just so long as you've got here.
Wǒ huì shuō Zhōngguó huà jiù hǎo le.
    (If) I could speak Chinese that would be great.

11.18 Good to eat

Phrases such as 'good to eat' are easily formed in Chinese:

hǎo-chī good to eat, delicious
hǎo-kàn good to look at, good-looking, pretty

Tīng means 'to listen to', and **hǎo-tīng** therefore means 'good to listen to', 'pleasant sounding'. On the same basis, **róngyi** 'easy' can be added to **dǒng** 'to understand' to make **róngyi-dǒng** 'easy to understand', 'easily understood'.

11.19 Soon

Kuài means 'fast', as we saw in 7.7. It has a secondary meaning of 'soon':

kuài èrshi nián le
    it will soon be twenty years
kuài wǔ diǎn le
    it's nearly 5 o'clock

11.20 Multi-functional again

Another word which can be either verb or noun (see 11.12) is **gōngzuò** 'to work' or 'work':

Tā hěn xǐhuan gōngzuò.
    She loves to work.
Tā hěn xǐhuan tā de gōngzuò.
    She loves her job.

11.21 City wall

In 5.18 we met **Chénghuáng**, the City God. **Chéng** means a defensive wall, and comes to mean 'city' because important cities were walled until very recent times. The expression **jìn chéng** 'to enter the city', 'to go into town', derives from 'to go inside the wall'.

11.22 Verb after verb

Whole series of verbal expressions can succeed each other in Chinese, provided they are in a logical sequence:

Tā <u>dàibiǎo Yīngguó</u> <u>dào Rìběn</u> <u>qù</u> <u>kāi huì</u>.
He's going to Japan to represent Britain at a conference.
Wǒ děi <u>jiē tā</u> <u>qù yīyuàn</u> <u>kàn tā àiren</u>.
I have to meet him to take him to the hospital to see his wife.

Exercise 66

Make a meaningful sentence from each jumbled set below, remembering that the general word order is subject-time-place-action.

1 A qù Zhōngguó
   B míngnián
   C tāmen
   D lǚyóu

2 A zài fànguǎnr
   B wǒmen
   C zuótiān
   D hē-le sān píng píjiǔ

3 A kāi huì
   B xīngqī liù
   C wǒmen
   D zái Běijīng Fàndiàn

4 A dào Měiguó qù
   B tāmen
   C wǔ yuè bā hào
   D liúxué

5 A jìn chéng qù
   B míngtiān
   C mǎi dōngxi
   D shéi

11.23 To heed

Tīng, as we saw above, means 'to listen to'. Like the English 'He won't listen to my advice', **tīng** has the extended meaning of 'to heed', 'to go along with':

Tīng nǐ de ānpái.
I'll go along with your arrangements.

Some new words

shíyóu	petroleum, oil
Shíyóubù	Ministry of Petroleum
gàosu	to tell, inform
qíshí	actually, in fact
búguò	however, but
yìzhí	(of time) all along
lèi	tired
sòng	to escort, see someone to
bīnguǎn	guest-house, hotel
yíqiè	everything, in everything

CONVERSATION 11C

Dr Jones is met at the airport by Mr Wang.

W   **Excuse me, are you Dr Jones?**

J   **Yes. Nín shi …?**
Yes. You are …?

W   **Wǒ xìng Wáng, dàibiǎo Shíyóubù lai huānyíng nín.**
My name is Wang, I've come to welcome you on behalf of the Petroleum Ministry.

J   **Xièxie, xièxie. Fēijī wǎn-diǎn le. Nín děng-le hěn jiǔ le ba?**
Thank you very much. The plane was delayed. You must have been waiting for a long while?

W   **Méi shìr. Nín dào-le jiù hǎo le. Tāmen méi gàosu wǒ nín huì shuō Zhōngguó huà.**
It doesn't matter. The main thing is that you have arrived. They didn't tell me you could speak Chinese.

J   **Zhǐ huì shuō ji jù. Wáng xiānsheng de Běijīng huà zhēn hǎo-tīng, yě róngyi-dǒng.**
I can only say a few words. Your Beijing accent sounds wonderful, and it's easy to understand too.

W **Shi ma? Qíshí wǒ shi Shànghǎi rén, búguò zài Běijīng zhù-le kuài èrshi nián le.**
Really? Actually I'm Shanghainese, but I've lived in Beijing for nearly twenty years now.

J **Yìzhí dōu zài Shíyóubù gōngzuò ma?**
Have you always worked in the Petroleum Ministry?

W **Shi a. Nín yídìng lèi le ba. Wǒ xiān sòng nín jìn chéng dào bīnguǎn xiūxi ba.**
Yes. You must be tired. I'll see you into town to your guest-house for a rest first of all.

J **Hǎo, yíqiè tīng nín de ānpái.**
Fine, I'll do whatever you've arranged.

Exercise 67

Translate into Chinese:

1 How long have you been studying English?
   About ten years, but I still can't speak it.

2 When do you practise taichi?
   Just before I go to bed.

3 Have you ever been to Japan?
   Yes, I used to go there once a year.

4 Will you do it or will he?
   We'll do whatever you say.

5 Is he coming to the meeting?
   No, he phoned and asked me to let you know that he can't come.

6 There are no buses today. How did you come?
   I came by taxi.

Chapter 12
New friends, old friends

- *A formal introduction*
- *Talking about an acquaintance*
- *Meeting an old friend*

12.1 'lái'

Lái has the basic meaning 'to come':

Lái, lái, lái, nǐ lai kànkan!
  Come over here and have a look!

Sometimes, though, **lái** is used as a substitute for other verbs with more specific meanings, rather as English uses 'do':

Tā bú huì zuò, wǒ lái.
  He can't do it, let me have a go.
Zài lái yí ge.
  Bring another one; 'Encore!'

12.2 Another verbal measure

The verbal measure words we have met so far are **cì** (see 9.16), **zhēn** and **tàng** (see 10.11). Another one is **xiàr**, which gives a sense of little time being expended on the verb:

Qǐng nǐ wèn yí xiàr.
> Please make a little enquiry.

Qǐng nǐ děng yí xiàr.
> Please wait a bit.

Tián yí xiàr biǎo.
> Just fill in the form.

Dǎ-le wǔ xiàr.
> Hit five times.

12.3 The adverb 'gāng'

Gāng means 'just', 'a moment ago':

Tā gāng zǒu.
> He has just gone.

Gāng liù diǎn.
> It's just six o'clock.

12.4 The bureau

Jú is a word meaning 'a bureau', 'an office'. It usually appears in combinations such as:

Gōngānjú
> Public Security Bureau (Police)

Lǚyóujú
> Tourist Bureau

Zhǎng means 'the head of an organisation or department':

júzhǎng
> bureau chief; director

Shíyóubù Bùzhǎng
> Minister for Petroleum

12.5   The manner of its doing

To comment on the way in which an action is performed, Chinese links the comment to the action verb with the marker **de:**

Tā zǒu de hěn kuài.
> He walks very quickly. (lit: He walks in a way that is very quick.)

Tā xué de hěn bù hǎo.
> He learns very badly.

The marker **de** in this pattern must come immediately after the verb, so that if an object has to be mentioned it is necessary to state it first, with or without stating the verb before it:

Tā (chī-)fàn chī de hěn kuài.
> He eats his food very quickly.

Exercise 68

Answer the following using the information provided, as in the example:

Tā Yīngyǔ shuō de zěnmeyàng? (*very beautifully*)

Tā Yīngyǔ shuō de hěn piàoliang.

1   Tā Hànyǔ xué de zěnmeyàng? (*very fast*)

2   Tā cài zuò de zěnmeyàng? (*extremely well*)

3   Nǐ zuótiān shuì-jiào shuì de zěnmeyàng? (*not very well*)

4   Tā zhào xiàng zhào de zěnmeyàng? (*very beautifully*)

12.6   Where did you get that idea?

We met **nǎr?** 'where?' in Chapter 5 (5.2 and 5.3). A variant form of **nǎr** is **nálǐ**, and **nálǐ** is often used as a polite self-deprecating response to praise or flattery, as much as to say 'Wherever did you get that idea?' 'How could that be the case?':

Nín zhèi ge cài zuò de zhēn hǎo.
> You've cooked this dish beautifully.

Náli, náli.
> I wish I had!

12.7 'duō?' = how?

Duō cháng? means 'how long?' and **duō** can be used with other adjectives in the same way:

duō dà?
> how big?

duō guì?
> how expensive?

12.8 Over the measure

Sān nián means 'three years'. To say 'more than three years' **duō** ('more/many/much') is used:

sān nián duō
> three years and a bit (but less than four)

but note:

sānshi duō nián
> over 30 (but less than 40) years

12.9 More results

In 10.13 and 11.8 we met result endings such as **wán**, **hǎo** and **kāi**. Here are two more, **cuò** showing that something results in an error, and **duì** showing that the result is correct:

shuōcuò
> to say something wrong, to mispronounce

zuòduì
> to do something right

12.10 Doing nothing but ...

We met **zhǐ** 'only' in 4.12. Note the following use as the first part of a negative sentence:

zhǐ shuō bú zuò
> just talking, not doing (i.e. All you're doing is talking, not getting on with things.)

zhǐ kàn bù chī
> just looking at it, not eating it

12.11 Toasting

The verb **jìng** means 'to respect', 'to salute', and it is often used when toasting someone:

Wǒ jìng nǐ (yì bēi)!
> Here's to you! Your health!

Some new words

jièshào	to introduce
gāoxìng	happy, delighted
liúlì	fluent
gōngfu	free/available time
liànxí	to practise
màn	slow
zìjǐ	self, oneself

CONVERSATION 12A

Mr Wang introduces Mr Young.

W   Lái, lái, lái, wǒ gěi nǐmen jièshào yí xiàr. Zhè wèi shì Léikè Gōngsī de Yáng dàibiǎo, gāng cóng Yīngguó lái. Zhè wèi shì Lǚyóujú de Lǐ Júzhǎng.

Come on, I'll introduce you. This is Mr Young, the representative of the Laker Company. He's just come from Britain. This is Bureau Chief Lee of the Tourist Bureau.

Y **Nín hǎo! Rènshi nín hěn gāoxìng.**
How do you do. I'm very pleased to know you.

L **Nín hǎo! Nín Hànyǔ shuō de zhēn liúlì.**
How do you do. Your Chinese is really fluent.

Y **Náli! Shuō de bù hǎo.**
I'm afraid not, I don't speak it well.

L **Xué-le duō cháng shíjiān le?**
How long have you been learning?

Y **Yì nián duō le. Méi gōngfu liànxi, xué de tài màn le.**
Over a year. I have no time to practise, so I learn too slowly.

L **Bú màn! Wǒ xué-le shí nián Yīngyǔ le, hái chángcháng shuōcuò.**
That's not slow. I've been learning English for ten years and still often get it wrong.

W **Éi, nǐmen zěnme zhǐ shuō-huà, bù hē-jiǔ? Lái, zài lái yì bēi. Wǒ jìng nǐmen: gānbēi!**
Hey, how come you're just talking and not drinking? Come on, have another glass. A toast to you both: Cheers!

Y/L **Gānbēi!**
Cheers!

W **Lái, chī diǎnr dōngxi. Jīntiān diǎnxin zuò de bú cuò.**
Come on, have something to eat. The titbits are pretty good today.

Y/L **Hǎo, wǒmen zìjǐ lái.**
Fine, we'll help ourselves.

12.12 Verb suffix 'zhe' (1)

The suffix **-zhe** is attached to activity verbs to indicate that the action is prolonged rather than over in one fell swoop:

Qǐng zuò.
Please sit down.
Qǐng zuò-zhe.
Please remain seated.
Qǐng nǐ tì wǒ ná yì bēi jiǔ.
Please take a glass of wine for me.
Qǐng nǐ tì wǒ ná-zhe zhèi bēi jiǔ.
Please hold this glass of wine for me. (**ná** = 'to take')

12.13 Verb suffix 'zhe' (2)

Another function of **-zhe** is to attach to a verb in subordinate position, giving the meaning 'When it comes to …', 'So far as … is concerned':

Tā kàn-zhe xiàng Rìběn rén.
When you come to look at him, he's like a Japanese.
Zhè ge cài chī-zhe hǎo-chī, kàn-zhe bù hǎo-kàn.
This dish isn't nice to look at, but it's good to eat.

Exercise 69

Translate into English:

1 Shéi zài mén wàitou zuò-zhe?

2 Tā chuān-zhe shénme?

3 Tā ná-zhe shéi de fēijī piào?

4 Tā děng-zhe nǐ ne.

5 Tā kàn-zhe hěn shòu.

12.14 To graduate

Bìyè literally means 'finish the course' and nicely translates 'to graduate', but it is used more widely in Chinese than in English, because it is not confined to universities:

xiǎoxué bìyè
to finish junior school

zhōngxué bìyè
  to finish middle school
dàxué bìyè
  to graduate from university

12.15 I used to think that …

The verb **yǐwéi** means 'to think', but it is usually used in the
sense 'I thought so, but now I know I was wrong':

Wǒ yǐwéi tā shi Déguó rén.
  I thought he was German (but he's actually …)
Wǒmen yǐwéi nǐ bù lái le.
  We thought you wouldn't come (but here you are).

12.16 Getting married

Jié-hūn is 'to marry':

Tāmen míngtiān zài Běijīng jié-hūn.
  They are getting married in Beijing tomorrow.

Jié-hūn is a verb + object construction, and 'X marries Y'
is **X gēn Y jié-hūn**.

Wáng xiáojie bù xiǎng gēn Lǎo Lǐ jié-hūn le.
  Miss Wang no longer wants to get married to Old Lee.

Some new words

shǒu	hand
jiǔbēi	wine glass
jiāo-shū	to teach
érzi	son
nǚ'ér	daughter
tóngxué	fellow student

CONVERSATION 12B

That person over there looks interesting. Young Zhang talks to Mr B:

B   **Ēi, Xiǎo Zhāng, nèi wèi chuān-zhe hóng mián'ǎo de xiáojie shi shéi?**
Hey, Young Zhang, who's that girl wearing the red jacket?

Z   **Něi wèi? Shi shǒu shang ná-zhe jiǔbēi de nèi wèi ma?**
Which one? That one with a wine glass in her hand?

B   **Bú shi, shì zài nàr zuò-zhe de nèi wèi.**
No, that one seated over there.

Z   **Òu, tā a, wǒ rènshi, xìng Liú.**
Oh, her. I know her, she's called Liu.

B   **Tā kàn-zhe xiàng Zhōngguó rén, kěshi Yīngyǔ zěnme shuō de nàme piàoliang a?**
She looks like a Chinese, but how come she speaks English so marvellously?

Z   **Tā shi Yīngguó huáqiáo. Lúndūn Dàxué bìyè yǐhòu, jiù dào Zhōngguó jiāo-shū lái le.**
She's an overseas Chinese from Britain. After graduating from London University she came to China to teach.

B   **Nǐ shi zěnme rènshi tā de?**
How did you get to know her?

Z   **Wǒ érzi gēn tā nǚ'ér tóngxué.**
My son and her daughter are in the same school.

B   **Òu, tā yǐjing yǒu nǚ'ér le, wǒ hái yǐwéi …**
Oh, she's already got a daughter. I was still under the impression that …

Z   **Yǐwéi tā méi jié-hūn, shì bu shi?**
You thought she wasn't married yet, right?

12.17 Yet more result verbs

Two verbs which we have met before can also be added to other verbs to show result: **jiàn** 'to see', 'to perceive', and **dào** 'to reach', 'to get as far as'.

kànjiàn   to see (lit: look at-see. The expression 'to have a look-see' has come into English from Chinese through Pidgin English)

xiǎngdào   to expect, anticipate (think so far as to get to this point)

Exercise 70

Fill in blanks with result verbs, as in the example:

Action	*Action + result*
Kàn, shānshang yǒu rén.	Zài nǎr? À, wǒ kàn<u>jiàn</u> le. Zài nàr!
1 Tīng, fēijī lái le.	Shì ma? À, wǒ tīng(…) le. Zhēn de lái le.
2 Shuō, nǐ hái xiǎng shuō shénme?	Méi you le. Wǒ yǐjing shuō(…) le.
3 Chī le ma?	Chī-le yì diǎnr, méi chī(…).
4 Qù mǎi le ma?	Qù le, kěshi méi mǎi(…).

12.18 Long time no see

The English expression 'long time no see' is actually a literal translation from the idiomatic Chinese **hǎo jiǔ bú jiàn** 'very long time no see', 'haven't seen you for ages'. Note the word order: when time has elapsed while something has *not* been happening, the period of time is placed *before* the verb.

Hěn jiǔ méi kànjiàn nǐ le.
   Not seen you for a long time.
Sān nián méi chī Zhōngguó fàn le.
   Haven't had Chinese food for three years.
Liǎng ge xīngqī méi kàn bào le.
   Haven't read a newspaper for two weeks.

Remember that when something *does* go on for a length of time, the length of time goes *after* the verb:

Chī-le sān nián Zhōngguó fàn.
   Had Chinese food for three years.

Exercise 71

Translate into English:

	Time duration	Time elapsed
1	xué-le sān nián	sān nián méi xué
2	tīng-le liǎng tiān	liǎng tiān méi tīng
3	liànxí-le sān ge yuè	sān ge yuè méi liànxí
4	xià-le wǔ ge xīngqī yǔ	wǔ ge xīngqī méi xià-yǔ

12.19 'shēntǐ'

Shēntǐ literally means 'the body', but it also means 'health'. It would be odd to translate **Tā shēntǐ hěn hǎo** as 'He has a good body'; it normally means 'He's very healthy'.

12.20 All things considered

The expression **hái kěyǐ** means 'passable'. In the same way **hái hǎo** and **hái bú cuò** mean 'not bad'. **Hái** imparts a slightly grudgingly conceded approval.

12.21 Away on business

Chūchāi is a verb + object expression meaning 'to be away on official business', 'to be on a business trip':

chū-le sān cì chāi
    was away three times on business

12.22 To see one another

Jiànmiàn is another verb + object (lit: see face (**miàn**)), but it works rather differently in that it needs **gēn** if it is to take an object:

gēn Lǎo Lǐ jiànmiàn
    to meet with Old Lee

12.23 To be in the role of

Dāng means 'to serve as', 'to be in the position of', 'to be in the role of':

Tā xiǎng dāng lǎoshī.
    She wants to be a teacher.
Tā kuài dāng bàba le.
    He'll soon be a father. (**bàba** = papa)

12.24 Comparison

We saw in 9.4 that a straightforward comparison can be modified with **yìdiǎnr** 'a little bit':

X bǐ Y kuài yìdiǎnr.
    X is a bit faster than Y.

The same kind of comparison can be modified with **duō le** 'a lot':

X bǐ Y dà duō le.

   X is a lot bigger than Y.

And further modification can be achieved by using a number and measure:

X bǐ Y guì sān kuài qián.

   X is three yuan more than Y.

Exercise 72

Make sentences expressing degree of comparison, as in the example:

Lǎo Wáng 32 suì, Xiǎo Lǐ 28 suì.

Lǎo Wáng bǐ Xiǎo Lǐ dà sì suì.

1   Lǎo Wáng chuān 40 hào de, Xiǎo Lǐ chuān 36 hào de.

2   Tā de biǎo 8.15, nǐ de biǎo 8.10.

3   Tā yǒu 200 ge, tā érzi yǒu 150 ge.

4   Yú mài wǔ kuài qián, jī mài bā kuài qián.

12.25 One after another

Měi, as we saw in Chapter 10, means 'each', 'every', so **měi tiān** means 'every day'. Another way to say 'every day' is **tiāntiān**; that is, the idea of 'every' can be shown by doubling the measure word:

Tā niánnián dōu lái.

   He comes every year.

Gègè dōu piàoliang.

   Every one is beautiful.

Note that it is common for the adverb **dōu** to be used with these doubled forms, and **dōu** must come after, not before, the doubling.

12.26 Simply must

To convey the idea 'simply must', Chinese often uses a double negative construction:

Bú qù bù xíng.
    simply must go (lit: if don't go, won't do)
Bú gěi bù xíng.
    just have to give

12.27 'dōu' = even

The adverb **dōu** has many uses. We have met it meaning 'all', 'both', and we saw in 12.25 above that it reinforces a doubled measure word. Another use is to give the meaning 'even':

Zhème dà de xīnwén, tā dōu bù zhīdao.
    He doesn't even know such an important piece of news as this.

Again **dōu** must come after, not before, the words it refers to (**zhème dà de xīnwén**).

Some new words

pèngjiàn	to bump into, to meet
zuìjìn	recently
fù	assistant, vice-, deputy
fù júzhǎng	deputy bureau chief
fù dàibiǎo	assistant representative
zhìshǎo	at least
gōngjīn	kilogram

CONVERSATION 12C

Meeting an old friend

L   **Èi, Lǎo Zhāng, hǎo jiǔ bú jiàn!**
Hey, Old Zhang, long time no see.

Z   **Shì nǐ a, Xiǎo Lǐ. Méi xiǎngdào zài zhèr pèngjiàn le.**
Oh, it's you, Young Lee. I didn't expect to bump into you here.

L   **Zuìjìn shēntǐ zěnmeyàng?**
How's your health been recently?

Z   **Hái kěyǐ. Hěn jiǔ méi kànjiàn nǐ le. Chūchāi le ma?**
It's OK. Haven't seen you for ages. Have you been away on business?

L   **Dào Shēnzhèn qù le bàn nián.**
Went to Shenzhen for six months.

Z   **Nà hǎo a. Zài Shēnzhèn pèngjiàn Wáng Jiànhuá le ba?**
That's great. You must have met Wang Jianhua in Shenzhen, I suppose?

L   **Wǒmen měi ge xīngqī dōu jiànmiàn. Tā dāng le fù júzhǎng le.**
We met every week. He's become an assistant bureau chief.

Z   **Shì ma? Rén hái shi lǎo yàngzi ma?**
Really? Is he still the same?

L   **Bǐ yǐqián pàng duō le; zhìshǎo pàng-le èrshi gōngjīn.**
Much fatter than before; at least 20 kilos heavier.

Z   **Hái nàme ài hē-jiǔ ma?**
Is he still as fond of drinking?

L   **Dāng-le fù júzhǎng, tiāntiān yǒu rén qǐng chī-fàn. Tā xiǎng bù hē dōu bù xíng!**
Since becoming assistant bureau chief, he gets invited out to dinner every day. He has no choice but to drink!

Exercise 73

Translate into Chinese:

1   He looks very tired this morning.

Yes, he didn't sleep very well last night.

2   Does she cook fish well?

She doesn't often cook fish. I'll do it.

3   Your spoken Chinese is excellent.

Far from it. I often make mistakes.

4   What is he holding in his hand?

It must be his passport.

5   We haven't had any chicken for three months.

All right, I'll go and buy one straight away.

6   Which T-shirt is more expensive: the yellow one or the blue one?

The blue one is $2 more than the yellow one.

Chapter 13
Asking for it

- *Making an international call and sending a fax*
- *An invitation to dinner*
- *Changing money*

13.1 Dialling up

Bō is the verb used for 'to dial' on a telephone:

zhí bō	to dial direct
bō (diànhuà) hàomǎ	to dial a (phone) number

13.2 Xiān ... zài ...

Xiān 'first' and **zài** 'next' are used to show the sequence of events. Both these words are adverbs which must be placed before verbs:

Wǒmen xiān qù Shànghǎi, zài qù Guǎngzhōu.
    We'll go to Shanghai first, and then to Guangzhou.

Exercise 74: Revision

How do you ...? Translate into English:

1   Qù huǒchēzhàn zěnme zǒu?

2   Zhèi ge cài zěnme zuò?

3   Zhèi ge dōngxi zěnme yòng?

4   Wèishēngjiān de mén zěnme kāi?

5   'Cheers!' Zhōngguó huà zěnme shuō?

6   Běijīng zěnme zhí bō?

13.3   To tell a fact

Gàosu means 'to tell a fact', 'to tell something'. In English the same word 'tell' is also used for 'to tell someone to do something', but Chinese does not then use **gàosu**. Note carefully the difference between the following:

Tā gàosu wǒ tā xìng Wáng.
   He told me he is called Wang.
Tā jiào wǒ lai kàn nǐ.
   He told me to come to see you.

13.4   Āiyā!

This is the most commonly heard exclamation. It is generally, but not always, used when something unpleasant happens like 'My goodness!', 'Oh dear!', 'Oh!' in English:

Āiyā, wǒ wàng-le dài hùzhào!
   Oh dear, I've forgotten to bring my passport!

13.5   To hit or not to hit?

'To make a telephone call' is **dǎ diànhuà** (lit: to hit the electric speech – see 10.10). The same verb **dǎ** is used in the expression **dǎ diànbào** 'to send a telegram' (lit: to hit the

167

electric report). But the newer expression **chuánzhēn** 'facsimile, fax' does not use **dǎ** but instead **fā** 'to send out'. So 'to send a fax' is **fā chuánzhēn**.

13.6 Machines and gadgets

Chuánzhēn is a fax, and 'a fax machine' is **chuánzhēnjī**. **Jī** 'machine' is added to many other words to indicate the physical machine/gadget/set. Thus:

zhàoxiàng	to photograph	**zhàoxiàngjī**	a camera
diànhuà	the telephone	**diànhuàjī**	a telephone
fēi	flying	**fēijī**	an aircraft
zǒng	general	**zǒngjī**	the switch-board

13.7 Trouble

The word **máfan** means 'trouble' or 'troublesome':

Nǐ shì bu shi yào zhǎo máfan?
    Are you looking for trouble?
Zuò Zhōngguó cài hěn máfan.
    Cooking Chinese food takes a lot of trouble.

Máfan is also a verb meaning 'to trouble', 'to bother', 'to inconvenience'. It is often used as a polite request, rather like the English 'Could I trouble you to …?'.

Máfan nǐ tì wǒ mǎi yì zhāng piào, hǎo ma?
    Could I bother you to buy a ticket for me?

Some new words

zǒngjī	switchboard, 'operator'
guójì	international
guójì diànhuà	international phone call
guójì (diànhuà)tái	international exchange
fāngbiàn	convenient
fúwù	to serve; service
zhōngxīn	a centre

CONVERSATION 13A

A hotel guest asks the switchboard operator about international phone calls.

S **Wéi, nǐ hǎo!**
   Hello!
G **Wéi, zǒngjī, qǐng wèn guójì diànhuà zěnme dǎ?**
   Hello, operator, could you tell me how to make an international call?
S **Hén fāngbiàn. Nín kěyǐ zài fángjiān zhí bō.**
   It's very convenient. You can dial direct from your room.
G **Shì ma?**
   Really?
S **Nín xiān bō guójìtái líng líng, zài bō nín yào de hàomǎ, jiù xíng le.**
   You first dial zero zero for the international exchange, then dial the number you want, and that's it.
G **Hǎo. Nǐ néng gàosu wǒ xiànzài Lúndūn jǐ diǎn zhōng ma?**
   Fine. Can you tell me what the time is in London now?
S **Lúndūn bǐ Shànghǎi wǎn bā xiǎoshí, xiànzài tāmen shi wǎnshang qī diǎn.**
   London is eight hours behind Shanghai: it's 7pm for them now.
G **Āiyā, tài wǎn le. Gōngsī xià-bān le. Nà ... wǒ zhǐ néng fā chuánzhēn le. Zhèr yǒu chuánzhēnjī ma?**
   Oh dear, it's too late. The office will have closed for the night. In that case ... I'll just have to send a fax. Do you have a fax machine here?
S **Yǒu, zài èr lóu fúwù zhōngxīn, èrshisì xiǎoshí dōu kāi.**
   Yes, it's in the business centre on the second floor and is open 24 hours.
G **Hǎo, máfan nǐ le.**
   Fine, sorry to trouble you.
S **Bú kèqi.**
   You're welcome.

13.8 Formal group names

We saw in 12.4 that **jú** means 'bureau' (as in **lǚyóujú** 'tourist
bureau'). A similar word is **chù** 'office', as in the term
wàishìchù 'foreign affairs office'. Yet another is **tuán** 'group', as
in **lǚyóutuán** 'a tourist group' and **dàibiǎotuán** 'a delegation'.

13.9 Leadership

Lǐngdǎo is another multi-functional word. It is a verb
meaning 'to lead', but it is also a noun meaning 'leadership',
'the leaders', 'the head'.

13.10 Polite address

Nín is a polite way of saying 'you', as we saw in 2.1. When
addressing more than one person politely it is common to use
the expression **nín jǐ wèi** (lit: you several gentlemen/ladies)
or **nín sān wèi** (you three gentlemen/ladies), etc.

13.11 'yìsi'

Yìsi means 'meaning', 'idea':

Wǒ bù dǒng zhèi jù huà de yìsi.
   I don't understand the meaning of this sentence.

Yìsi also means 'a token of affection', 'a mark of appreciation',
'a symbol of gratitude'. When giving someone a gift it is
polite to make light of it by saying:

Zhèi shi wǒ de yì diǎnr xiǎo yìsi.
   This is (just) a small mark of appreciation.

13.12 Just in the act of

To show that some action is happening or going on right
now, Chinese uses **zhèngzài** 'just ...ing', often adding **ne**
at the end of the sentence:

Tā zhèngzài dǎ diànhuà ne.
   She's telephoning.
Wǒmen zhèngzài chī-fàn ne.
   We're having dinner.

Exercise 75: Tā zhèngzài gànmá ne?

What's he doing at this very moment? Finish the following
sentences:

1   Tā zhèngzài (*drinking*).

2   Tā zhèngzài (*sleeping*).

3   Tā zhèngzài zìyóu shìchǎng (*shopping*).

4   Tā zhèngzài (*learning Chinese*).

13.13 That's settled!

Shuō 'to say', plus the result ending **dìng** 'fix', means
'to settle', 'to agree':

Shíjiān shuōdìng le, dìfang hái méi shuōdìng.
   The time is settled, but the place hasn't been agreed yet.

13.14 To dispatch

Pài means 'to send out', 'to dispatch', 'to deploy' people or
perhaps transport:

Qǐng nǐmen pài rén lái kànkan.
   Please send someone to have a look.
Wǒ pài chē qu jiē nǐ.
   I'll send a car to meet you.

Some new words

dùn	measure word for 'a meal'
biǎoshì	to express/show (feelings)
xīcān	Western food
xīcāntīng	restaurant serving Western food
Zhōngcān	Chinese food
Zhōngcāntīng	restaurant serving Chinese food
sòng	to send, deliver [further meaning of the word we met in Chapter 11]
qǐngtiě	invitation card

CONVERSATION 13B

A British delegation phones to invite the heads of the Chinese host unit to dinner.

H   **Wéi, Wàishìchù Lǐ chùzhǎng ma? Wǒ shi Yīngguó dàibiǎotuán de Hán Sēn.**
Hello, is that Mr Lee, the Head of the Foreign Affairs Office? This is Hansen of the British delegation.

L   **À, Hán Sēn xiānsheng, nǐ hǎo!**
Oh, Mr Hansen, how are you?

H   **Nǐ hǎo! Lǐ chùzhǎng, wǒmen tuánzhǎng xiǎng qǐng nín gēn júli de lǐngdǎomen chī dùn fàn. Bù zhīdao nín ji wèi shénme shíhou yǒu gōngfu?**
Hello. Mr Lee, the head of our delegation would like to invite you and the heads of your office to a meal. I wonder when you would all be free?

L   **Nǐmen bú yào kèqi le.**
No need to be so polite!

H   **Bú shi kèqi. Wǒmen yídìng yào biǎoshì yì diǎnr yìsi. Hòutiān wǎnshang fāngbiàn ma?**
This isn't out of politeness. We certainly must show how grateful we are. Would the evening of the day after tomorrow be convenient?

L   **Tāmen ji wèi lǐngdǎo zhèngzài kāi huì. Wǒ qu
    wèn yi xiàr. Qǐng nín děng yi deng … Wéi,
    hòutiān wǎnshang kěyǐ.**
    *The leaders are in a meeting. I'll go and ask them.
    Please hang on … Hello, that evening is OK.*

H   **Hǎo jíle. Nà, wǒmen jiù shuōdìng hòutiān
    wǎnshang liù diǎn bàn zài Guójì Fàndiàn liù
    lóu xīcāntīng.**
    *Super. So, we'll settle on the day after tomorrow,
    6.30pm in the Western restaurant on the 6th floor of
    the International Hotel.*

L   **Hǎo, xiān xièxie nǐmen.**
    Good. Let me thank you in advance.

H   **Bú xiè. Wǒ mǎshang pài rén sòng qǐngtiě lai.**
    *Not at all. I'll send someone over with the invitation
    cards straight away.*

13.15 Do a good turn

Bāng or **bāng-máng** means 'to do a good turn', 'to do a
favour', 'to help':

Qǐng nǐ bāng ge máng.
    Please give me a hand.
Bāng wǒ mǎi piào.
    Help me out by buying a ticket.
Qǐng nǐ bāng wǒ zhǎo yí wèi Zhōngwén lǎoshī hǎo ma?
    Please could you help me to find a Chinese teacher?

13.16 I'm afraid

Kǒngpà means 'I'm afraid' but has nothing to do with real
fear. In fact it mirrors the English non-fearful usage:

Zhèi ge dōngxi kǒngpa hěn guì ba.
    I'm afraid this must be very expensive.
Míngtiān kǒngpà bù xíng ba.
    I'm afraid tomorrow won't do.

13.17 If

Yàoshi means 'if' and is commonly followed in the second part of the sentence by **jiù** 'then':

Yàoshi xià-yǔ, nǐ qù bu qu?
   Will you go if it rains?
Yàoshi xià-yǔ, wǒ jiù bú qù le.
   If it does, I won't go after all.
Yàoshi tāmen yǒu chuánzhēn jiù hǎo le.
   It would be great if they had a fax.

13.18 On account of

Wèile means 'on account of', 'because of':

Tā xué Zhōngwén shi wèile qù Zhōngguó gōngzuò.
   He's learning Chinese on account of going to China
   to work.
Wèile huàn qián, wǒ děng-le sān ge xiǎoshí.
   I waited three hours in order to change money.

13.19 No way

Fázi means 'way', 'method'. **Méi fázi** is equivalent to the English 'There's nothing to be done about it'. It is often followed in Chinese by a verb:

Méi fázi yòng.
   There's no way to use it.
Jīntiān méi huǒchē, méi fázi qù.
   There's no train today, so there's no way of getting there.

Exercise 76: Lodging a complaint

Translate into English:

1   Fángjiān tài chǎo, wǒ méi fázi shuì-jiào.

2   Cài dōu lěng le, wǒmen méi fázi chī.

3   Cèsuǒ méi shuǐ, wǒmen méi fázi yòng.

4   Chōu-yān de (rén) tài duō, wǒmen méi fázi chī-fàn.

13.20 Another indefinite

Duōshao? normally means 'how many?', but like other question words (see for example **jǐ?** in 11.3) it can be used as an indefinite number rather than as a question:

Méi you duōshao rén xǐhuan dōngtiān qù nàr wánr.
There aren't many people who like going there for a visit in winter.

13.21 Ratios

When changing money, the rate can be expressed using **bǐ** 'compared to':

yī bǐ sì diǎn wǔ   1:4.5

The same device is used for giving football results:

sān bǐ yī   3–1

13.22 Must versus need not

We saw in Chapter 6 that **děi** means 'must', 'should', 'ought':

Zài nàr chī-fàn yídìng děi gěi xiǎofèi.
You certainly have to tip when you eat there. (**xiǎofèi** = small fee; tip)

Děi also combines with **bì**, meaning 'must', in **bìděi**:

Jīntiān xiàwǔ wǒ bìděi jìn chéng qu huàn qián.
    This afternoon I must go into town to change
    some money.

Beware that the negative form of **bìděi** is **bú bì** and that it
does not mean what you might logically expect, 'must not'.
Instead it means 'need not':

Zài nàr chī-fàn bú bì gěi xiǎofèi.
    There's no need to tip when you eat there.

13.23 Whatever, whoever, whenever

Question words can be used very effectively as '-ever'
words:

Tā yào duōshao, wǒmen jiù gěi duōshao.
    We'll give him however much he wants. (lit: He wants
    how much, we'll then give how much.)
Nǐ shuō něi ge hǎo, wǒ jiù mǎi něi ge.
    I'll buy whichever one you think is good.

Exercise 77

Fill in the blanks with question words, as in the example:

Nǐ yào mǎi <u>duōshao</u>, wǒmen jiù mài <u>duōshao</u>.

1   Nǐ xiǎng qǐng …, wǒmen jiù qǐng … .

2   Tā xiǎng chī …, wǒ jiù zuò … .

3   Nǐ shuō yīnggāi … zuò, wǒ jiù … zuò.

4   Nǐ shuō … hào qù, wǒmen jiù … hào qù.

13.24 Oh heck! Drat it!

Zāole is a mild expletive expressing annoyance or irritation:

Zāole, xià-yǔ le.
   Oh no, it's raining!

Some new words

dìdi	(younger) brother
xūyào	to need, require
Měiyuán	American dollars
wǔshi Měiyúan	US $50
or **wǔshi kuài**	
Měiyúan	
jǐngchá	the police
dǎomài	to profiteer
wàihuì	foreign exchange
xiànjīn	cash, ready money
lǚxíng	to travel
lǚxíng zhīpiào	traveller's cheque
yínháng	a bank
páijià	quoted price
gǎnxiè	to thank

CONVERSATION 13C

A young man asks a foreign tourist to change money.

Y   **Xiānsheng, qǐng nín bāng ge máng kěyǐ ma?**
    Can you help me, sir, please?

T   **Shénme shì?**
    What's the matter?

Y   **Wǒ dìdi chū guó liúxué, xūyào Měiyuán. Nín néng huàn yi diǎnr ma?**
    My brother is going abroad to study and needs some American dollars. Can you change me some?

→

T   **Huàn qián a! Kǒngpà bù xíng ba. Yàoshi jǐngchá …**
Change money! I'm afraid that won't do. If the police …

Y   **Méi guānxi. Wǒ bú shi dǎomài wàihuì de. Zhēn de shì wèile wǒ dìdi chū guó.**
It wouldn't matter. I'm not a money-changer. It really is on account of my brother going abroad.

T   **Nǐ yào Měiyuán xiànjīn, shì bu shi?**
You want cash, I suppose?

Y   **Shì a. Lǚxíng zhīpiào méi fázi yòng.**
Yes. There's no way traveller's cheques could be used.

T   **Wǒ méi dài duōshao xiànjīn. Nǐ děngdeng wǒ kànkan …** *[Takes out wallet]* **… yígòng zhǐ yǒu yì bǎi èrshi kuài.**
I haven't brought much cash. Hang on, let me see … I've only got $120 altogether.

Y   **Xíng. Jīntiān yínháng de páijià shi yī bǐ sì diǎn wǔ. Wǒ gěi nín yī bǐ wǔ ba.**
That'll do. The rate at the bank today is 1:4.5. I'll give you 1:5, shall I?

T   **Bú bì le. Yínháng gěi duōshao, nǐ jiù gěi duōshao ba.**
There's no need. Just give what the bank would give.

Y   **Nà tài gǎnxiè le. Yì Měiyuán huàn sì kuài wǔ Rénmínbì. Yì bǎi èr … Āiyā, zàole, jǐngchá lái le …**
Well, I'm very grateful. One American dollar gives ¥4.50 RMB. 120 … Oh, damn, here's the police …

Exercise 78

Translate into Chinese:

1 Can I dial direct to England?

   Yes, of course.

2 May I trouble you to take me to the station?

   No problem, get in.

3 Do I have to send this fax today?

   No need.

4 When shall we go to Japan?

   We'll go whenever you feel like going.

5 Where's your (younger) brother?

   He's sending a fax.

6 Thank you for your help.

   Don't mention it

Chapter 14

Oh where, oh where?

- *An invitation to a housewarming*
- *Asking for an address*
- *Interviewing for a driver*

14.1 They say that ...

Tīngshuō literally means 'listen say', and is used where in English we might say 'I've heard that ...', 'They say that ...':

Tīngshuō Lǎo Wáng bìng le.
I hear Old Wang's been taken ill.
Tīngshuō tāmen de diànhuà hàomǎ huàn le.
I've heard that their phone number has changed.

14.2 Last and next

In 8.10 we met **shàng** and **xià** for 'last' and 'next'. They are used with **xīngqī** ('week') and **yuè** ('month'), and seem to be equally happy with or without the measure word **gè**:

Tāmen shi shàng (ge) yuè shíbā hào lái de, dǎsuan xià (ge) yuè sì hào zǒu.
They came on the 18th of last month and are planning to leave on the 4th of next month.

Shàng xīngqī kāi-le sān cì huì, xià xīngqī hái děi kāi sān cì.
There were three meetings last week, and we have to hold three more next week.

14.3 Opposite

Duìmiàn means 'opposite', 'facing':

Bīnguǎn zài huǒchēzhàn (de) duìmiàn.
The hotel is opposite the railway station.
Tā jiā duìmiàn yǒu ge xiǎo gōngyuán.
There is a little park across from his house.

Exercise 79: Revision

Where is it? Translate into English:

1   Yínháng zài fàndiàn de dōngbianr.

2   Fúwù zhōngxīn jiù zài kāfēitīng duìmiàn.

3   Nán cèsuǒ zài xīcāntīng hòutou.

4   Wǒ de hùzhào zài nǐ yòubianr de nèi ge bāor li.

14.4 From A to B

The pattern used for indicating distance from one place to another makes use of **lí** 'separated from':

A lí B (hěn) jìn/yuǎn.
A is (very) close to/far from B.
Wǒ jiā lí gōngyuán hěn jìn.
My house is very near the park.

To state the actual measured distance, the verb **yǒu** is usually added to the pattern:

A lí B yǒu *distance.*
Lúndūn lí Běijīng (yǒu) duō yuǎn?
How far is it from London to Beijing?

Lúndūn lí Běijīng yǒu duōshao gōnglǐ?
How many kilometres is it from London to Beijing?
(**gōnglǐ** = kilometre)
Tā jiā lí jīchǎng zhǐ yǒu wǔ gōnglǐ.
His home is only 5km from the airport.

Exercise 80

True or false?

1   Lúndūn lí Luómǎ *(Rome)* chàbuduō yǒu wǔbǎi gōnglǐ.

2   Běijīng lí Tiānjin yǒu yìbǎi sānshi duō gōnglǐ.

3   Běijīng lí Shànghǎi bǐ Běijīng lí Guǎngzhōu yuǎn.

4   Yīngguó lí Zhōngguó bǐ Měiguó lí Zhōngguó yuǎn duō le.

14.5 For short

Chinese sometimes neatly shortens ideas which can be quite cumbersome to express in English. **Shàng-xià**, for instance, can stand for 'coming up and going down' or for 'going up and coming down' or for 'ascending and descending'. **Jìn-chū** similarly makes short work of 'entering and exiting':

Guójì Fàndiàn yǒu hěn duō diàntī, shàng-xià hěn fāngbiàn.
There are lots of lifts in the International Hotel: it's very easy to get up and down.
Wàitou yǒu jǐngchá, jìn-chū hěn máfan.
There's a policeman outside: it's quite tedious to get in and out.

14.6 'céng' versus 'lóu'

We met in 4.15 the use of **lóu** to mean a storey or floor of a building. **Lóu** also can mean 'a building' or 'a block'. To avoid confusion, the word **céng** (lit: a layer, a tier) is sometimes used for 'floor':

Tāmen gōngsī zài wǔ lóu (or wǔ céng).
    Their company is on the 5th floor.

When both buildings and floors are mentioned, **céng** is more likely to be used:

Tā jiā zài shíbā (hào) lóu sì céng 424 hào.
    His home is No. 424 on the 4th floor of Block 18.

14.7 Oh, yes, but ...

Reluctant concession can be shown by using the pattern:
XXX shì XXX, kěshi ...

A: **Nǐ de fángjiān méi diànhuà ma?**
    Isn't there a phone in your room?
B: **Yǒu shi yǒu, kěshi bù néng zhí bō.**
    Yes, but I can't dial direct.
A: **Nèi ge fàndiàn bù hǎo ma?**
    Isn't that hotel any good?
B: **Hǎo shi hǎo, kěshi tài guì le.**
    It's OK, but too expensive.

14.8 Service failure

The verb **tíng** means 'to stop'. It appears in two common expressions: **tíng diàn** 'power cut' and **tíng shuǐ** 'water shut-off':

Sān ge yuè méi xià-yǔ le. Zuìjìn cháng tíng shuǐ, yě cháng tíng diàn.
    It hasn't rained for three months. Recently there have been frequent water stoppages, and power cuts too.

14.9 Just about to

Zhèng xiǎng and **zhèng yào** both mean 'just about to', 'just thinking of':

Wǒ zhèng xiǎng qu kàn tā, tā jiù lái le.
Just as I was about to go and see him, he arrived.

14.10 Greater before lesser

When giving addresses in Chinese, give them in order from the larger to the smaller:

Zhōnghuá Rénmín Gònghéguó,
People's Republic of China,
Guǎngdōng shěng,
Guangdong province,
Guǎngzhōu shì,
Guangzhou city,
Zhōngshān lù,
Zhongshan Road,
145 hào,
No. 145,
sān lóu
3rd floor

Some new words

bān	to move
bān jiā	to move house
zhǎnlǎn	to exhibit; exhibition
fángzi	house
tiáojiàn	condition, conditions
biànfàn	a simple meal, 'pot-luck'
xīn	new
bǐ	pen
dìzhǐ	address
qū	district
xīwàng	to hope; hope

CONVERSATION 14A

Invitation to a housewarming

L   **Wéi, Wú Qiáng ma? Nǐ hǎo! Wǒ shi Lǐ Huá.**
    Hello, Wu Qiang? How are you? It's Lee Hua.

W   **Èi, Xiǎo Lǐ, hǎo jiǔ bú jiàn! Tīngshuō nǐmen yào bān jiā, shì ma?**
    Oh, Lee, long time no see! I heard you were moving house; is that right?

L   **Yǐjing bān le. Shàng yuè bā hào bān de.**
    We've moved already. We moved on the 8th of last month.

W   **Bāndào nǎr le?**
    Where did you move to?

L   **Jìng'ānlǐ, jiù zài Guójì Zhǎnlǎn Zhōngxīn duìmiàn.**
    Jinganli, right opposite the International Exhibition Centre.

W   **Nàme yuǎn a! Lí nǐmen gōngsī kǒngpà yǒu shí gōnglǐ ba. Fángzi zěnmeyàng?**
    So far away! It must be 10 kilometres from your work. What's the house like?

L   **Tiáojiàn hái kěyǐ. Jiù shi shàng-xià bù fāngbiàn: wǒmen zài shí céng.**
    The (living) conditions are not bad. It's just that it's not very convenient for getting up and down: we're on the 10th floor.

W   **Méi diàntī ma?**
    Isn't there a lift?

L   **Yǒu shi yǒu, kěshi cháng tíng diàn. Èi, Wú Qiáng, zhèi ge xīngqītiān zhōngwǔ yǒu gōngfu ma? Wǒmen xiǎng qǐng nǐ lái chī ge biànfàn.**
    Yes, but there are constant power cuts. Eh, Wu Qiang, are you free this Sunday lunchtime? We'd like to invite you around for a meal.

→

185

W　Hǎo a, wǒ zhèng xiǎng kànkan nǐmen de xīn jiā.
　　Oh good, I was just thinking that I'd like to see your
　　new home.
L　Nǐ nàr yǒu bǐ ma? Wǒ gàosu nǐ dìzhǐ: Cháoyáng
　　qū, Jìng'ānlǐ lù, 45 hào lóu, shí céng 1026.
　　Xīngqītiān zhōngwǔ shí'èr diǎn zěnmeyàng?
　　Have you got a pen there? I'll tell you the address:
　　1026, 10th floor, Building No. 45 Jinganli Road,
　　Chaoyang District. How about 12 noon on Sunday?
W　Hǎo, xīwàng dào shíhou bié tíng diàn!
　　Fine. I hope there won't be a power cut at the time!

14.11 Busy doing what?

Máng means 'busy' or 'to be busy with', and **Máng shénme?**
is a common way of asking 'Busy doing what?':

Tā zhèngzài máng chū guó de shì.
　　He's busy with the business of going abroad.

14.12 Engaged in

Zài is used to express 'engaged in', 'preoccupied with' over
a period of time:

Tā lái Zhōngguó yǐhòu, yìzhí zài liàn qìgōng.
　　Ever since coming to China he's been doing qigong.
Wǒ chángcháng zài xiǎng zhèi ge wèntí.
　　I'm always thinking about this problem.

14.13 To return

Huí means 'to return'. The addition of **lái** or **qù** shows
whether 'return' means 'come back' or 'go back':

Tā yǐjing huí Rìběn qu le.
　　She's already gone back to Japan.

186

Chūqu de rén duō, huílai de rén shǎo.
Many people go out, but few come back.

14.14 Long since

Zǎojiù literally means 'early as soon as that', and it very conveniently translates 'long since':

Wǒ zǎojiù zhǔnbèihǎo le. Nǐ shuō shénme shíhou zǒu jiù shénme shíhou zǒu.
I was ready long ago. We can go at any time you say.
Tā zǎojiù wàng-le wǒ shi shéi le.
She's long since forgotten who I am.

14.15 Rough estimates

Where English indicates approximate numbers by saying 'one or two', 'five or six', Chinese achieves the same effect by putting two numbers together:

Zuótiān zhǐ yǒu yì-liǎng ge rén méi lái.
There were only one or two who didn't come yesterday.
Tā dǎsuan zài Xiānggǎng wánr wǔ-liù tiān.
She decided to enjoy herself in Hong Kong for five or six days.

In the same way:

shísì-wǔ	14 or 15
èr-sānshí	20 or 30
qī-bābǎi	700 or 800

But note that there is one exception: it is not possible to use the same device for '9 or 10', because **jiǔ-shí** sounds like **jiǔshi** and so can be confused with '90'.

14.16 Compound verbal endings

Lái 'come' and **qù** 'go' when added to other verbs indicate the direction of the action to or away from the speaker (see

14.13). Other verb endings which give additional sense are
shàng 'up' and **xià** 'down', **chū** 'out' and **jìn** 'in' (see also
14.5), and **huí** 'back'. **Lái** and **qù** can be used with all of
these as well. It sounds complicated, but the following
examples show clearly how it works:

Tā cóng lóushang zǒuxiàlai le.
　　She walked down from upstairs.
Shān suīrán hěn gāo, kěshi qìchē háishi kāishàngqu le.
　　Although the mountain was high, the car still went up it.
Tā cóng wàiguó dàihuílai bù shǎo dōngxi.
　　She brought back lots of things from abroad.
**Tāmen de diànhuà yǒu wèntí, zhǐ néng dǎjìnqu, bù
néng dǎchūlai.**
　　Their phone is defective: you can only phone in, they
　　can't dial out.

Exercise 81

Fill in the blanks with verbal endings:

1　Tā míngtiān zǎochen qù, hòutiān wǎnshang huí(…).

2　Lóushang yào zhèi fèn bào, qǐng nǐ ná(… …).

3　Gěi tāmen de chuánzhēn yǐjing fā(… …) le.

4　Fángzi mǎihǎo le, wǒmen hòutiān bān(… …).

5　Wǒ bù néng yào tā de lǐwù, qǐng nǐ tì wǒ
　　sòng(… …) ba.

14.17 Inland and abroad

The opposite of **guówài** (lit: outside the country) 'abroad' is
guónèi (lit: inside the country) 'inland':

Guónèi dǎ tàijíquán de rén dāngrán bǐ guówài duō.
　　Of course there are more practitioners of taichi inside
　　China than abroad.

Zhèi xiē bíyānhú xiān zài guónèi zhǎnlǎn, míngnián zài sòngdào guówài qù.
These snuff bottles will first be exhibited in China, and then next year they'll be sent abroad.

14.18 More on 'huì'

Another use of the verb **huì**, which we met in 11.1, is to indicate future probability:

Jīntiān xiàwǔ bú huì xià-yǔ ba.
It won't rain this afternoon will it?
Wǒmen shi lǎo péngyou, tā yídìng huì bāng-máng.
We're old friends, he's sure to lend a hand.

Some new words

yánjiū	research; to research
jīngjì	economics
Jīngjì Tèqū	Special Economic Zone
jiàoshòu	professor
yìjiàn	opinion, idea
xiě	to write
xiě xìn	to write a letter
yóuzhèng biānmǎ	postcode; zip code
Yóujú	the Post Office
tuì	to return; to withdraw
tuìhuílai	to return to sender, send back
xiāngxìn	to believe
shì	to try

CONVERSATION 14B

Asking for an address

C   **Zuìjìn máng shénme?**
    What have you been busy at recently?

→

F	**Hái zài yánjiū Jīngjì Tèqū de wèntí. Éi, Fùdàn Dàxué de Táng jiàoshòu huí Shànghǎi le ma?**
	I'm still doing research into problems of the Special Economic Zones. Oh, has Professor Tang of Fudan University gone back to Shanghai?
C	**Zǎojiù huíqu le.**
	Some time ago.
F	**Wǒ yǒu yì-liǎng ge wèntí, hěn xiǎng tīngting Táng jiàoshòu de yìjiàn.**
	There are one or two matters on which I'd like to hear Professor Tang's opinion.
C	**Nǐ kěyǐ xiě xìn wèn tā a.**
	You could write and ask him, couldn't you?
F	**Duì. Nǐ yǒu tā de dìzhǐ ma?**
	Right. Do you have his address?
C	**Yǒu. Jiù zài zhèr. Hǎo, nǐ xiěxiàlai ba: Shànghǎi shì, 200435, Huáihǎi Běilù, 268 hào.**
	Yes, it's right here. OK, write it down: No. 268 Huaihai Road North, Shanghai Municipality, 200435.
F	**200435 shi shénme yìsi?**
	What does the 200435 mean?
C	**Nà shi yóuzhèng biānmǎ. Guónèi de xìn yàoshi bù xiěshang, Yóujú jiù gěi nǐ tuìhuílai.**
	That's the postcode. If you don't write it on an inland letter, the Post Office will return it to you.
F	**Bú huì ba?**
	Surely they wouldn't?
C	**Bù xiāngxìn, nǐ jiù shì yi shi!**
	If you don't believe it, try it!

14.19 That's right

Shìde 'That's right', 'Yes, sir' is the standard respectful reply to someone in authority.

14.20 Coming to rest

Normally phrases describing the location where something happens are introduced by **zài** and come before the verb (see 5.2). But when the location is where the verb's action comes to rest, the **zài** phrase, quite logically, comes after the verb:

Míngzi yīnggāi xiězai nǎr?
Where should I write my name?
Qìchē tíngzai wàitou kěyǐ ma?
Is it all right to park my car outside?
Tā shēngzai Zhōngguó, kěshi liǎng suì jiù dào-le Yīngguó.
She was born in China, but she moved to Britain when she was two years old.
Zhùzai zhèr de rén méi you bú rènshi tā de.
Everyone who lives here knows him.

Exercise 82: Place where/place whither

Translate into English:

1 Nǐ kěyǐ zài nǐ fángjiān xiě./Nǐ de dìzhǐ kěyǐ xiězai xíngli shang.

2 Tā zài wàitou tíng chē ne./Chē tíngzai wàitou le.

3 Tā cháng zài gōngyuán dǎ tàijíquán./Yǔ dǎzai tā shēn(tǐ) shang, hěn bù shūfu.

4 Wǒmen zài nǎr tián biǎo?/Wǒ de míngzi tiánzai nǎr?

14.21 Expecting a plural answer

When the answer to a question is likely to be in the plural, the questioner often puts in the adverb **dōu**:

Nǐ dōu xiǎng kàn shénme?
What things do you want to look at?
Tā dōu rènshi něi xiē rén?
Which people does she know?

14.22 Not dead but 'gone before'

Like people from many other cultures, Chinese are shy of mentioning death too directly, and there are lots of euphemisms which help to avoid the dread word **sǐ le** 'dead'. One very common one is **bú zài le** 'not present any more'.

14.23 Together

Yìqǐ means 'together':

Wǒmen wǔ ge rén zhùzai yìqǐ.
   The five of us live together.
Tāmen wǔ ge rén yìqǐ chū guó lǚyóu qu le.
   The five of them have gone abroad travelling together.

14.24 As soon as

The pattern **yī ... jiù** is used to convey the idea 'as soon as this, then that', or 'whenever this, then that'. Both words come immediately before the verbs in the two halves of the sentence:

Tāmen yì lái, wǒmen jiù zǒu.
   As soon as they come, we'll leave.
Tā yí kànjian jiǔbēi jiù xiǎng hē-jiǔ.
   Whenever he sees a glass he wants to have a drink.

14.25 Only then

Cái 'only then' is another very useful fixed adverb:

Zhèi jiàn shì tāmen zuótiān jiù zhīdao le. Wǒ jīntiān cái zhīdao.
   They knew about this matter as early as yesterday.
   I only knew of it today. (lit: I today only then knew.)
Nǐ jiǎo-le fèi cái néng zǒu.
   You can't leave until you've paid up. (lit: You're paid only then can leave.)

Go very careful! **Cái** will often be translated most easily by 'not until' in English, but there is no negative in the Chinese version.

Exercise 83

Fill in the blanks with either jiù or cái:

1   Yóujú jiǔ diǎn kāi mén. Tā bā diǎn bàn … dào le:
    tài zǎo le.

2   Wǒmen jiǔ diǎn kāi huì. Tā shí diǎn … dào:
    tài wǎn le.

3   Tā jiā lí huǒchēzhàn hěn yuǎn. Zǒu-lù qù, yì
    xiǎoshí … gòu.

4   Tā jiā lí huǒchēzhàn hěn jìn. Zǒu-lù qù, wǔ fēn
    zhōng … gòu le.

5   Lái Zhōngguó yǐhòu tā … zhīdao Běijīng yǒu
    zhème yí ge dà zhǎnlǎn zhōngxīn.

Some new words

kǒuyīn	accent
shēng	to be born
gēge	elder brother
sǎosao	elder brother's wife
ānquán	safe; safety
pángbiānr	beside; at the side
pàichūsuǒ	local police station
liúxia	to leave (name, address, etc.)
jiéguǒ	result; as a result
tōngzhī	to inform, let know

CONVERSATION 14C

An expatriate interviews for a driver:

F   **Nǐ jiào Zhāng Jūn, shì ma?**
      You're called Zhang Jun, right?

D   **Shìde.**
      Yes.

F   **Jīnnián duōshao suì le?**
      How old are you this year?

D   **Èrshiwǔ.**
      25.

F   **Shénme dìfang rén?**
      Where are you from?

D   **Sìchuān rén.**
      Sichuan.

F   **Nǐ shuō-huà zěnme méi you Sìchuān kǒuyīn a?**
      How come you don't have a Sichuan accent?

D   **Wǒ shēngzai Sìchuān, kěshi liǎng suì jiā jiù
      bāndào Běijīng lái le.**
      *I was born in Sichuan, but my family moved to
      Beijing when I was two.*

F   **Jiā li dōu yǒu shénme rén?**
      Who are there in your family?

D   **Fùqin bú zài le. Xiànzài zhǐ yǒu mǔqin, gēge,
      gēn sǎosao.**
      *My father has passed away. Now there are only my
      mother, my elder brother and his wife.*

F   **Dōu zhùzhai yìqǐ ma?**
      Do you all live together?

D   **Shìde.**
      Yes.

F   **Yǐqián dōu zài nǎr gōngzuò-guo?**
      Where else have you worked?

D   **Zhōngxué yí bìyè jiù xué kāi-chē, yìzhí kāi
      chūzū, qùnián cái huàndào Měiguó yínháng.**
      *As soon as I finished secondary school I learned how
      to drive, and I drove a taxi right up until last year
      when I went to work for an American bank.*

F   **Yàoshi gōngsi de chē wǎnshang tíngzai nǐ jiā, ānquán ma?**
    If the company car were parked at your place at night, would it be safe?

D   **Méi wèntí. Wǒ jiā pángbiānr jiù shi pàichūsuǒ.**
    No problem. Next door is the police station.

F   **Hǎo. Nǐ liúxia dìzhǐ ba. Jiéguǒ wǒmen huì tōngzhī nǐ.**
    Fine. Leave your address. We'll let you know the result.

Exercise 84

Translate into Chinese:

1   Where is the International Exhibition Centre?

    It's just opposite the Xinhua Hotel.

2   How far is your house from the railway station?

    I think it's about five kilometres.

3   Do you have his address in Beijing?

    Yes, here it is: 29 Yongding Road, 3rd floor, Beijing 100826.

4   When was it that he went back to Shanghai?

    He went back as soon as he received (**jiēdào**) your fax.

5   Mr Wang said that there's nothing to be done about it.

    Tell him you're a friend of mine, I am sure he would help.

6   Can I sit next to you, Miss Lee?

    Yes, of course, but I have to leave in a minute.

Chapter 15
Lost and found

- *At the post office*
- *Asking for directions in town and on the road*

15.1 From A to B again

As we know from 6.7, **lù** means 'road' or 'route'. It is often used with a number and measure in the 'from A to B' pattern (see 14.4) to mean 'a journey of':

Shànghǎi lí Nánjīng yǒu sānbǎi gōnglǐ lù.
    Shanghai is 300km from Nanjing.
Tā jiā lí dàxué zhǐ yǒu shí fēn zhōng de lù.
    His home is a journey of only ten minutes from
    the University.
Fàndiàn lí huǒchēzhàn, zuò dìtiě sān zhàn lù.
    It is three stops on the underground from the hotel to
    the railway station.

15.2 Even the most ...

We met **zuì** 'most' in 9.22. Used with the adverb **yě** it means 'even the most ...':

Chī dùn fàn zuì kuài yě děi bàn xiǎoshí.
>To eat even the fastest meal takes half an hour. [To eat a meal even at the fastest rate …]

Dǎ guójì diànhuà zuì shǎo yě děi yìbǎi kuài qián.
>To make an international phone call costs at least ¥100.

Exercise 85

Translate into English:

1   Tā zuì zǎo yě děi míngtiān dào.

2   Tā jiā lí gōnggòngqìchēzhàn zuì shǎo yě děi zǒu èrshi fēn zhōng.

3   Běijīng bā yuè zuì rè yě bú huì dào sìshi dù.

4   Cóng Zhōngguó lái de xìn, zuì kuài yě yào yí ge xīngqī.

15.3 Ordinal numbers

Ordinal numbers (the first, the second, the third, etc.) are easily formed by prefixing **dì-** to a number:

wǔ ge rén   five people
dì-wǔ ge rén   the fifth person

There are a few cases where Chinese does not use **dì-** even though the English seems to call for it. So:

the second floor   **èr lóu**
the No. 44 (bus)   **sìshisì lù**

15.4 This having been done … again

In 11.16 we met sentences of the 'Having eaten I will go' type, where the main action is contained in 'I will go' and the dependent clause 'Having eaten' is marked in Chinese by *verb*-**le** (*object*):

Wǒ chī-le zǎofàn jiù chūqu le.
Having had breakfast I went out.

Such dependent clauses can be used regardless of whether the main action is in the past, the present or the future:

Tā fā-le chuánzhēn jiù huí jiā le.
He went home after sending the fax.
Tā měi tiān xià-le bān dōu qu mǎi dōngxi.
She goes shopping every day after work.
Wǒ xià-le fēijī jiù xiān qu kàn Chángchéng.
Having got off the plane I will first go to see the Great Wall.

Exercise 86

Using the suggestions in brackets, answer the following questions in Chinese:

1   Tā shi shénme shíhou qù de?

    (After we gave her the money)

2   Tā shénme shíhou zǒu?

    (After watching the news)

3   Nǐ shénme shíhou qu kàn tā?

    (After I post these letters)

4   Tā měi tiān shénme shíhou chī zǎofàn?

    (After doing his taichi)

15.5 By sea and by air

The different ways to send a letter are:

píngxìn	surface mail
guàhàoxìn	registered mail
hángkōngxìn	airmail

Hángkōng by itself means 'aviation', and **hángkōng gōngsī** is the term for 'an airline'. British Airways is called in Chinese **Yīngguó Hángkōng Gōngsī** or **Yīngháng** for short.

15.6 Overload

Chāozhòng means 'overweight'. It is short for **chāoguò zhòngliàng** (lit: exceed weight):

Zhèi fēng xìn chāozhòng le. Sān kuài liù.
  This letter is overweight. It'll cost ¥3.60.
  (**fēng** is the measure word for letters)
Duìbuqǐ, nín de xíngli chāozhòng le.
  I'm sorry, your baggage is overweight.

15.7 Continents

Yàzhōu	Asia
Fēizhōu	Africa
Ōuzhōu	Europe
Měizhōu	America
Dōngnányà	South-east Asia
Dōng'ōu	Eastern Europe
Xī'ōu	Western Europe
Nán'ōu	Southern Europe
Běi'ōu	Northern Europe

15.8 'Duō' and 'shǎo' as adverbs

Duō and **shǎo** can be used before verbs as adverbs meaning 'more' and 'less/fewer':

Qǐng nǐ duō mǎi yì diǎnr.
  Please buy a little more.
Wǒ yīnggāi shǎo chī yì diǎnr.
  I should eat a bit less.
Tā shǎo gěi-le wǒ yì zhāng.
  He gave me one sheet fewer.

15.9 Bank notes and stamps

Both bank notes and stamps take the measure word **zhāng**.
Note the following formula for describing them:

Wǒ yào shí zhāng wǔshi kuài de, èrshi zhāng shí kuài de.
I'll have ten ¥50s and twenty ¥10s.
Qǐng nǐ gěi wǒ wǔ zhāng liǎng kuài de, shí zhāng yì máo de.
Please give me five ¥2 and ten 10-cent (stamps).

Some new words

guò	to go over/through/past/across
mǎlù	road, main road (in a city)
jì	to post (a letter)
chēng	to weigh
míngxìnpiànr	postcard
yóupiào	(postage) stamp

CONVERSATION 15A

A tourist looks for the post office:

T **Qǐng wèn fùjìn yǒu yóujú ma?**
Excuse me, is there a post office nearby?

P **Méi you, lí zhèr zuì jìn de yě yǒu sān zhàn lù.**
No, even the nearest one is three stops away.

T **Zài nǎr a?**
Where?

P **Nǐ zhīdao Yǎbǎo Lù ma?**
Do you know Yabao Road?

T **Bù zhīdao.**
No.

P **Cóng zhèr zuò sìshisì lù wǎng nán zǒu, dì-sān zhàn jiù shi Yǎbǎo Lù, xià-le chē, guò mǎlù jiù shi yóujú.**

Go south from here on the 44, and the third stop is
Yabao Road. Get off the bus, go across the road, and
that's the post office.

T   **Hǎo, xièxie nín.**
Fine, thank you.

[In the post office]

T   **Qǐng wèn jì Yīngguó de hángkōngxìn duōshao
qián?**
*Excuse me, how much is it to send an airmail letter
to Britain?*
C   **Nálai kànkan.**
Let me have a look at it.
T   **Wèishénme?**
Why?
[Reluctantly hands the letter to the clerk]
C   **Děi chēng yí xiàr ... Méi chāozhòng, liǎng kuài.**
It has to be weighed ... It's not overweight, ¥2.
T   **Jì Ōuzhōu, Měizhōu de míngxìnpiànr duōshao
qián?**
How much to send postcards to Europe and America?
C   **Guójì hángkōng dōu shi yí kuài liù.**
Overseas airmail is all ¥1.60.
T   **Hǎo, wǒ děi duō mǎi ji zhāng yóupiào. Qǐng nǐ
gěi wǒ shí zhāng liǎng kuài de, èrshi zhāng yí
kuài liù de.**
*OK, I have to buy a few more stamps. Please give me
ten ¥2 ones and twenty ¥1.60 ones.*

15.10 Losing the way

Mí means 'confused' and **mílù** is 'confused about the road',
'lost the way':

Zài shān li zǒu, cháng mílù.
One often loses the way when walking in the mountains.
Qǐng wèn něi biānr shì běi a? Wǒ mílù le.
Excuse me, which way is north? I've lost my way.

15.11 Ambassadors and embassies

The word for an ambassador is **dàshǐ** and an embassy building is called a **dàshǐguǎn:**

Zhōngguó [zhù Yīng(guó)] Dàshǐ
  The Chinese Ambassador [to Britain]
Yīngguó [zhù (Měi(guó)] Dàshǐguǎn
  The British Embassy [in America]
  (**zhù** = to stay, be stationed)

15.12 Stressing adjectives with 'shì'

Adjectives, as we know, also act as verbs, so that **dà** doesn't only mean 'big'; it also means 'to be big'. For this reason we do not often find the verb 'to be' (**shì**) used with an adjective, but **shì** can be used to show emphasis:

Tā hěn piàoliang.
  She's very beautiful.
Tā shì hěn piàoliang.
  She really is very beautiful.
Tā shì xiǎng dāng dàshǐ.
  He really does want to be ambassador.

15.13 Good to eat ... again

In 11.18 we met **hǎo** and **róngyi** used before verbs to make phrases like 'good to eat' and 'easy to understand'. Sometimes **hǎo** and **róngyi** are used interchangeably: **hǎo- zhǎo** and **róngyi-zhǎo** both mean 'easy to find'.

Note that this type of phrase can take a negative form as well:

Nèi tiáo lù chē duō, bù hǎo-zǒu.
  That road has a lot of traffic, it's not easy to go on.

Exercise 87

Translate into Chinese:

1 Chinese food is good to eat but difficult to prepare.

2 His house is in the mountains and very hard to find.

3 One (ticket) is not enough, please buy some more.

4 He's too fat, he ought to have one fewer bowl of rice each day.

15.14 At the end of

Tóu literally means 'head', but we have also met it in words like **qiántou** and **hòutou**, and other place-words use it too:

Tā jiā jiù zài zhèi tiáo lù de dōngtóur.
His home is at the east end of this road.

15.15 Bound to be

Kěndìng can mean 'bound to be', 'sure to', but it is also a verb meaning ' be certain about it', 'affirm':

Tā shi bu shì zài dàshǐguǎn gōngzuò, wǒ bù néng kěndìng.
I can't be positive whether he works at the embassy or not.

Tā zhèi jiàn xíngli kěndìng chāozhòng le.
I'm sure that this piece of luggage of hers is overweight.

15.16 Go careful!

The word **xiǎoxīn** (literally: 'little heart') means 'careful', 'go careful':

Zài guówài lǚxíng, chī dōngxi děi tèbié xiǎoxīn.
When travelling abroad one should be especially careful about what one eats.

Xiǎoxīn! Qiántou yǒu jǐngchá.
Careful, there's a policeman ahead.

15.17 It'd be better if ...

The pattern **háishi ... ba** translates 'it would be better if', 'had better':

Tāmen dōu bú rènshi lù, háishi nǐ qù ba.
None of them know the way, it'd be better if you went.

Zuò huǒchē tài màn, wǒmen háishi zuò fēijī ba.
It's too slow by train, we'd better go by air.

Exercise 88

Give your advice in Chinese:

1 (Dàjiā dōu shuō chōu-yān bù hǎo), *you'd better give it up.*

2 (Jīntiān tài wǎn le), *we had better do it tomorrow.*

3 (Fēijīpiào bù róngyi-mǎi), *you'd better go by train.*

4 (Xìn tài màn), *we had better send them a fax.*

Some new words

hónglǜdēng	traffic lights
hóngdēng	red light
lǜdēng	green light
gǎn	to dare
rénxíngdào	pavement
rénxínghéngdào	pedestrian crossing

CONVERSATION 15B

A foreign tourist asks a policeman the way:

T   **Tóngzhì, wǒ mílù le. Zhè shi shénme dìfang?**
     Comrade, I've lost my way. What is this place?

P   **Nǐ yào qù nǎr?**
     Where do you want to go?

T   **Yīngguó Dàshǐguǎn. Yǒu rén gàosu wǒ jiù zài
     zhè fùjìn.**
     *The British Embassy. Someone told me it's in this
     neighbourhood.*

P   **Shì lí zhèr bù yuǎn.**
     It really is quite close.

T   **Zài něi tiáo lù shang?**
     On what road?

P   **Guānghuá Lù.**
     Guanghua Road.

T   **Hǎo-zhǎo ma?**
     Is it easy to find?

P   **Hěn róngyi: dào qiántou hónglǜdēng wǎng yòu
     guǎi, dì-sān tiáo jiù shi Guānghuá Lù.**
     *Very easy: turn right when you get to the traffic lights
     ahead, and the third street is Guanghua Road.*

T   **Dàshǐguǎn zài lù de něi tóur?**
     Which end of the street is the Embassy?

P   **Hǎoxiàng shi zài xītóur, wǒ bù gǎn kěndìng.**
     *I think it's at the west end, but I can't be certain
     about that.*

T   **Méi guānxi, dào nàr wǒ zài wèn rén. Duō xiè!**
     *It doesn't matter, I will ask someone again when I get
     there. Many thanks.*

P   **Bú kèqi. Ěi, xiǎoxīn qìchē! Bié zài zhèr guò
     mǎlù. Nǐ háishi zǒu rénxínghéngdào ba.**
     *You're welcome. Hey, mind the traffic! Don't cross the
     road here, you'd better use the pedestrian crossing.*

T   **Hǎo, hǎo, hao.**
     Oh, fine, OK.

15.18 'huài' and 'huài le'

Huài means 'bad', 'evil', 'rotten':

Hǎo rén zuò hǎo shì, huài rén zuò huài shì.
Good people do good things, bad people do bad ones.

Huài le means 'become bad', 'gone rotten', 'gone wrong':

Zāole! Yú gēn ròu dōu huài le, bù néng chī le.
Curses! The fish and meat have both gone bad, and have become uneatable.
Duìbuqǐ, wǒ lái wǎn le. Wǒ de biǎo huài le.
I'm sorry I'm late. My watch has gone wrong.

15.19 The missing person

As we saw in 9.1, **gěi** introduces a prepositional phrase before the verb and means 'for'. Sometimes the object of **gěi** is so well understood that it can be left out:

Máfan nǐ gěi (wǒ) xiě yí xiàr.
May I trouble you to write it (for me)?
Nǐ bù shūfu, yīnggāi qǐng dàifu gěi kànkan.
If you aren't well, you should ask the doctor to have a look (for you).

15.20 What's the matter?

Zěnme le? means 'What's the matter?':

Tā zěnme le?
What's the matter with him?
Chē zěnme le? Zěnme bù zǒu le?
What's wrong with the bus? Why won't it go any more?

Exercise 89: New situation 'le'

Translate into English:

1 Tā de shǒu zěnme le?

2 Tā bìng le, bù néng lái le.

3 Nǐ zěnme méi mǎi piào? Duìbuqǐ, wǒ wàng le.

4 Diàntī huài le, wǒmen zǒushàngqu ba.

15.21 'Dà' as an emphasiser

Dà means 'big', 'great', and it is used with certain expressions to give them intensity. So, since **rè tiānr** means 'hot weather', **dà rè tiānr** means 'sizzling hot weather'. **Báitiān** means 'in daylight', so **dà báitiān** means 'in broad daylight':

Dà rè tiānr bié chūqu le.
  Don't go out in this boiling hot weather.
Nǐ zěnme dà báitiān zài jiā li shuì-jiào a?
  How come you're asleep at home in broad daylight?

15.22 Running sounds together

It is quite possible to have more than one particle at the end of a sentence, and sometimes one can fuse with the other. By fusion **le + a** becomes **la**, and **ne + a** becomes **na**:

Tā zhēn lái la?!
  She's really arrived?!
Hái méi chi-fàn na?!
  Still not eaten?!

15.23 What's to be done?

Bàn means 'to see to things', 'to manage', and **Zěnme bàn?** (literally: How to do it?) means 'What's to be done?':

Qìchē, huǒchē, fēijī dōu méi you, nǐ shuō zěnme bàn? Wǒ yě méi fázi.
> There are no buses, trains or aircraft, what do you think we can do?
> I have no way out of this either.

15.24 Turn back

Wǎng, as we saw in 6.4, means 'towards': **wǎng qián zǒu** 'go forwards'. **Wǎng huí zǒu** means 'to turn back':

Qiántou lù huài le, wǒmen zhǐ néng wǎng huí zǒu.
> The road ahead is damaged, there's nothing for it but to turn back.

15.25 Follow the road

Shùnzhe means 'following':

Shùnzhe zhèi tiáo dà lù wǎng dōng zǒu, yídìng néng dào Zhōngguó.
> Go east along this highway and you will certainly be able to get to China.

15.26 'Shàng' again

We have met **shàng** many times, most commonly matched by its opposite **xià**. **Shàng** has an additional function as a verb ending which indicates that an action or state of affairs is being initiated:

chuānshang mián'ǎo
> to put on a jacket
> [cf. **chuān mián'ǎo** to wear a jacket]

dàishang yǎnjìngr
>to put on glasses
>[cf. **dài yǎnjìngr** to wear glasses]

xiěshang míngzi
>to write one's name in/on
>[cf. **xiě míngzi** to write one's name]

qíshang zìxíngchē
>to get on a bicycle
>[cf. **qí zìxíngchē** to ride a bicycle]

Some new words

xiū or **xiūlǐ**	to mend, repair, fix
hòulúnr	rear wheel
hūrán	suddenly
zhuàn	to revolve, turn
lùkǒur	intersection
shízìlùkǒur	crossroads
fāngxiàng	direction

CONVERSATION 15C

A cycling tourist asks the way from a bicycle repairer:

T **Lǎo shīfu, wǒ de chē huài le. Máfan nín gěi xiūlǐ yí xiàr.**
   Maestro, my bike's broken down. Could I ask you to mend it for me?

S **Zěnme le?**
   What's wrong?

T **Bù zhīdao wèishénme, hòulúnr hūrán bú zhuàn le.**
   I don't know why, but the back wheel suddenly stopped going round.

S **Wǒ kànkan … wèntí bú dà.**
   Let me see … No great problem.

T **Mǎshang néng xiūhǎo ma?**
   Can you fix it straight away?

→

S   **Shí fēn zhōng ba. Dà rè tiānr, nǐmen shàng nǎr qù a?**
     It'll take about 10 minutes. Where are you off to in such heat?

T   **Lúgōu Qiáo.**
     To the Marco Polo Bridge.

S   **Shàng Lúgōu Qiáo zěnme zǒu zhèi tiáo lù a?**
     How come you're on this road if you're going to that bridge?

T   **Wǒmen zǒucuò la? Āiyā! Nà zěme bàn na?**
     Have we gone wrong, then? Oh dear! So, what do we do about it?

S   **Bú yàojǐn. Nǐmen xiān wǎng huí zǒu, dào dì-èr ge shízìlùkǒur zài wǎng zuǒ guǎi, shùnzhe dà lù yìzhí xiàqu jiù dào le.**
     Nothing to worry about. First go back the way you came, then turn left at the second crossroads, keep on down the highway and you'll be there.

T   **Lúgōu Qiáo zài něi ge fāngxiàng a?**
     Which direction is the bridge in?

S   **Zài xī biānr. [Points] Nǐmen wǎng zuǒ guǎi jiù shi wǎng xī guǎi. Hǎo le, xiūhǎo le. Qíshang shìshi.**
     West … Turn left and that's turning west. OK, it's mended. Get on and try it.

T   **Duō xiè nín la, lǎo shīfu!**
     Many thanks, maestro!

Exercise 90

Translate into Chinese:

1   Excuse me, is there a post office near here?

    Yes, there's one just in Xinhua Road.

2   How much does it cost to send an airmail letter to Europe?

    International airmail letters all cost ¥2.

3   Excuse me, where is the nearest police station?

    Turn right at the traffic lights. It's at the second crossroads.

4   What's wrong with your telephone?

    I don't know why, but now you can only phone in, we can't dial out.

5   Is the fax machine out of order?

    No, there is a power cut.

6   Which road shall we take?

    Better take the main road, the minor roads are difficult at night.

Chapter 16
Time is money

- *Buying fruit in the market*
- *Buying an air ticket*
- *Rushing for the train*

16.1 All there is

In answer to the question **Tā yǒu shénme?** 'What has he got?' you might well hear the emphatic **Tā shénme dōu yǒu** 'He's got everything' (lit: He whatever all has got). The negative answer in the same vein would be **Tā shénme dōu méi yǒu** 'He hasn't got anything'. Similarly:

Shéi xǐhuan chī Sìchuān cài?
　　Who likes Sichuan food?
Shéi dōu xǐhuan.
　　Everyone likes it.
Shéi dōu bù xǐhuan.
　　No one likes it.

Any of the question words you have learned can be used in this 'all-inclusive' way. In the negative form you have the choice of using either **dōu** or **yě**.

Exercise 91

Answer the following questions in the way indicated:

1   Nǐ xiǎng mǎi něi ge? (*all of them*)

2   Nǎr yǒu Zhōngguó fànguǎnr? (*everywhere*)

3   Nǐ shénme shíhou yǒu gōngfu? (*any time*)

4   Zuótiān wǎnshang nǐ qu kàn shéi le? (*no one*)

16.2   Per unit

There are two ways in which you can ask 'How much for each one?': **Duōshao qián yí ge?** or **Yí ge duōshao qián?** 'How much for one?'. The first of these is probably more commonly used:

Píjiǔ duōshao qián yì píng?
    How much is beer a bottle?

16.3   Going metric

China has decided to adopt the metric (**gōng**) system, but long before she did so she had met with metric measures and had devised a way of translating them. Wherever possible, old Chinese 'market' terms were retained, with the word **gōng** prefixed:

jīn	a catty (0.5 kg)	**gōngjīn**	a kilogram
lǐ	a Chinese mile (0.5 km)	**gōnglǐ**	a kilometre

16.4   Import-export

jìnkǒu	(lit: enter mouth) import
chūkǒu	(lit: exit mouth) export

Tā zài jìn-chūkǒu gōngsī gōngzuò.
    She works for an import-export company.

16.5 Stressing a statement

The little word **kě** is used to give emphasis, just as in English we use 'really', 'certainly', 'in no way':

Jīntiān kě zhēn lěng.
>It's really cold today.

Wǒ kě méi you qián.
>There's no way I've got any money.

16.6 'duìbuqǐ'

We met **duìbuqǐ** right at the beginning of the course.
It means 'sorry', 'pardon me', 'excuse me', and it is made up of three parts:

duì	to face, to match up with
bù	not
qǐ	to rise up

Literally, then, **duìbuqǐ** means 'face not rise up', and it does not stretch the imagination too far to see that that means 'face you but cannot rise up'; that is, 'I am prostrate before you (with shame)'.

The positive form of this negative phrase is **duìdeqǐ** ('face you can rise up') and it means 'to not let someone down', 'to treat someone fairly', 'to be worthy'. There are many other examples of constructions where two verbs have **de** or **bu** sandwiched between them, and sometimes their meanings are not readily apparent, but all of them have the 'can/cannot' idea in common:

mǎideqǐ	to be able to afford (to buy)
mǎibuqǐ	to be unable to afford (to buy)
chīdeqǐ	to be able to afford to eat
chībuqǐ	to be unable to afford to eat

16.7 The four seasons

Chūntiān	spring
Xiàtiān	summer
Qiūtiān	autumn
Dōngtiān	winter

16.8 Guaranteed

Bāo has the meaning 'guaranteed', 'assured', 'absolutely certain to':

Chī-le wǒ de yào, sān tiān bāo hǎo.
> When you've taken my medicine you're guaranteed to be well in three days.

16.9 Twice, thrice, fourfold

The word **bèi** is used to indicate multiples:

Tā bǐ nǐ kuài sān bèi.
> He's three times faster than you are.

Zhōngguó bǐ Rìběn dà èrshiwǔ bèi.
> China is 25 times bigger than Japan.

Note that by a quirk of language **yí bèi** and **liǎng bèi** usually mean the same thing:

Duō yí bèi = duō liǎng bèi = twice as many

16.10 Another particle 'ma'

Ma is used at the end of a statement to point out rather patronisingly that something is very obvious:

Tā shi Yīngguó huáqiáo ma, Yīngyǔ dāngrán hǎo le.
> Of course her English is good: she's a British Overseas Chinese.

Some new words

shuǐguǒ	fruit
píngguǒ	apple
xiāngjiāo	banana
tiāo	to pick, choose
xīgua	water melon
Xīnjiāng	Xinjiang (Autonomous Region)
piányi	cheap
zhǎng	to rise (of price or rivers)
jìjié	season
bù tóng	different, not the same

CONVERSATION 16A

A tourist buys fruit in the market:

S **Xiānsheng, mǎi diǎnr shuǐguǒ ba; wǒmen zhèr shénme dōu yǒu.**
Buy some fruit, sir; we've got all kinds here.

T **Píngguo zěnme mài?**
How much are the apples?

S **Yí kuài bā yì jīn.**
¥1.80 a catty.

T **Xiāngjiāo ne?**
And the bananas?

S **Sān kuài èr. Zhè shi jìnkǒu xiāngjiāo, zuò fēijī lái de, nín yào duōshao?**
¥3.20. These are imported bananas, they came in by air. How many do you want?

T **Wǒ kě chībuqǐ jìnkǒu shuǐguǒ.**
There's no way I can afford to eat imported fruit.

S **Nà nín tiāo ge xīgua ba.**
Then how about choosing a water melon?

T **Qiūtiān dōu kuài guòqu le, zěnme hái yǒu xīgua a?**
Autumn is nearly over, how come there are still water melons?

S   **Zhè shi Xīnjiāng lái de, bāo tián, bù tián bú yào qián!**
These are Xinjiang melons, guaranteed sweet, and if they aren't I won't want your money!

T   **Duōshao qián yì jīn a?**
How much a catty?

S   **Piányi, liǎng kuài bā.**
Very cheap, ¥2.80.

T   **Shénme? Liǎng kuài bā? Xiàtiān cái mài qī máo, zěnme sān ge yuè zhǎng-le sì bèi!**
What? ¥2.80? In summer they only cost 70 cents, how can they have gone up fourfold in three months?

S   **Jìjié bù tóng le ma! Dào-le chūntiān jiu gèng guì le. Nín tiāo něi ge?**
But it's a different season, don't you see? Come the spring they'll be even more expensive. Which one do you choose?

T   **Wǒ něi ge yě bù gǎn tiāo, háishi děngdao míngnián xiàtiān zài chī ba.**
I daren't take any of them, I'd better wait till next summer and have some then.

16.11 Difficult

Nán and **kùnnán** both mean 'difficult'. **Kùnnán** can also be used as the noun 'difficulty':

Qǐng rén bāngmáng hěn (kùn)nán.
    It's very hard to get someone to help.
Wǒmen zuì dà de kùnnán jiù shi rén tài duō.
    Our greatest difficulty is that there are too many people.

Note that only **nán** (not **kùnnán**) can be used as an adverb:

Hànyǔ bù nán-xué.
    Chinese isn't hard to learn.

Exercise 92: Revision

Give the opposite of the following:

1	hǎo	6	pàng	11	piányi
2	duō	7	zǎo	12	róngyi
3	hēi	8	kuài	13	nuǎnhuo
4	dà	9	duì	14	xǐhuan
5	lěng	10	yuǎn		

16.12 Can/cannot verbs (1)

Result verbs can be split by **bu** or **de** just like **duìbuqǐ/duìdeqǐ** in 16.5, and again this gives 'unable to/able to' meanings. So **mǎidào** 'to succeed in buying' can be split into **mǎdedào** 'can be bought' and **mǎibudào** 'cannot be bought'. Similarly:

kàndejiàn/kànbujiàn	able to/unable to see
zuòdewán/zuòbuwán	able to/unable to finish doing
bàndechéng/bànbuchéng	able to/unable to succeed in doing (**chéng** = to succeed, complete)

Zài Lúndūn mǎidedào Zhōngguó píjiǔ ma?
    Can Chinese beer be bought in London?
Zhèi jiàn shì sān tiān zuòbuwán.
    This thing could not be finished in three days.
Fēijī zài nǎr? Tài yuǎn le, wǒ kànbujiàn.
    Where's the plane? It's too far away, I can't see it.

Here are paired sentences which show up some interesting nuances of meaning:

You can buy it in China.	(1) **Nǐ kěyǐ zài Zhōngguó mǎi.**
	(2) **Nǐ zài Zhōngguó mǎidedào.**

(1) might be used in a context such as 'You can buy it in China and save yourself the trouble of buying it elsewhere.'
(2) means 'You can buy it in China, it is available there.'

He says that I can't see it. (1) **Tā shuō wǒ bù néng kàn.**

(2) **Tā shuō wǒ kànbujiàn.**

(1) means that I am not allowed to see it.

(2) means that I am unable to see it or incapable of seeing it.

16.13 In time or not in time

Another common can/cannot verb pair with **de/bu** is
láidejí/láibují. Láidejí means 'to make it in time', 'to be
able to catch it':

Tāmen wǔ diǎn bàn xià-bān, nǐ xiànzài qù hái láidejí.
They come off duty at 5.30, if you go now you will
catch them.
Huǒchē yǐjing kāi le, láibují le.
The train has already started, you won't catch it.

Exercise 93

Fill in the blanks with result verbs:

1   Zhème duō shì, wǒ jīntiān zuò(... ...).

2   Wǒmen zhǐ yǒu èrbǎi kuài qián, chī(... ...) zhème
    guì de yú.

3   Tā bú dài yǎnjìngr, shénme dōu kàn(... ...).

4   Zhǐ yǒu shíwǔ fēn zhōng le, wǒmen zuò chē qù ba,
    zǒu-lù lái(... ...) le.

5   Qù Xīnjiāng de rén bù duō, fēijīpiào yídìng
    mǎi(... ...).

16.14 Don't worry

Fàngxīn literally means 'let your heart relax'. It will translate as 'Don't worry', 'rest assured', 'be at ease' and so on:

Tā yí ge rén chū guó lǚxíng; tā mǔqin hěn bú fàngxīn.
    She went travelling abroad on her own; her mother was very worried.
Nǐ fàngxīn ba, wǒmen yídìng láidejí.
    Don't worry, we'll make it in time.

16.15 'hǎole': then it'll be all right

Jīntiān nǐ zhème máng, wǒ qù hǎole.
    You're so busy today, I'll go (and that'll do it).
Yàoshi nǐ bú fàngxīn, gěi tā dǎ ge diànhuà hǎole.
    If you're worried, phone him up and that'll sort it out.

Some new words

mǎn	full
hétong	contract
qiān	to sign (a contract)
yùnqi	luck
hángbān	flight
wèizi	seat, place
qǐfēi	take-off (of plane)
zhǒng	kind of, sort of (measure word)
míxìn	superstition

CONVERSATION 16B

A western tourist buys an air ticket:

T **Xiáojie, wǒ xiǎng mǎi fēijīpiào.**
    Miss, I'd like to buy an air ticket.
C **Qù nǎr? Něi tiān zǒu a?**
    Where are you going? Which day are you travelling?

T Hā'ěrbīn, shí'èr hào, xià xīngqī sì.
Harbin, the 12th, next Thursday.

C Hā'ěrbīn yǒu jiāoyìhuì, kǒngpà hěn kùnnán.
There's a trade fair on in Harbin, I'm afraid it'll be difficult …

[She checks.]

Bù xíng, quán mǎn le.
It's no good, they're all full.

T Āiyā, zhè zěnme bàn a? Piào mǎibudào, wǒ de hétong jiu qiānbuchéng le.
Oh dear, what's to be done? If I can't get a ticket, my contract can't be signed.

C Nín shénme shíhou qiān hétong a?
When are you to sign the contract?

T Shísān hào xiàwǔ.
On the afternoon of the 13th.

C Nà nín shísān hào shàngwǔ zǒu yě láidejí a. Wǒ kànkan … éi, nín yùnqi zhēn hǎo, shísān hào 6176 hángbān hái yǒu wèizi.
Well then, if you travel on the morning of the 13th you'll still be in time. Let me see … aha, your luck's good, there are still seats on flight 6176 on the 13th.

T Shì ma? Jǐ diǎn néng dào Hā'ěrbīn?
Really? What time can I get to Harbin?

C Shàngwǔ shí diǎn wǔshí qǐfēi, zhōngwǔ shí'èr diǎn bàn dào.
Take-off at 10.50 a.m., arrival 12.30 midday.

T Kěshi … shísān hào shi ge xīngqīwǔ a! Wǒ pà …
But … the 13th is a Friday. I'm afraid …

C Zhōngguó méi zhèi zhǒng míxìn, nín zuò wǒmen fēijī fàngxīn hǎole.
There's no such superstition in China, on our planes you can just stop worrying.

16.16 A bit more ...

'Do it a bit quicker', 'Hit it a bit harder' and so on are
expressed in Chinese using the pattern *verb + adjective +*
(yì) diǎnr.

Wǒ de Hànyǔ bù xíng, qǐng nín shuō màn (yì) diǎnr.
    My Chinese is no good, please speak a bit slower.
Xià-yǔ le, wǒmen zǒu kuài (yì) diǎnr ba!
    It's raining, let's walk a bit faster!
Tài xiǎo le, qǐng nǐ zuò dà (yì) diǎnr kěyǐ ma?
    It's too small, can you make it a bit bigger?

Exercise 94

Use the 'verb + adjective + (yì) diǎnr' pattern.

What would you say to someone if

1   he is speaking too fast?

2   she is selling too expensively?

3   he is always late?

4   she doesn't do her work well?

16.17 From now to then

The same word **lí** 'separated from', which we met in 14.4
and 15.1 in connection with distances, can also be used
for time:

Xiànzài lí qǐfēi shíjiān hái yǒu bàn xiǎoshí.
    There is still half an hour to take-off time.
Lí kāi huì zhǐ yǒu yí gè xīngqī le.
    There's only one week until the meeting takes place.

16.18 Can/cannot verbs (2)

Another 'success' word for can/cannot verbs is **kāi**, which basically means 'to open' but as a success word conveys an idea of 'detachment' or 'separation':

Zhèi píng píjiǔ kāibukāi.
> This bottle of beer can't be opened.

Wǒ zhèngzài kāi huì zǒubukāi, wǎnshang qu kàn nǐ, xíng ma?
> I'm in a meeting and can't leave; is it all right if I go to see you this evening?

Yìbǎi kuài yì zhāng de Rénmínbì, wǒ zhǎobukāi.
> A ¥100 note, I can't give change for that.

16.19 Forget it!

Suàn means 'to calculate', but the colloquial expression **suànle** or **suànle ba** has the special meanings of 'let it be!', 'let it pass!', 'that'll do!', 'forget it!':

Tiānqi zhème huài, suànle, bié qù Chángchéng le.
> The weather's so bad, let's forget it, we won't go to the Great Wall after all.

Suànle ba, bié gēn tā shuō le, shuō-le yě méi yòng.
> Give up, don't talk to her any more; it wouldn't be any good if you did.

Some new words

gǎn	to catch, catch up with
gǎnbushàng	to be unable to catch up
dòng	to move
zǒubudòng	to be unable to move along
zháojí	worried, uptight, anxious
gāofēng	a high peak
gāofēng shíjiān	peak time
wēixiǎn	danger, dangerous

CONVERSATION 16C

Rushing for the train

P   **Shīfu, wǒ yào gǎn qī diǎn sìshiwǔ de huǒchē, néng bu néng kāi kuài diǎnr?**
Driver, I want to catch the 7.45 train, can you drive a bit faster?

D   **Nín kànkan, chē zhème duō, zǒubudòng a!**
Just look, there's so much traffic, we can't move!

P   **Lí kāi chē zhǐ yǒu èrshi fēn zhōng le, yàoshi gǎnbushàng zhèi bān chē …**
It's only 20 minutes to departure, and if I don't catch this one …

D   **Nín bié zháojí, dà lù zǒubudòng, wǒmen huàn xiǎo lù.**
Don't worry, since the main road is clogged we'll change onto the minor roads.

P   **Gāofēng shíjiān xiǎo lù yě zhème jǐ … Xiǎoxīn!**
At peak hour the minor roads are just as crowded … Watch out!

D   **Méi shìr. Zhè xiē zìxíngchē zhēn tǎoyàn!**
No problem. These bicycles are a real nuisance!

P   **Shīfu, tài wēixiǎn le, háishi kāi màn diǎnr ba!**
Driver, it's too dangerous, you'd better drive slower!

D   **… Hǎo le, chēzhàn dào le, hái yǒu bā fēn zhōng, kěndìng láidejí.**
… We're all right, we've got to the station and there are still eight minutes. You're sure to be in time.

P   **Xièxie nǐ a, shīfu.** *[Pays fare.]* **Zhè shi yìbǎi.**
Thank you, driver … Here's a hundred.

D   **Āiyā, yìbǎi? Wǒ zhǎobukāi a …**
Oh dear, a hundred? I can't change it …

P   *[Looks at watch.]*
Suànle, bú bì zhǎo le. Zàijiàn!
Forget it, no need to make change. Goodbye!

Exercise 95

Translate into Chinese:

1 How are the bananas sold?

   ¥2.60 a catty, two catties for ¥5.

2 Are all fruit getting more expensive?

   Yes, apples now cost ¥1.20 a catty: three times more than they were last year.

3 I'm afraid that you won't get there in time if you take the train.

   It can't be helped: I can't afford an air ticket.

4 What can we do if we miss the 6.45 train?

   Don't worry, there is another one at 6.55.

5 The plane is about to take off; please hurry up.

   What did you say? Could you speak more slowly?

6 Where are you going this summer?

   I shall go wherever is cheap.

Chapter 17
What's it like?

- *Describing missing luggage*
- *Problems with the hotel room*
- *Describing symptoms to the doctor*

17.1 Colour shades

Chinese uses the words **shēn** (deep) and **qiǎn** (shallow) for 'dark' and 'light' of certain colours:

shēn lán   dark blue
qiǎn lǜ   light green

17.2 Brands and trademarks

Páir (or **páizi**) means 'a label', 'a tag', 'a plate', but is also commonly used for a brand or trademark:

xíngli páir
  luggage tag/label
Nín yào shénme páir de jiāojuǎnr?
  What brand of film do you want?

17.3 The 'bǎ' construction (1)

We have mostly used the *Subject + Verb + Object (S-V-O)*
sentence pattern, because this is the basic one for Chinese.
But sometimes it is necessary to put the *object* in front of the
verb rather than after it, in order to stress what it is that is
done to the object. To do this, **bǎ**, a word which means 'to
grasp', 'to take', is used. So instead of *S-V-O* the pattern
becomes *S-bǎ-O-Verbal phrase*, as much as to say 'Subject
takes the object and does something to it'. Here are some
examples:

Qǐng nǐ bǎ zhèi zhāng piào gěi <u>Wáng xiānsheng</u>.
 Please give this ticket to Mr Wang.
Tā bǎ dōngxi bān<u>zǒu le</u>.
 He moved the things out.
Qǐng nǐ bǎ chē kāi<u>dào wǒ jiā lai</u>.
 Please drive the car over here to my house.
Bié bǎ xíngli fàng<u>zai nàr</u>.
 Don't put the luggage there.

What is common to all these is that, if the object had not
been moved, it would have competed with other things (the
underlined phrases) for the position after the verb, and the
desired stress would have been lost in the clutter. Note that
the object is always a definite one ('the' rather than 'a').

Exercise 96

Translate into English:

1 Tā yǐjing bǎ qián gěi wǒ le.

2 Wǒ kěyǐ bǎ zhèi ge bāor fàngzai zhèr ma?

3 Shéi bǎ wǒ de zhàoxiàngjī názǒu le?

4 Qǐng nǐ bǎ zhèi ge nádào lóushang qu.

17.4 Have a go

Shì means 'to try', and the expression **shìshi kàn** means 'try it and see'. Some other expressions are constructed in the same way, for instance:

Wènwen kàn.
>   Let's ask and see.

Bǐbǐ kàn.
>   We'll compare them and see.

Exercise 97

Translate into English:

1 Nǐ shìshi kàn: dà hào zěnmeyàng?

2 Dàjiā xiǎngxiǎng kàn: něi ge fázi hǎo?

3 Wǒ wàngle fàngzai nǎr le. Wǒ qu zhǎozhǎo kàn.

4 Huǒchē shénme shíhou dào, nǐ qu wènwen kàn.

Some new words

chá	to check, look into, investigate
jiàngluò	to land (of an aircraft)
xiāngzi	suitcase, box, trunk
huī	grey
lúnzi	wheel
jìde	to remember
hòu	thick (in dimension)
yīfu	clothes
jìxù	to continue, go on

CONVERSATION 17A

An airline passenger asks a ground stewardess about his missing luggage:

P   **Xiáojie, máfan nǐ tì wǒ chá yí xiàr xíngli hǎo ma?**
    *Could I trouble you to check for my luggage
    for me, miss?*

G   **Nín zuò de shi něi ge hángbān?**
    Which flight were you on?

P   **CA109, cóng Xiānggǎng lái de.**
    CA109 from Hong Kong.

G   **109 yǐjing jiàngluò yí ge bàn xiǎoshí le, xíngli
    zǎojiù chūlai le.**
    *It's already an hour and a half since 109 landed, and
    the luggage came out ages ago.*

P   **Kěshi méi you wǒ de xiāngzi.**
    But my case wasn't there.

G   **Nín de xiāngzi shi shénme yánsè de?**
    What colour is your case?

P   **Shēn huīsè de, yǒu lúnzi.**
    It's dark grey, with wheels.

G   **Duō dà?**
    How big?

P   **Gēn nèi biānr nèi ge hóng xiāngzi yíyàng dà.**
    The same size as that red case over there.

G   **Shénme páir de?**
    What make?

P   **Wǒ bú jìde le, hǎoxìang shi Fǎguó zuò de.**
    *I don't remember, but I've an idea that it was
    French made.*

G   **Nín bǎ xíngli páir gěi wǒ, wǒ qu gěi nín
    chácha kàn.**
    *Give me your luggage ticket and I'll go and check
    for you.*

→

[Five minutes later]

G   **Dùibuqǐ, méi yǒu.**
    I'm sorry, it's not there.

P   **Āiyā, nà zěnme bàn? Tiānqi zhème lěng, wǒ de hòu yīfu dōu zài xiāngzi li ne.**
    Oh dear, what can I do? It's so cold, and my thick clothes are all in the case.

G   **Nín xiān tián zhāng biǎo, wǒmen zài jìxù gěi nín zhǎo.**
    First fill in a form, then we'll go on looking for it for you.

17.5 To such an extent that

We have met several ways of qualifying adjectives:

Xīgua <u>hěn</u> guì.
> Water melons are very expensive.

Xīgua <u>zhēn</u> guì.
> Water melons are really expensive.

Xīgua guì <u>jíle</u>.
> Water melons are extremely expensive.

More complicated qualifying phrases can easily be dealt with by using the marker **de**, which gives the sense of 'in such a way that' or 'to such an extent that':

Xīgua guì de méi rén mǎideqǐ.
> Water melons are so expensive that no one can afford to buy them. [Water melons are expensive to such an extent that no one can afford to buy them.]

Tiānqi lěng de shéi dōu bù xiǎng chūqu.
> The weather is so cold that no one wants to go out.

Exercise 98

Fuse two together, as in the example:

A   Tiānqi tài rè le.   B   Wǒ bù xiǎng chī-fàn.
Tiānqi rè de wǒ bù xiǎng chī-fàn.

1   A   Tā tài lèi le.   B   Tā zǒubudòng le.
2   A   Yǔ tài dà le.   B   Wǒmen bù néng chūqu le.
3   A   Zhōngguó cài tài   B   Shéi dōu xiǎng chī.
        hǎo chī le.
4   A   Tā de xiāngzi   B   Shí ge rén dōu
        tài dà le.   bānbudòng.

17.6 Don't bring that up again!

Tí means 'to lift up', and **Bié tí le!** is just like the English
'Don't bring that up again!', 'Don't even mention it!'

Zuótiān chī de hǎo ba?
Bié tí le, nàr de cài yòu guì yòu nán-chī.
  You ate well yesterday, I suppose?
  Don't talk about it, the food there was both expensive
  and not good.
Nǐ de Hànyǔ hěn liúlì le ba?
Bié tí le, wǒ sān ge yuè méi liànxi le.
  Your Chinese must have become very fluent, surely?
  Don't even mention it, it's been three months since I
  practised it.

17.7 It would be better if I didn't …

The pattern **bu** + *verb* + **háihǎo, yi** + *verb* is used to give the
meaning 'It would be better if I didn't …, because no sooner
do I than …':

Zhèi ge wèntí bù xiǎng hái hǎo, yì xiǎng wǒ jiu zháojí.
It would be better not to think about this problem,
because as soon as I do I get anxious.
Dàifu gěi wǒ de yào bù chī hái hǎo, yì chī dùzi gèng téng le.
It would have been better if I hadn't taken the medicine
the doctor gave me, because no sooner had I taken it
than my stomach ached even worse.

17.8 'nòng'

The basic meaning of **nòng** is 'to play around with', but it
has an all-purpose use something like the verbs 'to make',
'to get' and 'to do' in English:

Shéi bǎ wǒ de zìxíngchē nònghuài le?
Who's damaged my bike?
Tā méi bǎ zhèi jiàn shì nòng qīngchu.
He didn't get this clear.

17.9 Free of charge

Miǎnfèi means 'gratis', 'free of charge':

Zài zhèr kàn yí cì dàifu duōshao qián?
Wánquán miǎnfèi.
How much does it cost here for a consultation
with the doctor?
It's absolutely free.

17.10 Hospitality

The word for 'a reception' is **zhāodàihuì**. **Zhāodài** means 'to
serve', 'to entertain':

Chī, zhù bú bì gěi qián, jiāoyìhuì miǎnfèi zhāodài.
There is no need to pay for food or accommodation, the
Trade Fair provides it all free of charge.

232

17.11 To set out from home

Chūmén literally means 'to go out of the door', and it has an extended meaning of 'to set out from home':

Tā měi tiān zǎochen qī diǎn bàn chūmén.
He leaves home every morning at 7.30.

17.12 Can/cannot with 'liǎo'

Liǎo means 'to finish', 'to settle', 'to dispose of' and forms a partnership with many other verbs in can/cannot patterns:

chūdeliǎo/chūbuliǎo:
Hěn duō shì hái méi zuòwán, qī diǎn zhōng chūbuliǎo mén.
There are a lot of things I haven't finished doing, I cannot leave at 7 o'clock.

chīdeliǎo/chībuliǎo:
Tā chīdeliǎo yí ge dà xīgua ma?
Can he eat a whole large water melon?

zuòdeliǎo/zuòbuliǎo:
Zhèi jiàn shì yí ge rén zuòbuliǎo.
This thing can't be done by one person.

Some new words

ānjìng	quiet
kōngtiáo	air-conditioning
chuānghu	window
fēng	wind, breeze
gōngchǎng	factory
(hēi)yān	(black) smoke
chuī	to blow
tào	a suit (measure for clothes)
xīzhuāng	a (western-style) suit
zāng	dirty
dāying	to respond; agree to
xǐ	to wash
kāishǐ	to begin

CONVERSATION 17B

A hotel guest talks with his Chinese friend:

C À, zhèi fángjiān zhēn bú cuò, yòu ānjìng yòu liángkuai.
Ah, this room is not bad at all, it's quiet and cool.

G Nǐ zuótiān lái jiu hǎo le.
You should have come yesterday!

C Wèishénme?
Why is that?

G Zuótiān zhèi qū tíng diàn, méi you kōngtiáo, rè de wǒ yí yè méi shuìhǎo.
This district had a power cut yesterday, there was no air-conditioning and it was so hot that I didn't sleep well all night.

C Nǐ kěyǐ bǎ chuānghu dǎkāi ya, lóu zhème gāo, yídìng yǒu fēng.
You could open the window, this building is so high there'd certainly be a breeze.

G Bié tí le, bù kāi chuānghu hái hǎo, yì kāi chuānghu duìmiàn gōngchǎng de hēiyān quán chuījìnlai le, bǎ wǒ nèi tào bái xīzhuāng dōu nòng zāng le.
Don't talk about that, it would have been better not to have opened it, because as soon as I did, all the smoke from the factory opposite blew in and made my white suit filthy.

C Nǐ méi zhǎo jīnglǐ ma?
Didn't you send for the manager?

G Zhǎo le, tā dāying miǎnfèi tì wǒ xǐgānjing.
I did, and he agreed to have it washed for me free of charge.

C Nà hái bú cuò. Ēi, nǐ kuài huàn yīfu ba, Dàshǐguǎn de zhāodàihuì qī diǎn kāishǐ.
That's not so bad. Hey, hurry up and change, the Embassy reception starts at 7 o'clock.

G Nǐ yí ge rén qù ba, wǒ de xīzhuāng hái méi xǐhǎo ne, chūbuliǎo mén.
You go on your own, my suit is still not ready, so I can't go out.

17.13 Ailments

Téng means 'sore', 'ache', 'pain':

tóuténg	headache
dùziténg	stomach-ache
yáténg	toothache
hóulóngténg	sore throat
késou	cough

17.14 Parts of the face

yǎnjing	eyes (not to be confused with **yǎnjìngr** 'glasses')
bízi	nose
ěrduo	ears
zuǐ	mouth

17.15 Getting through

Tōng means 'to get through', 'to communicate', 'to penetrate':

lù bù tōng le	the road is impassable
bízi bù tōng	blocked-up nose
diànhuà dǎbutōng	to be unable to get through on the phone

17.16 To be a bit …

Yǒu yì diǎnr or **yǒu diǎnr** 'to be a little bit', 'to have a little bit' can be used in front of an adjective or auxiliary verb:

Wǒ jīntiān yǒu yì diǎnr bù shūfu.
> I'm a little unwell today.

Mǎibudào piào, tā xīn li yǒu diǎnr zháojí.
> She can't get a ticket and she's feeling a bit anxious.

Zhèi zhǒng píngguǒ yǒu (yì) diǎnr guì.
> This kind of apple is rather costly.

235

(cf. **Zhèi zhǒng píngguǒ (bǐ nèi zhǒng) guì yì diǎnr.**
   This kind of apple is a bit more costly than that kind.)
Tā hǎoxiàng yǒu diǎnr bù gāoxìng.
   He seems a bit unhappy.
(cf. **Tā hǎoxiàng hěn gāoxìng.**
   He seems very happy: **yǒu (yì) diǎnr** is only used for
   things which are undesirable.)

Exercise 99: Not quite opposite

Make a contrasting statement using yǒu (yì) diǎnr, *as
in the example:*

Zhèi jiàn shì hěn róngyi.

Nèi jiàn shì <u>yǒu diǎnr kùnnán</u>.

1 Jīntiān hěn nuǎnhuo. → Zuótiān …

2 Zhèr de dōngxi hěn piányi. → Nàr de dōngxi …

3 Gōngyuán lǐtou hěn ānjìng. → Gōngyuán wàitou …

4 Tā de yīfu hěn gānjing. → Tā àiren de yīfu …

5 Zài Běijīng qí zìxíngchē hěn ānquán. → Zài Lúndūn
   qí zìxíngchē …

17.17 The 'bǎ' construction (2)

Quite often the use of **bǎ** stresses the result of an action or
gives a sense of deliberateness to it, sometimes even a sense
as strong as the English 'He went and …':

Qǐng nǐ bǎ xíngli dǎkāi.
   Please open your luggage.
Qǐng nǐ bǎ zuǐ zhāngkāi.
   Please open your mouth. (**zhāng** = to stretch open)
Kuài bǎ yīfu chuānshang.
   Hurry up and put your clothes on.
Tā yǐjing bǎ chē xiūhǎo le.
   He's already mended the car.
Tā bǎ wǒ de biǎo dǎhuài le.
   She went and smashed my watch.

Exercise 100

Fill in the blanks along the lines suggested:

1 Shéi bǎ zhèi píng jiǔ hē … le? (*finish drinking*)

2 Wǒ yǐjing bǎ yīfu xǐ … … le. (*wash clean*)

3 Qǐng nǐ bǎ dìzhǐ liú … . (*leave*)

4 Tā yǐjing bǎ fàn zuò … le. (*make ready*)

17.18 The verb 'ràng'

Ràng means 'to let', 'to allow', 'to cause':

Tā zěnme le? Ràng wǒ kànkan.
What's happened to him? Let me see.
Dàifu bú ràng tā zuò fēijī.
The doctor wouldn't let her fly.
Wǒmen xiān gàosu tā ba, bié ràng tā zháojí.
Let's tell her first, we shouldn't let her be worried.

17.19 Another step in time

In 7.1 we saw that 'the day before yesterday' is **qiántiān**. Chinese can go one further step backwards by using **dàqiántiān**, where English only has the clumsy term 'the day before the day before yesterday'. Logically enough, **dàhòutiān** means 'the day after the day after tomorrow'.

17.20 Not much good

We have seen in 11.3 and 13.20 that question words can be used as indefinites. Here are more examples of indefinites, used in the negative:

Zhèi zhǒng yào méi shenme yòng.
This medicine isn't much use.

Jīntiān de xīgua bù zenme tián.
The water melons aren't very sweet today.

17.21 Further uses of 'kāi'

We have met **kāi** mostly in its basic meaning of 'to open', 'to start' (cf. 16.18). Note these other uses:

kāi zhīpiào	to write a cheque
kāi yàofāng	to write out a prescription

Some new words

juéde	to feel
gǎnmào	influenza, 'flu
shì-biǎo	to take someone's temperature
fāyán	inflammation
xiāohuà	digestion
shàngyī	upper garments
jiěkāi	to open up
Hǎinán	Hainan (island province off South China)
zhēnjiǔ	acupuncture (and moxibustion)
Zhōngyào	Chinese medicine
kāishuǐ	boiled water

CONVERSATION 17C

A tourist with 'flu sees the doctor:

D   **Qǐng zuò, nǎr bù shūfu?**
     Sit down, what's the problem?

T   **Tóuténg, késou, bízi bù tōng, juéde tèbié lèi, hǎoxiàng shi gǎnmào.**
     My head aches, I've got a cough, my nose is blocked up, I feel extremely tired; I think it's 'flu.

D   **Shénme shíhou kāishǐ de?**
When did it start?

T   **Qiántiān wǎnshang.**
The night before last.

D   **Xiān shìshi-biǎo ba.**
Let me take your temperature first.

T   **Fāshāo ma?**
Have I got a fever?

D   **Yǒu yì diǎnr, 37 dù 4. Qǐng nǐ bǎ zuǐ zhāngkāi. Ā-a-a … Èn, hóulóng yǒu diǎnr fāyán. Xiāohuà zěnmeyàng?**
A little, 37.4°. Please open your mouth. Aaah … Hmm, your throat is a bit inflamed. How's your digestion?

T   **Hái hǎo, kěshi méi wèikǒu.**
It's OK, but I have no appetite.

D   **Qǐng nǐ bǎ shàngyi jiěkāi, ràng wǒ tīngtīng … Méi shenme, jiù shi gǎnmào le.**
Please open up your upper clothing and let me listen … Nothing much, it is only the 'flu.

T   **Dàifu, wǒ dàhòutiān děi qù Hǎinán, yòng zhēnjiǔ shì bu shi kěyǐ ràng gǎnmào kuài diǎnr hǎo?**
Doctor, in three days time I have to go to Hainan: could acupuncture get 'flu cured quicker?

D   **Gǎnmào jiù shi xūyào duō xiūxi, zhēnjiǔ yě méi shenme yòng. Wǒ gěi nǐ kāi ji zhǒng Zhōngyào, hòutiān zài lai kàn. Ò, bié wàng-le duō hē kāishuǐ!**
What 'flu needs is lots of rest, acupuncture won't be much use. I'll write you out some prescriptions for Chinese medicine, and you come back to see me the day after tomorrow. Oh, don't forget to drink plenty of boiled water!

Exercise 101

Translate into Chinese:

1 Will you please give this letter to Mr Wang?

Yes, I will.

2 What time will the plane land in Hong Kong?

I don't know. I'll go and ask.

3 Is he very busy today?

Yes, he is so busy that he hasn't had his lunch
(**wǔfàn**) yet.

4 Did you find her?

No, I had the address wrong.

Chapter 18
The high life

- *Ordering a meal*
- *Buying a painting*
- *Planning a night out*

18.1 Do whatever you like

We met question words in their '-ever' forms in 13.23. Here are some more examples where using question words twice gives the idea 'Do whatever you like':

Xǐhuan <u>shénme</u> jiù chī <u>shénme</u>.
   Eat whatever is liked.
Xiǎng mǎi <u>něi</u> ge jiù mǎi <u>něi</u> ge.
   Buy whichever is wanted.
Yīnggāi zhǎo <u>shéi</u> jiù zhǎo <u>shéi</u>.
   Call on whoever ought to be called on.
<u>Nǎr</u> hǎowánr jiù qù <u>nǎr</u>.
   Go wherever is good fun.
Nǐ yào <u>duōshao</u> wǒ jiù gěi (nǐ) <u>duōshao</u>.
   I'll give you however much you want.

18.2 Foreigner

Wàiguó (lit: outside country) means 'foreign', and a **wàiguó rén** is a 'foreigner'. **Lǎo wài** (lit: old outside) is a rather informal version of the word; so **lǎo wài** is to **wàiguó rén** as 'Aussie' is to 'Australian'.

18.3 Culinary seasoning

Táng 'sugar' makes things **tián** 'sweet'.
Cù 'vinegar' makes things **suān** 'sour'.
Yán 'salt' makes things **xián** 'salty'.
Làjiāo 'chilli' makes things **là** 'peppery-hot'.

18.4 The more ... the better

Yuè ... yuè ... is used to mean 'the more ... the more ...':

Qǐng dàifu mǎshang lái, yuè kuài yuè hǎo.
 Ask the doctor to come at once, the quicker the better.
Zhōngguó cài, wǒ yuè chī yuè xiǎng chī.
 The more I eat Chinese food, the more I want to eat it.

When only one idea is involved, as in 'gets more and more X', Chinese uses the pattern **yuè lái yuè X** 'the more time goes by the more X':

Dōngxi yuè lái yuè guì le.
 Things get more and more expensive.

Exercise 102

Translate into English:

1 Qǐng nǐ míngtiān shàngwǔ lái, yuè zǎo yuè hǎo.

2 Wǒ yuè zháojí yuè bú huì shuō.

3 Wèishénme tā yuè chī yuè shòu?

4 Xué Zhōngwén de rén yuè lái yuè duō le.

18.5 Cuisine

Chǎo 'to stir-fry' is a well-known Chinese cooking technique. Some standard dishes are:

chǎo qīngcài/jīdīng/ròupiàn ...
    stir-fried green vegetables/diced chicken/sliced pork ...

Hóngshāo (lit: red-cooked) is another technique, based on braising in soy sauce:

hóngshāo jī/ròu/yú/dòufu ...
    red-cooked chicken/pork/fish/beancurd ...

Here are some other common dishes:

làzi jīdīng	diced chicken with chilli
tángcù páigu	sweet-and-sour spare ribs
suānlà tāng	sour-and hot soup

18.6 'lái': to cause to come

Lái of course basically means 'to come', but it is also used as 'to cause to come', 'to bring':

Gěi wǒmen lái liǎng píng píjiǔ.
    Bring us two bottles of beer.

18.7 Suit yourself

Suíbiàn has a range of meanings, from 'easy-going' to 'please yourself' and 'at your convenience'. Note that sometimes the word can be split, as in the third example here:

Suíbiàn zuò, bié kèqi!
    Please sit as you please, no need to stand on ceremony.
Nín suíbiàn gěi duōshao dōu xíng.
    It's fine to give as much as you please.

Wǒmen shénme shíhou qù? Suí (nǐ) biàn.
What time shall we go? It's up to you.

18.8 Despite

Bié kàn literally means 'don't look at', and is used where English might say 'regardless of' or 'despite':

Bié kàn tā nàme yǒu-qián, zhǐ yǒu yí tào xīzhuāng.
Despite being so rich, he only has one suit.

18.9 Ain't it the truth!

In 16.5 we met **kě**, meaning 'certainly', 'really'. It forms part of the emphatic colloquial expression **Kě bú shì ma**, 'Not half!':

Tā yú zuò de zhēn hǎo!　　　**Kě bú shì ma!**
　She cooks fish beautifully!　　　I couldn't agree more!

Some new words

diǎn cài	order a (restaurant) meal
yǒu-míng	famous, renowned
mǐfàn	(cooked) rice
jiǎozi	filled dumplings
bǎo	full, replete
è	hungry, starving
xíguàn	custom; to be accustomed to
kuàizi	chopsticks

CONVERSATION 18A

A Chinese host orders a meal for his foreign guest:

H　**Nǐ xǐhuan chī shénme jiù diǎn shénme, bié kèqi.**
　Order whatever you like to eat, don't restrain yourself at all.

G   **Wǒ bú huì kèqi, kěshi wǒ zhèi ge 'lǎo wài'
    kànbudǒng càidān, háishi máfan nǐ ba.**
    *I don't even know how to be polite! But silly old
    foreigner that I am, I can't read the menu, so I'd
    better trouble you.*

H   **Zhèr de <u>làzi jīdīng</u> hěn yǒu-míng, nǐ néng
    chī là de ma?**
    *The diced chicken with chilli here is very famous,
    can you take hot foods?*

G   **Néng, wǒ ài chī là de, yuè là yuè hǎo.**
    Yes, I love hot things, the hotter the better.

H   **<u>Tángcù páigu</u> zěnmeyàng?**
    What about sweet-and-sour spare ribs?

G   **Hǎo jíle.**
    Super.

H   **Zài lái yí ge <u>hóngshāo yú</u>, yí ge <u>chǎo qīngcài</u>, yí
    ge <u>suānlà tāng</u> …**
    *And then we'll have red-cooked fish, stir-fried green
    vegetables, hot-and-sour soup …*

G   **Tài duō le ba?**
    Isn't that too much?

H   **Bù duō. Nǐ xiǎng chī mǐfàn, háishi xiǎng
    chī jiǎozi?**
    It's not a lot. Would you rather have rice or dumplings?

G   **Suíbiàn, dōu xíng. Zhōngwǔ méi chībǎo,
    wǒ kě zhēn è le.**
    *It doesn't matter, either will do. At lunch I didn't have
    enough and I'm really hungry now.*

H   **Ò, duì le, nǐ xíguàn yòng kuàizi ma?**
    Oh, by the way, are you used to using chopsticks?

G   **Méi wèntí, bié kàn wǒ Zhōngwén bù xíng,
    kuàizi yòng de hái kěyǐ. Zhōngguó cài bú yòng
    kuàizi bù hǎo-chī.**
    *No problem. Despite my poor Chinese, I'm not bad
    with chopsticks. Chinese food is only good with
    chopsticks.*

H   **Kě bú shì ma!**
    You're absolutely right!

18.10 How terrific!

Dūo or **duōme** and the particle **a** enable you to 'exclaim' over something:

Tiānqi duō hǎo a, chūqu wánr wánr ba.
How lovely the weather is! Let's go out to play.
Zhè cài zuò de duōme piàoliang a!
How beautifully the dish is cooked!

Exercise 103

Turn the sentences into exclamations, as in the example:

Lúndūn dōngxi guì. → Lúndūn dōngxi duōme guì a!

1 Tā Fǎyǔ shuō de hǎo.

2 Xué Zhōngwén bù róngyi.

3 Yàoshi wǒmen yǒu chuánzhēn jiù fāngbiàn le.

4 Kànjiàn hóngdēng bù tíng hěn wēixiǎn.

18.11 What a shame!

Kěxī means 'it's too bad', 'what a pity':

Zhème hǎo de bīnguǎn, kěxī lí gōngchǎng tài jìn le.
Such a nice hotel, what a pity it's too close to the factory.
Zhème hǎo de bīnguǎn méi rén zhù, duōme kěxī a!
Such a nice hotel, what a shame that no one stays there.

18.12 Painting a painting

'To paint' is **huà** and 'a painting' is **huàr**, so the Chinese and the English seem to echo each other:

huà huàr   to paint a painting

18.13 'duì' again

Note the use of the word **duì** ('towards') in the following cases where English uses 'in' or 'about':

Tā duì guójì wèntí hěn yǒu-yánjiū.
She's very knowledgeable about international problems.
Tà duì zuò Zhōngguó cài méi you xìngqù (or **bù gǎn xìngqù**).
He has no interest in cooking Chinese food.
(**xìngqu** = interest)

18.14 Large numbers

So far we have met numbers up into the hundreds only. The word for 'a thousand' is **qiān**. Beyond that, English then counts thousands ('ten thousand', 'a hundred thousand') but Chinese has a word **wàn** which means 'ten thousand' and it is this which is the base word for higher figures. Compare the two systems carefully:

yìqiān	1,000
yíwàn	10,000
shíwàn	100,000
yìbǎiwàn	1,000,000
yìqiānwàn	10,000,000
yíwànwàn	100,000,000

Wànwàn is now usually replaced by the word **yì**.

Exercise 104

Read off the following figures:

1	1,500	4	678,400,000
2	24,678	5	1,154,260,000
3	186,395		

18.15 Apologies

Duìbuqǐ is the common way of saying 'sorry', and it will stand you in good stead. You can make it a little more heart-felt by adding **hěn** in front: **hěn duìbuqǐ** 'I'm very sorry'. A more formal expression, equivalent perhaps to 'I very much regret that ...', is **fēicháng bàoqiàn**.

18.16 Haggling

The word for 'price' is **jiàqian**. In many markets and in some shops, bargaining for the price is still the practice, and the word for 'to bargain' is **jiǎng-jià** (literally: talk price):

Tā hěn huì jiǎng-jià.
　　She's very good at bargaining.

18.17 Not even one measure

The simple sentence **Nǐ bú pàng** means 'You're not fat'. Much more emphatic is **Nǐ yì diǎnr yě bú pàng**
 or (using **dōu** instead of **yě**) **Nǐ yì diǎnr dōu bú pàng**
'You one bit even not fat', i.e. 'You aren't even a bit fat':

Tā yí ge rén dōu bú rènshi.
　　She doesn't even know one person.
Wǒ yí cì Zhōngyào dōu méi chī-guo.
　　I haven't taken even one dose of Chinese medicine.

18.18 'kāi' again

In 17.21 we met **kāi zhīpiào** 'to write a cheque'. **Kāi** is similarly used in **kāi zhèngmíng** 'to issue a certificate':

Bié wàng-le qǐng yīyuàn gěi nǐ kāi ge zhèngmíng.
　　Don't forget to ask the hospital to issue you with
　　a certificate.

18.19 Plastic acceptability

Xìnyòngkǎ are 'credit cards'; shōu means 'to receive', 'to accept':

Nǐmen shōu bu shōu xìnyòngkǎ?
Do you take credit cards?

Some new words

fú	(measure for paintings)
héhuā	lotus flower
shānshuǐ	scenery, landscape (lit: hills and water)
Wànlǐ Chángchéng	the (10,000 li) Great Wall
nóng	dense, heavy, thick
Hè!	(exclamation of surprise or wonder)
Yìnxiàngpài	Impressionist school
nèiháng	expert
yúnhǎi	sea of clouds
guóyíng	state-operated, state-run
chūjìng	to leave the country

CONVERSATION 18B

A tourist buys a painting from a shop assistant:

S **Nín kàn zhèi fú héhuā duō piàoliang a!**
See how beautiful this lotus flower painting is!

T **Wǒ bǐjiào xǐhuan shānshuǐ … Zhèi fú 'Wànlǐ Chángchéng' huà de bú cuò. Kěxī yánsè tài nóng le.**
I rather prefer landscapes … This 'Great Wall' is painted rather well. What a pity that the colour is too heavy.

S **Nín duì Zhōngguó huàr hěn yǒu-yánjiū a!**
You're very knowledgeable about Chinese paintings!

T **Náli, zhǐ shi yǒu-xìngqù … Hè, zhèi fú 'Huángshān' hǎo a! Wánquán shi Yìnxiàngpài.**
Oh, I wouldn't say that, it's just that I'm interested …
→

249

> *Hey, this 'Huang Shan' is good! It's completely Impressionist.*

S   **Nín zhēn nèiháng!**
> *You're really expert!*

T   [Pointing at the price tag]
Zhè shi jiàqian ma? Liǎngwàn liùqiān wǔ? Tài guì le ba!
> *Is this the price? 26,500? That's terribly expensive!*

S   **Yì diǎnr yě bú guì. Nín kàn zhè yúnhǎi huà de duō hǎo a, hái zài dòng ne!**
> *It's not at all expensive. Look how well done the sea of clouds is, it's still moving!*

T   **Néng piányi diǎnr ma?**
> *Can you make it a bit cheaper?*

S   **Fēicháng bàoqiàn, wǒmen guóyíng shāngdiàn bù jiǎng-jià.**
> *I much regret that we state-run shops do not bargain.*

T   **Dài chūjìng yǒu wèntí ma?**
> *Any problems with taking it out of the country?*

S   **Méi wèntí, nín fàngxīn, wǒmen gěi nín kāi zhèngmíng.**
> *No problem. Don't worry, we will issue you with a certificate.*

T   **Nǐmen shōu bu shōu xìnyòngkǎ?**
> *Do you take credit cards?*

S   **Shōu, shōu.**
> *Certainly we do.*

18.20 Busy at

Mángzhe means 'busy at', 'busy with':

mángzhe xué Hànyǔ
    busy studying Chinese
mángzhe kàn péngyou
    busy visiting friends
mángzhe kāi huì
    busy in meetings

18.21 Apart from …

Chúle X yǐwài means 'apart from X':

Wǒ de péngyou chúle nǐ yǐwài dōu qù-guo Zhōngguó.
Apart from you, all my friends have been to China.
Chúle hóngshāoròu yǐwài tā hái xiǎng chī tángcù páigu.
He wants to have sweet-and-sour spare ribs as well as
red-cooked pork.

18.22 'shòu'

Shòu means 'to be at the receiving end of', 'to suffer'.
Shòu kǔ is 'to suffer hardship', **shòu lèi** 'to be put to a lot
of trouble', and **shòu huānyíng** is 'to be well received','to be
welcomed', 'to be popular':

Zhōngguó cài zài Yīngguó hěn shòu huānyíng.
Chinese food is very popular in Britain.

18.23 Verb + 'xiàqu'

Xiàqu literally and commonly means 'to go down', but it has
an extended usage when added to a verb, meaning then 'to
go on *verb*-ing':

Wǒ yǐjing bǎo le, zhēn de chībuxiàqu le.
I'm already full, I really can't eat any more.
Suīrán hěn nán, kěshi wǒ hái xiǎng xuéxiàqu.
Although it's very hard, I still want to go on
studying it.
**Gōngchǎng gěi de qián zhème shǎo, shéi dōu
zuòbuxiàqu le.**
The factory pays so little money, no one can
carry on working there.

18.24 Simply must

'You simply must do this' in Chinese can be expressed as 'If you don't do this, it won't do' **Fēi ... bù kě** (**fēi** means 'not'):

Gōngānjú de rén shuō, wǒmen míngtiān fēi chūjìng bù kě.
The Public Security Bureau man says that we just have to leave the country tomorrow.
Wǒ fēi bǎ Hànyǔ xuéhǎo bù kě.
I simply must master Chinese.

Exercise 105

Make it stronger!

Huángshān fēngjǐng nàme hǎo, <u>nǐ yīnggāi qu kànkan</u>.

Huángshān fēngjǐng nàme hǎo, <u>nǐ fēi qu kànkan bù kě</u>.

1   Nàme hǎochī de Běijīng kǎoyā, <u>wǒ yídìng yào chī</u>.

2   Wǎnshang hěn lěng, <u>děi guānshang chuānghu</u>.

3   Zhèi jiàn shì <u>bù néng bú gàosu tā</u>.

4   Qǐng tāmen kāi zhèngmíng <u>děi gěi qián</u>.

18.25 You and me

Wǒmen, as you know (2.1), means 'we', 'us'. There is another word **zánmen** which means 'we', 'us' but (unlike **wǒmen**) it always includes both the speaker and the person(s) being spoken to.

18.26 Transliterations

Most languages accommodate foreign words in some way, often savaging the pronunciation in the process. (Think of what English does to 'Paris', ignoring its original 'Paree' sound.) Chinese is no exception, and there are lots of foreign borrowings:

Kǎlā-OK	Karaoke
Dísīkē	Disco

18.27 Huòzhě

Huòzhě means 'or', but it does not appear in questions, only in statements. ('Or' in questions is of course háishi.)

Qǐng nǐ míngtiān huòzhě hòutiān lái yíxiàr.
Please come over tomorrow or the day after.
Huòzhě nǐ lái, huòzhě wǒ qù, dōu kěyǐ.
Either you come or I'll go, either will do.

Some new words

diànshì	television
tán shēngyì	talking/negotiating business
biéde	other
jiémù	programme
píndào	(television) channel
liánxùjù	serial, 'soap opera'
gùshi	story, plot
yǎn	to act
kū	to weep
xiào	to laugh
huódòng	activity, to 'do something'
chàng-gēr	to sing (songs)
diànyǐngr	films, movies
sànbù	to stroll, go for a walk

CONVERSATION 18C

*A foreign businessman and his Chinese friend plan
'a wild night out':*

C   **Lái Zhōngguó yǐhòu, cháng kàn diànshì ma?**
*Since coming to China, have you often watched
television?*

F   **Měi tiān mángzhe tán shēngyì, chúle xīnwén
yǐwài, hěn shǎo kàn biéde jiémù.**
*I'm busy every day talking business; apart from the
news I rarely watch any other programmes.*

C   **Èr Píndào de liánxùjù hěn shòu huānyíng,
kàn-guo méi you?**
*The serial on Channel Two is very popular. Have you
seen it?*

F   **Kàn-guo liǎng cì jiù kànbuxiàqu le.**
I watched it twice, but couldn't go on watching it.

C   **Wèishénme? Gùshi yòu hǎo, yǎn de yòu hǎo.
Wǒ měi tiān fēi kàn bù kě.**
*Why not? The plots are good, and it's well acted. I
just have to watch it every day.*

F   **Wǒ jiù pà kàn rén kū, hǎoxiàng liánxùjù li
zǒngshi yǒu rén zài kū.**
*I just hate to see people cry, and it seems that in soap
operas there are always people crying.*

C   **Duì le, kū de shíhou shì bǐ xiào de shíhou duō.**
You're right, there's more crying than laughing.

F   **Shíjiān hái zǎo, zánmen chūqu
huódònghuódòng ba.**
It's still early, let's go out and do something, shall we?

C   **Hǎo a. Qù Kǎlā-OK zěnmeyàng?**
Great. How about going to Karaoke?

F   **Wǒ duì chàng-gēr kě shi yì diǎnr xìngqù dōu
méi you.**
I haven't got the slightest interest in singing.

254

C   **Kàn diànyǐng huòzhě tiào dísīkē yě xíng a.**
    *To see a film or go disco-dancing would be
    all right too.*

F   **Wǒ bù xiǎng qù rén duō de dìfang.**
    I don't want to go where there are lots of people.

C   **Nà ...**
    Well, ...

F   **Qù gōngyuán sànsanbù hǎo bu hǎo?**
    How about going for a walk in the park?

Exercise 106

Translate into Chinese:

1   What would you like to eat?

    It's up to you. I'll eat whatever you order.

2   Have you got used to the weather here?

    Yes, I have. Now I feel the hotter it is the better.

3   What a beautiful park this is!

    You can say that again.

4   Are you interested in photography?

    No, not a bit.

5   What was the price of that Chinese painting
    you bought?

    ¥18,500.

6   Why are you so busy practising taichi every day?

    I simply must master it before going back to
    Britain.

Chapter 19

Happy endings

- *Describing what went wrong*
- *A celebration dinner*
- *Talking about learning Chinese*

19.1 Within an inch of

Chà(yì)diǎnr means 'came very close to':

Jīntiān zǎochen wǒ chàdiǎnr méi gǎnshang huǒchē.
This morning I very nearly missed my train.
Chūguó nèi tiān tā chàdiǎnr wàng-le dài hùzhào.
On the day he left the country he nearly forgot to take his passport.

19.2 To have an accident

Chū shì means 'to have an accident':

Chē kāi de tài kuài le, chàdiǎnr chū shì.
The car was being driven too quickly, there was almost an accident.

19.3 The passive

Chinese does not use the formal passive construction as much as English does. The example sentence in 19.2 has an English passive, 'was being driven', but no clear indication of passive in Chinese. Compare the following two sentences, which have the same form in Chinese, although in English one is active and the other passive:

Tā hái méi xǐ ne.
> He still hasn't washed it. (active)

Xīzhuāng hái méi xǐ ne.
> The suit still hasn't been washed. (passive)

The formal passive most commonly uses the word **bèi** which may or may not introduce the agent (the person/thing carrying out the action):

Xìn bèi tuìhuílai le.
> The letter was returned.

Xìn bèi Yóujú tuìhuílai le.
> The letter was returned by the Post Office.

Where the agent is included, **bèi** may be replaced by **jiào** or **ràng**; and in these same cases **gěi** is sometimes inserted in front of the verb. So the passive pattern has quite a few permutations:

Xìn bèi/jiào/ràng Yóujú (gěi) tuìhuílai le.

Exercise 107

Translate into English:

1   Xíngli yǐjing sòngdao nín de fángjiān le.
2   Chuánzhēn mǎshang jiù fāchūqu.
3   Wǒ zhèi ge xiāngzi zài jīchǎng bèi jiǎnchá le sān cì.
4   Dàibiǎotuán bèi qǐngdào shí lóu qù le.
5   Diànshìjī jiào tā érzi gěi nònghuài le.

19.4 To lose

Diū means 'to lose', 'to mislay':

Zhàoxiàngjī diū le, zhǎobudào le.
    The camera is lost and can't be found.
Chēpiào yào náhǎo, bù néng diū.
    You must hold on tight to your ticket, you mustn't lose it.

19.5 Leaving aside X, there's still Y

XXX bù shuō, hái YYY is the pattern for setting one
consideration aside but being left with another:

Fángjiān tài rè bù shuō, hái nàme zāng.
    Forget about the fact that the room is too hot,
    it's also so dirty.
Jiàqian guì bù shuō, hái hěn nán mǎidào.
    As well as being high-priced, it's also hard to get hold of.

19.6 Spending time or money

Just as the one verb 'spend' works for both time and money
in English, so there is one verb **huā** in Chinese which does
the same:

Tā huā-le yí ge xīngqī de shíjiān shōushi xíngli.
    She spent a whole week packing her luggage.
Zhèi cì lǚxíng yígòng huā-le liǎngqiān kuài.
    On this trip I've spent altogether ¥2,000.

19.7 Luckily

'Fortunately', 'luckily', 'by good chance' can all be translated
by the word **xìngkuī**:

Nǐ kàn yǔ zhème dà, xìngkuī wǒmen méi chūqu.
    Look how hard it's raining, fortunately we didn't go out.

19.8 It has to be said that ...

The verb **yě**, which we usually translate as 'also', is sometimes used to means 'it has to be said that ...', 'admittedly ...':

Zhōngguó rén yě tài ài chī le.
> It must be admitted that Chinese people are overfond of eating.

Suīrán tā hěn xiǎoxīn, kěshi yě yǒu chū shì de shíhou.
> Although she is very careful, there are indeed times when she has accidents.

19.9 In no time at all

Yí xiàr means 'in no time at all', 'in a trice', 'all at once':

Tā zhīdao wèntí zài nǎr, yí xiàr jiù xiūhǎo le.
> He knew where the problem lay, and had it mended in no time.

Some new words

dù-jià	to spend one's holidays
Màngǔ	Bangkok
qiánbāor	wallet, purse
tōu	to steal
chóngxīn	anew, afresh, all over again
shēnqǐng	to apply for
qiānzhèng	visa
běnlái	originally
shǒuxù	procedures, formalities
xiǎotōur	thief
zhuādào	to arrest, catch
bèn	stupid
yīnwei	because

CONVERSATION 19A

A foreign resident returns from holiday and meets his Chinese friend:

C **Dù-jià huílai la?! Wánr de hǎo ba?**
You're back from holiday! Did you enjoy yourself?

F **Bié tí le. Chàdiǎnr huíbulái le.**
Don't talk about it. I nearly couldn't get back.

C **Zěnme le? Chū-le shénme shì?**
What? What happened?

F **Dào Màngǔ de dì yī tiān, wǒ de hùzhào, qiánbāor jiù bèi tōu le.**
On the first day I got to Bangkok, my passport and wallet were stolen.

C **Nà kě máfan le.**
You were in real trouble!

F **Kě bú shì ma! Qián diū le bù shuō, hái děi chóngxīn shēnqǐng hùzhào, qiānzhèng, xìnyòngkǎ ...**
Too right! Forget the money I lost, but I also had to apply again for passport, visa, credit cards ...

C **Huā-le bù shǎo shíjiān ba?**
It must have cost you a lot of time.

F **Běnlái bàn zhèi xiē shǒuxù zuì shǎo yě děi liǎng ge xīngqī. Xìngkuī dì èr tiān jǐngchá jiù bǎ xiǎotōur zhuàdào le.**
Actually it should take at least two weeks to go through the procedures. Luckily the police caught the thief the next day.

C **Zhème kuài?**
So quickly?

F **Nèi ge xiǎotōur yě tài bèn le, yòng wǒ de xìnyòngkǎ qu mǎi dōngxi, yí xiàr jiù bèi zhuādào le.**
That thief was really too stupid, he went shopping with my credit card and was caught in no time.

C **Hùzhào, qiánbāor dōu zhǎodào le ma?**
Did you find your passport and wallet?

> F **Dōu zhǎodào le. Fàndiàn hái miǎnfèi zhāodài**
>   **wǒ zhù-le yí ge xīngqī, yīnwei shi zài tāmen nàr**
>   **diū de.**
>   *Yes. And the hotel gave me a week's free stay because*
>   *it was there that I lost them.*

19.10 On the one hand … and on the other

Fāngmiàn means 'aspect' and the expression **yì fāngmiàn …**
yì fāngmiàn … has the sense of 'on the one hand … and on
the other …':

Zhèi jiàn shì yì fāngmiàn shi yīnwei tā bù xiǎoxīn, yì
fāngmiàn yě shi yīnwei tiānqi bù hǎo.
   This thing happened because on the one hand he wasn't
   careful, and on the other the weather wasn't good.
Tā yì fāngmiàn xiǎng qù Zhōngguó, yì fāngmiàn yòu pà
lǚxíng tài lèi.
   On the one hand she wants to go to China, but on
   the other she is also afraid that the travelling will
   be too tiring.

19.11 Welcome and farewell

Huānyíng means 'to welcome' (see Chapter 1), and its
opposite 'to bid farewell' is **huānsòng**. **Huān** means 'joyous'.

Exercise 108

Give the opposite of the following:

1	gānjìng	5	wàngle	8	chūguó
2	bǎo	6	qǐfēi	9	bìděi
3	ānquán	7	jìnkǒu	10	chūjìng
4	fàngxīn				

19.12 Formal address

When talking formally to a group of people, such as when addressing a meeting, the group is addressed as **gè wèi** 'everybody':

Gè wèi dàibiǎo ...
   Delegates, ...
Gè wèi péngyou ...
   Dear friends, ...
Gè wèi guìbīn, gè wèi xiānsheng, gè wèi nǚshì ...
   Distinguished guests, ladies and gentlemen, ...
   (nǚshì is the equivalent of 'Ms')

19.13 percentages

Percentages and fractions are both expressed in the same way:

bǎi fēn zhī shí	10%
bǎi fēn zhī liùshiwǔ	65%
bǎi fēn zhī sìshijiǔ diǎn bā	49.8%
sān fēn zhī yī	$1/3$
shí fēn zhī yī	$1/10$

Exercise 109

Say it in Chinese:

1   $1/4$
2   $1/25$
3   17%
4   0.8%
5   99.9%

19.4 The parties concerned

A number of expressions share the common element **fāng** 'side', 'party':

wǒ fāng	my (our) side
nǐ fāng	your side
Yīng fāng	the British side
Zhōng fāng	the Chinese side
mǎi fāng	the buying party
mài fāng	the selling party
shuāng fāng	both sides

19.15 It is indeed so

To show strong agreement with something someone else has said, or to make a strong definitive statement, the pattern **shi ... de** is used. Compare the following pairs of statements:

Wǒ bú qù.
　　I'm not going.
Wǒ shi bú qù de.
　　I'm certainly not going.
Zhǎo gōngzuò hěn kùnnán.
　　It is very hard to find work.
Zhǎo gōngzuò shi hěn kùnnán de.
　　It is indeed the case that work is hard to find.

19.16 Here's a toast to ...

Gānbēi of course means 'bottoms up' and is the standard way of toasting. 'To drink to ...' is **wèi ... gānbēi**:

Wèi wǒmen de yǒuyì gānbēi.
　　Let's drink to our friendship.
Wèi Zhōng-Yīng liǎng guó rénmín de yǒuyì gānbēi.
　　A toast to friendship between the peoples of China and Britain.

19.17 Good wishes

Here is a useful list of expressions of good wishes:

zhù	to wish
zhù nǐ/gè wèi/dàjiā ...	I wish you/all of you/everybody ...
... shēntǐ jiànkāng	good health
... wànshì rúyì	contentment in all you do
... jiànkāng chángshòu	health and long life (birthday greeting)
... shēngrì kuàilè	birthday happiness
... Shèngdàn kuàilè	Happy Christmas
... Xīnnián kuàilè	Happy New Year
... yílù píng'ān	a peaceful journey (farewell to traveller)
... yílù shùnfēng	a following wind (farewell to traveller)

19.18 Style

Notice how in the following Conversation 19B the speakers drop into a semi-formal style, using resounding set phrases which add grandeur and colour to an occasion.

Some new words

yànhuì	a feast, banquet
qìngzhù	to celebrate
qiāndìng	to sign (a treaty/contract)
hé	and
zǒngjīnglǐ	general manager
qiàtán	to hold (business) talks
jiàzhí	value, worth
zēngjiā	to increase
xīnkǔ	hard work, toil
zhídé	to be worth it
jīnhòu	henceforth
hézuò	co-operation
xìnxīn	confidence, belief
zhàogù	consideration, care

CONVERSATION 19B

Manager Wang hosts a celebration dinner for Mr Laker:

W Jīntiān de yànhuì yì fāngmiàn shi wèile
qìngzhù zánmen qiāndìng-le xīn hétong, yì
fāngmiàn yě shi wèile huānsòng nín hé gè wèi
Yīngguó péngyou.
*Today's banquet is on the one hand to celebrate our
signing the new agreement, and on the other to say
farewell to you and all our British friends.*

L Fēicháng gǎnxiè Wáng zǒngjīnglǐ. Zhèi cì
qiàtán suīrán shíjiān hěn cháng, kěshi hétong
jiàzhí bǐ shàng cì zēngjiā-le bǎi fēn zhī èrshí,
dàjiā de xīnkǔ shi zhídé de.
*We are extremely grateful to General Manager Wang.
Although the talks this time have taken a long while,
the value of the contract has increased 20% over last
time, and everyone's hard work has really been worth it.*

W Xīwàng xià cì zēngjiā de gèng duō.
I hope that next time it will increase even more.

L Wǒ duì shuāng fāng jīnhòu de hézuò shi yǒu
xìnxīn de.
*I have great confidence in the future co-operation of
our two sides.*

W Lái, xiān wèi wǒmen de xīn hétong gān yì bēi!
Come on, let's first drink a toast to our new contract!

L Gānbēi! ... Wǒ yào tèbié gǎnxiè Zhōngguó
péngyou duì wǒmen de zhāodài hé zhàogù, wǒ
jìng dàjiā yì bēi, zhù gè wèi shēntǐ jiànkàng,
wànshì rúyì, gānbēi.
*Cheers! ... I would especially like to thank our
Chinese friends for their hospitality and care, and I
drink a toast to you all, and wish you good health and
success in all you do. Cheers!*

W and others
Gānbēi!
Cheers!

19.19 Making fun

The expression **kāi wánxiào** means 'to make a joke' or 'to poke fun', 'to take the mickey', so it can be either wholly pleasant or perhaps a little hurtful:

Tā hěn xǐhuan kāi wánxiào.
  She loves making jokes.
Tā shi gēn nǐ kāi wánxiào de, bié zháojí.
  He's just making fun of you, don't worry.

19.20 How could that be?

Zěnme huì … ne? is a useful way to express incredulity or great surprise:

Xiàtiān zěnme huì xià-xuě ne?
  How could it be snowing in the summertime?
Sìchuān rén zěnme huì bú ài chī là de ne?
  How could a Sichuanese not like spicy food?

Exercise 110

Convert to 'How could it be?'

Mǎgē Bōluó shì Xībānyá rén.

Mǎgē Bōluó zěnme huì shì Xībānyá rén ne?

1 Yì nián yǒu sānbǎi liùshiliù tiān.

2 Yīngguó rén bù hē xiàwǔ chá.

3 Zuò huǒchē bǐ zuò fēijī wēixiǎn.

4 Chī Zhōngguó cài róngyi pàng.

19.21 Never ever

Cónglái means 'all along', 'always'. It combines with **méi** and **guò** to mean 'has never at any time':

Wǒ cónglái méi pèngjiàn-guo zhème bèn de rén.
I have never met such a stupid person.
Tā cónglái méi kàn-guo Zhōngguó diànyǐngr.
He has never ever seen a Chinese film.

Similarly, **cónglái bù** means 'never does':

Tā cónglái bú kàn Zhōngguó diànyǐngr.
He never watches Chinese films.

Exercise 111: Often and never

Answer the questions in 'I have never done it before' style:

Tā cháng chī Zhōngguó cài. Nǐ ne?

Wǒ cónglái méi chī-guo Zhōngguó cài.

1   Tā cháng qù Zhōngguó. Nǐ ne?

2   Tā cháng yòng Zhōngwén xiě xìn. Nǐ ne?

3   Wǒ chángchang pèngjiàn zhèi zhǒng shì. Nǐ ne?

4   Tā zǒngshi bù xiǎoxīn, cháng diū dōngxi. Nǐ ne?

19.22 From time to time

Yǒu shíhou or **yǒu de shíhou** means 'sometimes', 'from time to time', 'now and then'. Like other adverbs of time, it comes before the verb:

Tā yǒu shíhou xǐhuan yí ge rén chūqu sànbù.
She sometimes likes to go out for a stroll on her own.
Xué wàiyǔ yǒu shíhou juéde róngyi, yǒu shíhou juéde kùnnán.
Learning a foreign language sometimes seems easy, and at others hard.

Some new words

běn	(measure for books)
shū	book
shèngxia	to remain over

kè	a lesson
Hànzì	Chinese characters
pīnyīn	to spell out sounds
Hànyǔ pīnyīn	Hanyu pinyin (the official Chinese system of romanisation used in this book)
jiǎng	to expound, explain, speak
zhēnzhèng	true, real
liǎojiě	to understand

CONVERSATION 19C

A student of Chinese talks to a Chinese friend:

F **Zhèi běn shū kuài xuéwán le ba?**
   You'll soon have finished studying this book, won't you?

S **Kuài le. Zhǐ shèngxia zuì hòu yí kè le.**
   Soon. There only remains the last lesson.

F **Nǐ xiànzài yígòng rènshi duōshao Hànzì le?**
   How many characters do you know altogether now?

S **Yí ge dōu bú rènshi.**
   I don't know even one.

F **Bié kāi wánxiào le, nǐ Hànyǔ shuō de zhème liúlì, zěnme huì bú rènshi Hànzì ne?**
   Don't pull my leg, how could you not know any characters when you speak Chinese so fluently?

S **Shì zhēn de. Wǒ shi yòng Hànyǔ pīnyīn xué de, cónglái méi xué-guo Hànzì.**
   It's the truth. I learned through Hanyu pinyin, I've never learned any Chinese characters.

F **Nà duō bu fāngbiàn a!**
   How inconvenient that must be!

S **Shì a, yǒu shíhou dào-le cèsuǒ ménkǒur dōu bù gǎn jìnqu.**
   Yes, sometimes when I get to the door of the toilets I daren't go in.

F **Wèishénme?**
   Why is that?

S **Yīnwei bú rènshi páizi shang xiě de shi náncèsuǒ háishi nǔcèsuǒ.**

*Because I don't know whether what is written on the
sign is Men's Toilet or Women's Toilet.*

F   **Nǐ dǎsuan shénme shíhou kāishǐ xué ne?**
    When do you intend to start learning?

S   **Mǎshang jiù kāishǐ, xià yí kè jiǎng de
    jiù shi Hànzì.**
    *I'm going to start immediately. It's characters which
    will be talked about in the next lesson.*

F   **Tài hǎo le, xué-le Hànzì cái néng zhēnzhèng
    liǎojiě Zhōngwén!**
    *Excellent. You cannot truly understand Chinese until
    you have learned characters!*

Exercise 112

Translate into Chinese:

1   How long did you wait for your visa?

    It usually takes about six months, but fortunately I
    knew people in the Embassy, so I got it at once.

2   How come you are not wearing a suit today?

    Don't even mention it – all my clothes have
    been stolen.

3   Have car imports increased this year?

    Yes, they have increased by 7.5%.

4   There are too many people on the road, will you
    please drive a bit slower?

    Don't worry, I have never had an accident
    while driving.

5   It says in the paper that more than 70% of men
    students are smokers.

    How could there be so many?

6   Why do you want to study Chinese?

    For one thing, I am very interested in learning
    foreign languages, and for another, I would like to
    have a real understanding of China.

Chapter 20
Writing

- *How Chinese characters were created*
- *Organising characters*
- *Some useful characters*

20.1 How Chinese characters were created

Chinese characters have been created in various ways
over the centuries, but the earliest ones were simple pictures
of objects.

人 is the character for 'person', 'Man'. It derives clearly
enough from a picture of a man 亻
木 'a tree', 'wood' was a simple sketch of a tree 朳
山 'mountain', 'hill' ♔
目 'eye' 🦞

Some abstract ideas could be indicated by an extension of
the picture principle:

上 'above' and 下 'below' derived from ⌣ and ⌢
一 'one' 二 'two' and 三 'three'.

A further extension was the 'logical' one, where new characters were logically put together from existing ones:

明 'bright' was formed by putting the sun 日 and the moon 月 together.

旦 'dawn' was shown by a picture of the sun 日 rising above the horizon.

尖 'sharp' consists of 小 'small' above 大 'big'.

信 'trust', 'belief' is composed of 'a person' 人 and his 'word' 言

Over time, as writing materials and fashions changed, these original pictures became stylised in different ways. Here are some simple characters, showing how they have developed from the oldest forms on the left to the regular modern forms on the right:

𡴌	𡴌	𡴌	子	子	child
𣱱	𣱱	𣱱	水	水	water
𢇁	𢇁	𢇁	絲	丝	silk
𣎵	果	果	果	果	fruit
𧇂	𧇂	𧇂	虎	虎	tiger

The most common way of forming characters has been to build them from a meaningful 'radical' element and a sound-indicating 'phonetic' element. The characters for types of tree and things made of wood usually contain the 'wood radical' 木, the same character which started out as a picture of a tree 木. For example, 松 is a 'pine tree', 棍 is a 'stick', 柴 is 'firewood', and 森 is a 'forest'. 氵 represents 'water' (the full character for which is 水) and appears in characters for liquids: 河 is a 'river', 油 is 'oil', and 汗 is 'sweat'. There are many other radical elements, such as 钅 for metals (full character 金), 车 for vehicles, 石 for minerals, 艹 for plants (full character 草), 鱼 for fish and 虫 for insects.

The 'phonetic' element is added to the 'radical' to give a pronunciation guide. For example, the character 工 means 'work' and is pronounced **gōng**. It appears in a number of other characters, where it gives a clue to pronunciation: 功 means 'merit', 攻 means 'to attack', and both of these characters are pronounced **gōng**. Alas, there are also some characters which contain 工 but which are no longer pronounced **gōng** (江 for instance is nowadays pronounced **jiāng**), and there are many more characters which are pronounced **gōng** but which do not contain 工, so you cannot put too much faith in these pronunciation guides. Still, they are a useful aid to character learning, and the 'radical + phonetic' system is still the method used to create new characters today.

There are dozens of words pronounced **shì**, but they are easily distinguished from each other when written down in characters. Here are a few of them:

是 to be　　事 business　　市 market

士 scholar　　室 room　　视 to see

试 to try　　示 to show　　世 a generation

The first advantage of characters, then, is that they serve to make clear what in speech can be quite muddling. The second advantage is that Chinese people who can read and write all use the same writing system, regardless of which kind of Chinese they speak. A Cantonese speaker is unintelligible to a Shanghainese listener, and vice versa, but when they write things down they understand each other perfectly, because they both use standard written Chinese, which does not take account of their different pronunciations and dialect peculiarities. So the written language allows China to have communication where there might otherwise be misunderstanding.

20.2 Organising characters

Looking up words in English dictionaries is very simple: we have an alphabet which has a fixed order, and we organise our words in that same order. Chinese has no alphabet, and therefore has no such obvious way of organising a dictionary. Some dictionaries are arranged by rhyme, some by topic in much the same way as a Thesaurus, some by complicated numerical systems arbitrarily assigned to characters. Some recent dictionaries have used romanisation and been arranged in alphabetical order, but the most frequently used method has been to arrange characters by their radical elements. In the late seventeenth century a table of 214 radicals was compiled and all characters were classified under one or other of the 214, which were in a set order like the twenty-six letters of the ABC.

To look up a character in a dictionary, you first identify the radical and then count the number of additional pen strokes used in writing the character. So, to look up the character 城 , you first decide that the left-hand side (土 'earth') is the radical, then look that up in the chart of radicals and find that it is the 32nd of the 214, then count the additional strokes in the remainder of the character (成), finding that there are six of them. The character (it is pronounced **chéng** and means 'city') will be found in the sixth subsection of the 32nd section of the dictionary, along with a few other characters which also have six strokes added to the 'earth' radical.

One of the reforms carried out after the foundation of the People's Republic of China in 1949 was the simplification of the Chinese script. For the most part, this consisted of cutting down the number of strokes used to write complex characters:

錢 'money' was simplified to 钱
國 'country' became 国
視 'to see' became 视

Some of the simplifications were more swingeing:

邊 'side' was cut down to 边

聽 'to listen' reduced to 听

龍 'dragon' was slimmed down to 龙

The new simplified characters could not be forced into the 214 categories, and new radical tables had to be devised. Unfortunately, each new dictionary that has been published seems to have followed a different table, so that the old standard was not replaced by anything so universal and dictionary-searching has accordingly tended to become more rather than less complicated. The old full-form characters are still used in Hong Kong, in Taiwan and among most of the Overseas Chinese communities.

Until this century, Chinese was written from top to bottom and from the right to the left of the page, so that the writer started at the top right-hand corner of what would be the last page in a western book, wrote in a column down to the bottom, then started at the top again, and so on until he finished the page at the bottom left-hand corner. Another result of the reforms was that nowadays it is becoming more common to write across the page from left to right, starting at what all western writers would agree to be the front of the book. Newspapers sometimes mix the two systems, having some text reading across and some down.

Each character, however complicated or simple, takes up the same space on the page. You can think of them as being written in squares all of the same size. There is a set order for writing the strokes of a character, most of them starting at the top left-hand corner and working downwards and to the right, ending usually in the bottom right-hand corner of the imaginary square. Here, for example, is the order for writing 中 **zhōng** 'middle':

丨 冂 口 中 (4 strokes altogether)

个 **gè**, the measure word for people and many other objects, is very simple:

丿 人 个 (3 strokes)

东 **dōng** 'east':

一 七 玍 东 东 (5 strokes)

南 **nán** 'south':

一 十 广 卢 卢 声 南 南 南 (9 strokes)

国 **guó** 'country' is a little trickier:

丨 冂 冂 冋 用 国 国 国 (8 strokes)

你 **nǐ** 'you' is split into a left and a right side:

丿 亻 亻 价 价 你 你 (7 strokes)

20.3 Some useful characters

We cannot possibly hope to teach you to read and write in this book, but it is not too hard to introduce a few characters which are frequently met with and which are useful for everyday life in China. Remember that each character is meaningful and read as one syllable of speech.

Let's start with a very important pair:

男 **nán** man, male

女 **nǔ** women, female

男 厕 (所) **náncè(suǒ)** men's toilet

女 厕 (所) **nǔcè(suǒ)** women's toilet

推 **tuī** push

拉 **lā** pull

开 **kāi** open

关 **guān** closed

出 口 **chūkǒu** exit

入 口 **rùkǒu** entrance

有 人 **yǒu rén** occupied

无 人 **wú rén** vacant

不 准 **bù zhǔn** … not permitted to …

不 准 停 车 **bù zhǔn tíng chē** no parking

禁 止 **jìnzhǐ** … strictly forbidden to …

禁 止 吸 烟 **jìnzhǐ xī yān** no smoking

游 客 止 步 **yóukè zhǐ bù** out of bounds to visitors

出 入 请 下 车 **chū rù qǐng xià chē** please
                  dismount at the gate

一 二 三 **yī, èr, sān** one, two, three

四 五 六 **sì, wǔ, liù** four, five, six

七 八 九 十 **qī, bā, jiǔ, shí** seven, eight, nine, ten

百 千 万 亿 **bǎi, qiān, wàn, yì** 100, 1,000, 10,000,
                   100,000,000

元 **yuán** dollar, yuan

角 **jiǎo** dime, ten cents

分 **fēn** cent

人民币 **Rénmínbì** Renminbi

公斤 **gōngjīn** kilogram

公里 **gōnglǐ** kilometre

东西南北 **dōng, xī, nán, běi** east, west, south, north

中国 **Zhōngguó** China

北京 **Běijīng** Beijing

上海 **Shànghǎi** Shanghai

天津 **Tiānjin** Tianjin

南京 **Nánjīng** Nanjing

西安 **Xī'ān** Xian

成都 **Chéngdū** Chengdu

桂林 **Guìlín** Guilin

广州 **Guǎngzhōu** Guangzhou (Canton)

香港 **Xiānggǎng** Hong Kong

台湾 **Táiwān** Taiwan

台北 **Táiběi** Taipei

公用电话 **gōngyòng diànhuà** public telephone

邮电局 **Yóudiànjú** Post Office

医院 **yīyuàn** hospital

人民医院 **Rénmín Yīyuàn** The People's Hospital

银行 **yínháng** bank

中国银行 **Zhōngguó Yínháng** The Bank of China

外汇兑换 **wàihuì duìhuàn** foreign exchange

派 出 所 pàichūsuǒ police station

火 车 (站) huǒchē(zhàn) train (station)

地 铁 (站) dìtiě(zhàn) underground (station)

售 票 处 shòupiàochù ticket office

公 共 汽 车 (站) gōnggòngqìchē(zhàn) bus
(station/stop)

出 租 汽 车 (站) chūzūqìchē(zhàn) taxi (rank/station)

机 场 jīchǎng airport

首 都 机 场 Shǒudū Jīchǎng Capital Airport

饭 店 fàndiàn hotel

北 京 饭 店 Běijīng Fàndiàn The Peking Hotel

百 货 商 店 bǎihuò shāngdiàn department store

营 业 时 间 yíngyè shíjiān hours of business

收 款 台 shōukuǎntái cashier's desk

To progress beyond what this book can teach you, you will need to study characters in earnest. This chapter has just been a 'taster'; if you would like to learn systematically how to read and write, try the *Character Text for Colloquial Chinese* by P C T'ung, Department of East Asia, School of Oriental and African Studies, University of London, Thornhaugh Street, Russell Square, London WC1H 0XG. It is available in two versions, one in full and one in simplified characters.

Wán 完 The End

Key to exercises

Chapter 2

Exercise 1:   1 Holland 2 Denmark 3 India 4 Ireland
5 Mexico 6 Malaysia 7 Scotland

Exercise 2:   1 True 2 False: Zhou Enlai was born in
Jiangsu Province. 3 True 4 False: Shaw was born in Dublin.
5 False: Picasso was Spanish.

Exercise 3:   1 Tā shi Běijīng rén ma? 2 Tā shi Ài'ěrlán rén
ma? 3 Tā xìng Lǐ ma? 4 Tā jiào Wáng Zhōng ma? *[Note
that it would be possible to use* ba *instead of* ma *in all these
examples, so there are two correct answers to each.]*

Exercise 4:   1 Nà shi wǒ fūren. 2 Zhè bú shi wǒ de
míngzi. 3 Zhè shi wǒ de péngyou, Lǐ Dàwěi. 4 Nà shi tā
de míngpiàn.

Exercise 5:   1 We are all friends. 2 They are all called Yang.
3 Are you German too? 4 I'm British. They are all British too.

Exercise 7:   1 Wǒ xìng Lǐ. Wǒ shi Yīngguó rén. 2 Nǐ shi
Běijīng rén ma? 3 Wǒmen dōu jiào tā Lǎo Wáng. 4 Tā
fūren yě shi Měiguó rén. 5 Zhè bú shi wǒ de míngpiàn.
6 Tā de péngyou dōu shi Xiānggǎng rén.

Chapter 3

Exercise 8:   1 Tā xìng shénme? 2 Tā jiào shénme míngzi?
3 Tā shi něi guó rén? 4 Nà shi shénme? 5 Tā shi shéi de
péngyou?

Exercise 9:   1 yě 2 yě 3 dōu 4 jiù 5 yě, dōu

Exercise 10:   1 yāo-líng-sì 2 jiǔ-jiǔ-jiǔ 3 líng-yāo-sān-èr-
bā qī-wǔ liù-èr liù-yāo 4 líng-yāo-qī-yāo èr-sān-sì wǔ-liù-
bā-jiǔ 5 líng-yāo-bā-yāo wǔ-sān-sān liù-sì-qī-èr

Exercise 12:   1 *A*: Tā xìng shénme? *B*: Tā xìng Wáng. 2 *A*:
Nǐ de diànhuà hàomǎ shi duōshao?/Nǐ de diànhuà duōshao
hào? *B*: Líng-yāo-èr-yāo sì-bā-liù wǔ-qī-sān-jiǔ. 3 *A*: Zhè
shi shéi de hùzhào? *B*: Wǒ péngyou de. 4 *A*: Nǐ zhīdao tā

shi něi guó rén ma? *B*: Zhīdao, tā shi Fǎguó rén. 5 *A*: Lín jīnglǐ shi Shànghǎi rén ma? *B*: Bú shi, tā shi Rìběn Huáqiáo. 6 *A*: Wéi, shì Zhāng xiānsheng ma? *B*: Shì. Nín shi …?

Chapter 4

Exercise 13:   1 ge   2 bēi   3 jiān   4 –   5 ge *or* wèi

Exercise 14:   1 Wǒ bù xiǎng zhù Běijīng Fàndiàn.   2 Tāmen dōu méi you hùzhào.   3 Nǐmen bú yào shuāngrénfáng ma? 4 Nín méi you míngpiàn ma?   5 Wǒmen de fángjiān dōu bú dài wèishēngjiān.

Exercise 15:   1 There's no phone in my room.   2 There are two bathrooms on the third floor.   3 Are there any Chinese companies in London?   4 At their place there's tea and coffee too.

Exercise 16:   1 Tā shì bu shi Běijīng rén?   2 Tā yǒu méi you Zhōngguó péngyou?   3 Tā xiǎng bu xiang hē hóngchá? 4 Tā rèn(shi) bu rènshi Zhāng Dépéi?   5 Nàr rè bu re?

Exercise 18:   1 *A*: Nǐmen yǒu liǎng jiān dānrénfáng ma? *B*: Méi you. Wǒmen zhǐ yǒu yì jiān shuāngrénfáng.   2 *A*: Nín zhù jǐ tiān? *B*: Wǔ tiān.   3 *A*: Nǐmen xiǎng hē shénme? *B*: Liǎng bēi chá, yì bēi kāfēi.   4 *A*: Wǒmen de fángjiān tài rè le! *B*: Nín xiǎng huàn yì jiān ma?   5 *A*: Zhèr zhǔn hē-jiǔ ma? *B*: Duìbuqǐ, bù zhǔn. Hē-jiǔ, chōu-yān dōu bù zhǔn.   6 *A*: Nàr de fēngjǐng piàoliang ma? *B*: Piàoliang. Nàr de rén yě piàoliang.

Chapter 5

Exercise 19:   1 Lǐ xiānsheng zài ma?   2 Yǒu rén zài jiā ma? 3 Wèishēngjiān zài yī lóu.   4 Tā zài lǐtou.   5 Kāfēitīng zài zuǒbianr.   6 Běijīng Fàndiàn jiù zài qiántou.

Exercise 20:   1 Wǔ máo (qián).   2 Yí kuài èr (máo). 3 Shíbā kuài.   4 Sìshiwǔ kuài wǔ (máo).   5 Liùshiqī kuài sān (máo).   6 Jiǔshijiǔ kuài jiǔ máo jiǔ.

Exercise 21:   1 shéi   2 jǐ   3 nǎr   4 shénme   5 duōshao   6 nǎr

Exercise 22:   1 xībianr   2 dōngbianr   3 nánbianr 4 běibianr   5 nánbianr *or* dōngnánbianr

Exercise 24:   1 *A*: Wéi, Wáng xiānsheng zài ma? *B*: Duìbuqǐ, tā bú zài.   2 *A*: Tāmen dōu zài nǎr? *B*: Tāmen dōu zài kāfēitīng.   3 *A*: Qǐngwèn, cèsuǒ zài nǎr?   *B*: Zài èr

lóu. 4 *A*: Zhèi ge cháhú duōshao qián?   *B*: Shíliù kuài wǔ.
5 *A*: Tā jiā zài nǎr? *B*: Zài gōngyuán (de) dōngbianr.
6 *A*: Kànkan nín de wǎnbào kěyǐ ma?   *B*: Kěyǐ, nǐ kàn ba.

Chapter 6

Exercise 25:   1 Wǎng qián zǒu. 2 Wǎng dōng guǎi.
3 Wǎng zuǒ guǎi. 4 Qiántou bù zhǔn (wǎng) yòu guǎi.
5 Qù gōngyuán.

Exercise 26:   1 He has gone/went to Shanghai. 2 Miss Li
has arrived in Beijing. 3 They all know it now. 4 She has
gone/went to the park.   5 Have you read the evening paper?

Exercise 27:   1 ge/wèi 2 ge/jiān 3 hào 4 lù
5 fènr   6 kuài

Exercise 28:   1/4 Wǒ xǐhuan mǎi dōngxi, wǒ xiǎng qù
bǎihuò dàlóu. 2/3 Wǒ xǐhuan hē chá, wǒ xiǎng qù
kāfēitīng. 3/1 Wǒ xǐhuan rè de dìfang, wǒ xiǎng qù
Xībānyá. 4/2 Wǒ xǐhuan kàn fēngjǐng, wǒ xiǎng qù Guìlín.
[*Guilin is in Guangxi Province; city and surrounding scenery are
renowned for their beauty.*]

Exercise 29:   1 rèshuǐ 2 Xīzhàn 3 Yuǎndōng Gōngsī
4 Chē yàoshi 5 Yǒuyìmén 6 bíyānhú méi you shìchǎng

Exercise 30:   1 I want to go to the Friendship Store to buy
something. 2 He wants to come to England to study.
3 I am thinking of going to the north to see friends. 4 Would
you like to go to the park to relax?   5 I would like to go to
the free market to have a look around.

Exercise 32:   1 *A*: Qǐng wèn, Yǒuyì Shāngdiàn zài nǎr?
B: Nǐ kàn, jiù zài nàr. Jiù zài nèi ge dà fàndiàn hòutou.
2 *A*: Tóngzhì, qǐng wèn, qù Běijīng Dàxué zěnme zǒu?
B: Hěn yuǎn. Wǒ yě bù zhīdao zěnme zǒu. 3 *A*: Qǐng wèn,
zhè chē dào Tiān'ānmén ma? *B*: Dào. Hái yǒu liǎng zhàn.
4 *A*: Tāmen dōu qù Zhōngguó le ma? *B*: Dōu qù le.

Chapter 7

Exercise 33:   1 Yī-bā-sì-èr nián bā yuè èrshibā hào/rì
2 Yī-jiǔ-yī-yī nián shí yuè shí rì/hào 3 Yī-jiǔ-bā-jiǔ nián liù
yuè sì hào/rì 4 Yī-jiǔ-jiǔ-líng nián shíyī yuè shíwǔ hào/rì
5 Èr-líng-yī-líng nián yī yuè sānshiyī hào/rì

Exercise 34:   1 She has already left for China.   2 I have already bought that thing.   3 We already know each other. 4 The train has already arrived.   5 Today is the fifth already.

Exercise 35:   1 hē chá de rén   2 mài bíyānhú de shāngdiàn 3 qù Tiānjin de huǒchēpiào   4 qù Tiān'ānmén de chē   5 zuò fēijī de rén

Exercise 36:   1 Míngtiān liù hào.   2 Jīntiān xīngqī sì. 3 Hòutiān èrshisān hào.   4 Jīntiān shí yuè èr hào.

Exercise 37:   1 Jiǔ diǎn zhōng.   2 Liǎng diǎn bàn. 3 Bā diǎn wǔ fēn.   4 Sì diǎn sān kè.

Exercise 38:   1 I have a friend who is from Hong Kong. 2 He wants to invite me to go for a drink.   3 She asks/asked me how much money I have.   4 I know an Overseas Chinese who owns ten Chinese restaurants.

Exercise 40:   1 *A*: Nǐ shénme shíhou qù Rìběn?   *B*: Jiǔ yuè wǔ hào/rì.   2 *A*: Tā xīngqī liù lái ma?   *B*: Bù lái, tā xīngqī tiān lái.   3 *A*: Qǐng wèn, xiànzài jǐ diǎn le?   *B*: Shí diǎn shí fēn.   4 *A*: Xīngqī liù nǐ jǐ diǎn zhōng xià bān?   *B*: Shí'èr diǎn bàn.   5 *A*: Nǐ rènshi Huáyuán Gōngsī de Lǐ jīnglǐ ma?   *B*: Bú rènshi, kěshi wǒ yǒu ge hǎo péngyou rènshi tā.   6 *A*: Huǒchē jǐ diǎn zhōng dào?   *B*: Yǐjing dào le.

Chapter 8

Exercise 41:   1 Shǒudū Fàndiàn bǐ Huáyuán Fàndiàn dà. 2 Píjiǔ bǐ kuàngquánshuǐ guì.   3 Shānshang bǐ shānxia liángkuai.   4 Lóushang de zhōng bǐ lóuxia de (zhōng) kuài.

Exercise 42:   1 to stay for three weeks 2 to have Chinese food for two years 3 to be on duty/working for eight hours 4 to be on a plane for 15 hours 5 to ride a bike for twenty minutes

Exercise 43:   1 … tā méi (you) qián le.   2 … tā bù xiǎng chī le.   3 … bù máng le.   4 … bù jǐ le.

Exercise 44:   1 The weather isn't good there, and things are expensive too.   2 On the mountain the scenery is beautiful and the weather is cool.   3 The Capital Hotel is well-situated and its rooms are large.   4 The Dahua Restaurant is a long way away but its roast duck is excellent.

Exercise 45: 1 hóng 2 hóng 3 hēi 4 lán

Exercise 47: 1 *A*: Jiānádà dōngtiān zěnmeyàng? *B*: Lěng jí le. 2 *A*: Xiānggǎng sān yuè hěn nuǎnhuo ma? *B*: Hěn nuǎnhuo, bǐ Shànghǎi nuǎnhuo. 3 *A*: Nǐ (de) péngyou dài yǎnjìngr ma? *B*: (Tā) bú dài. 4 *A*: Nǐ chuān jǐ hào de? *B*: Wǒ bù zhīdao. Kěnéng shi 42 hào. 5 *A*: Nǐ xǐhuan shénme yánsè de? *B*: Wǒ xǐhuan huáng (yánsè) de.

Chapter 9

Exercise 48: 1 Tā yào zuò fēijī qù Zhōngguó. 2 Qǐng nǐ bié zài zhèr chōu-yān. 3 Qǐng nǐ gěi wǒ mǎi fènr wǎnbào. 4 Nǐ kěyǐ tì wǒmen qǐng Wáng xiānsheng lái ma?

Exercise 49: 1 Shànghǎi bǐ Běijīng nuǎnhuo yì diǎnr. 2 Tiān'ānmén bǐ Yǒuyì Shāngdiàn jìn yì diǎnr. 3 Lǎo Lǐ de biǎo bǐ huǒchēzhàn de zhōng kuài yì diǎnr. 4 Zuò gōnggòngqìchē qù bǐ qí chē qù kuài yì diǎnr.

Exercise 50: 1 Bíyānhú gēn xiǎo mián'ǎo yíyàng guì. 2 Tiān'ānmén gēn Bǎihuò Dàlóu yíyàng yuǎn. 3 Zuò chē qù gēn qí chē qù yíyàng kuài. 4 Xiǎo Wáng gēn Xiǎo Lǐ yíyàng pàng.

Exercise 51: 1 Tāmen zài xiūxi ne. 2 Tāmen zài tiào-wǔ ne. 3 Tāmen zài lóuxia hē-jiǔ ne. 4 Tāmen zài kàn tiānqi yùbào ne. 5 Tāmen méi(you) zài chōu-yān.

Exercise 52: 1 chōu-yān de rén 2 chī-sù de rén/bù chī ròu de rén 3 xǐhuan hē chá de rén 4 xiǎng qù Zhōngguó de rén/xiǎng dào Zhōngguó qù de rén 5 zǎochen dǎ tàijíquán de rén

Exercise 54: 1 *A*: Qǐng nǐ tì wǒ xuǎn yí ge. *B*: Hǎo. Wǒ xiǎng hóng de zuì hǎo. 2 *A*: A Nǐmen liǎng ge rén yíyàng gāo ma? *B*: Bù, tā bǐ wǒ gāo yì diǎnr. 3 *A*: Wǒmen qǐng tā chī kǎoyā hǎo bu hao? *B*: Bù xíng. Tā shi chī-sù de. 4 *A*: Tā zài gànmá ne? *B*: Tā zài xiūxi ne. 5 *A*: Wǒ xiǎng xué tàijíquán; nǐ kěyǐ tì wǒ zhǎo wèi lǎoshī ma? *B*: Méi wèntí.

Chapter 10

Exercise 55: 1 He isn't here; he's gone to the park. 2 He's not at home; he's gone to the (company) office.

3 He didn't come to work; he went shopping. 4 Has he also gone for a drink?

Exercise 56: 1 *A* Chī le. *B* Hái méi (chī) ne. 2 *A* Lái le. *B* Hái méi (lái) ne. 3 *A* Jié le. *B* Hái méi (jié) ne. 4 *A* Mǎi le. *B* Hái méi (mǎi) ne.

Exercise 57: 1 *A*: Were you drinking yesterday? *B*: Yes. *A*: How many bottles did you have? 2 *A*: Did you go to see friends? *B*: Yes. *A*: How many did you see? 3 *A*: Did you go to Japan? *B*: Yes. *A*: How many days did you stay there? 4 *A* Have you bought any quilted jackets? *B* Yes. *A* How many have you bought? 5 *A* Have you done your taichi? *B* Yes. *A* How many minutes did you do?

Exercise 59: 1 yí (ge) xīngqī yí cì 2 yí ge yuè liǎng cì 3 yì nián sān tàng 4 yì tiān sì zhēn

Exercise 61: 1 *A*: Wéi, wǒ kěyǐ gēn Lǐ Xiānsheng shuō-huà ma? *B*: Duìbuqǐ, tā yǐjing huí guó le. 2 *A*: Zuótiān nǐ dǎ-le duōshao ge diànhuà? *B*: Yígòng yìbǎi èrshisān ge. 3 *A*: Bào shang yǒu shénme xīnwén? *B*: Bào shang shuō jīnnián yǒu hěn duō rén yào chū guó. 4 *A*: Nǐ chīwán le ma? *B*: Hái méi ne. Wǒ hēwán tāng jiù lái. 5 *A*: Tā fā shāo le ma? *B*: Sānshibā dù liù. Wǒmen zhǎo dàifu lái ba? 6 *A*: Nǐmen cháng chī Zhōngguó fàn ma? *B*: Cháng chī. Chàbuduō yí ge yuè liǎng cì.

Chapter 11

Exercise 62: 1 Qù-guo. 2 Zhù-guo. 3 Méi lái-guo. 4 Méi shuō-guo.

Exercise 63: 1 Shì yī-jiǔ-bā-liù nián shí yuè qù de. 2 Shì zài Xiānggǎng mǎi de. 3 Tā shi zuò fēijī lái de. 4 Tā shi qùnián qī yuè zǒu de.

Exercise 64: 1 wán *or* hǎo 2 wán 3 hǎo 4 kāi

Exercise 65: 1 He has been living in Shanghai for three years. 2 We have been studying Chinese for two years. 3 She has already bought ten T-shirts. 4 He has already been talking for five hours. 5 I have already taken 200 photos.

Exercise 66: 1 C B A D 2 B C A D 3 C B D A 4 B C A D 5 D B A C

Exercise 67:   1 Nǐ xué-le duō jiǔ (de) Yīngwén le? Chàbuduō shínián le, kěshi wǒ hái bú huì shuō. 2 Nǐ shénme shíhou dǎ tàijíquán? Shuì-jiào yǐqián. 3 Nǐ qù-guo Rìběn ma? Qù-guo, wǒ yǐqián měi nián qù yí tàng/cì. 4 Shì nǐ zuò háishi tā zuò? Wǒmen tīng nǐ de. 5 Tā lái kāi huì ma? Bù lái. Tā dǎ diànhuà jiào wǒ gàosu nǐ tā bù néng lái. 6 Jīntiān méi you gōnggòngqìchē, nǐ shi zěnme lái de? Wǒ shi zuò chūzūqìchē lái de.

Chapter 12

Exercise 68:   1 Xué de hěn kuài. 2 Zuò de hǎo jíle. 3 Shuì de bú tài hǎo. 4 Zhào de hěn piàoliang.

Exercise 69:   1 Who is sitting outside the door? 2 What is she wearing? 3 Whose air ticket is he holding? 4 He is waiting for you. 5 She looks very thin.

Exercise 70:   1 jiàn 2 wán 3 wán 4 dào

Exercise 71:   1 (having) studied for 3 years + didn't study for 3 years 2 (having) listened for 2 days + didn't listen for 2 days 3 (having) practised for 3 months + didn't practise for 3 months 4 (having) rained for 5 weeks + didn't rain for 5 weeks

Exercise 72:   1 Lǎo Wáng bǐ Xiǎo Lǐ dà sì hào. 2 Tā de biǎo bǐ nǐ de (biǎo) kuài wǔ fēn zhōng. 3 Tā bǐ tā érzi dūo wǔshi ge. 4 Jī bǐ yú guì sān kuài qián.

Exercise 73:   1 Tā jīntiān zǎoshang kàn-zhe hěn lèi. Shì a, tā zuótiān wǎnshang méi shuì-hǎo/shuì de bù hǎo. 2 Tā (zuò) yú zuò de hǎo ma? Tā bù cháng zuò yú, wǒ lái ba. 3 Nǐ Zhōngguó huà shuō de tài hǎo le. Náli, wǒ cháng shuō-cuò. 4 Tā shǒu shang ná-zhe shénme ne? Yídìng shi tāde hùzhào. 5 Wǒmen sān ge yuè méi chī jī le. Hǎo, wǒ mǎshang qu mǎi yì zhī. 6 Něi jiàn dàbèixīnr guì? Huáng de háishi lán de? Lán de bǐ huáng de guì liǎng kuài qián.

Chapter 13

Exercise 74:   1 How do I get to the station? 2 How do you cook this dish? 3 How is this thing used? 4 How do you open the toilet door? 5 How do you say 'Cheers!' in Chinese? 6 How do you dial direct to Beijing?

Exercise 75: 1 ... hē-jiǔ ne. 2 ... shuì-jiào ne.
3 ... mǎi-dōngxi ne. 4 ... xué Zhōngguó huà ne.

Exercise 76: 1 The room is too noisy, there is no way I can get to sleep. 2 The food is all cold, we can't eat it. 3 There's no water in the toilet, we can't use it. 4 There are too many people smoking, we can't eat here.

Exercise 77: 1 shéi (*or* něi wèi), shéi (*or* něi wèi)
2 shénme, shénme 3 zěnme, zěnme 4 jǐ, jǐ

Exercise 78: 1 Wǒ kěyǐ zhí bō Yīngguó ma? Dāngrán kěyǐ.
2 Máfan nǐ sòng wǒ dào huǒchēzhàn hǎo ma? Méi wèntí, shànglai ba! 3 Wǒ jīntiān děi fā zhèi ge chuánzhēn ma? Bú bì. 4 Wǒmen shénme shíhou qù Rìběn? Nǐ xiǎng shénme shíhou qù, wǒmen jiù shénme shíhou qù. 5 Nǐ dìdi zài nǎr ne? Tā zhèngzài fā chuánzhēn ne. 6 Xièxie nǐ de bāng-máng. Bú kèqi.

Chapter 14

Exercise 79: 1 The bank is to the east of the hotel.
2 The business centre is just opposite the café. 3 The men's toilet is behind the western restaurant. 4 My passport is in the bag on your right.

Exercise 80: 1 False 2 True 3 False 4 True

Exercise 81: 1 lai 2 shàngqu 3 chūqu 4 jìnqu 5 huíqu

Exercise 82: 1 You can write it in your room./Your address can be written on the luggage. 2 He is outside parking./The car has been parked outside. 3 He often practises taichi in the park./The rain falling on him made him very uncomfortable. 4 Where shall we fill in the forms?/Where should I fill in my name?

Exercise 83: 1 jiù 2 cái 3 cái 4 jiù 5 cái

Exercise 84: 1 Guójì Zhǎnlǎn Zhōngxīn zài nǎr? Jiù zài Xīnhuá Fàndiàn duìmiàn. 2 Nǐ jiā lí huǒchēzhàn (yǒu) duō yuǎn? Wǒ xiǎng chàbuduō (yǒu) wǔ gōnglǐ. 3 Nǐ yǒu tā de Běijīng dìzhǐ ma? Yǒu, jiù zài zhèr: Běijīng 100826, Yǒngdìng Lù èrshijiǔ hào, sān lóu. 4 Tā shi shénme shíhou huí Shànghǎi qù de? Tā yì jiēdào nǐ de chuánzhēn jiù huíqu le. 5 Wáng xiānsheng shuō méi fázi. Gàosu tā nǐ shi wǒ de péngyou: tā yídìng huì bāng-máng. 6 Lǐ xiáojie, wǒ kěyǐ zuòzai nǐ pángbiānr ma? Dāngrán kěyǐ, kěshi wǒ mǎshang jiù děi zǒu.

Chapter 15

Exercise 85:   1 The earliest he could arrive would be tomorrow.   2 His house is at least 20 minutes walk from the bus stop.   3 It won't get hotter than 40° in Beijing in August. 4 Letters from China take at least a week.

Exercise 86:   1 Wǒmen gěi-le tā qián, tā jiù qù le.   2 Tā kàn-le xīnwén jiù zǒu.   3 Wǒ jì-le xìn jiù qù (kàn tā).   4 Tā dǎ-le tàijíquán jiù chī zǎofàn.

Exercise 87:   1 Zhōngguó cài hǎo-chī kěshi bù hǎo-zuò. 2 Tā jiā zài shān li, hěn bù hǎo-zhǎo.   3 Yì zhāng bú gòu, qǐng nǐ duō-mǎi ji zhāng.   4 Tā tài pàng le, měi tiān yīnggāi shǎo-chī yì wǎn fàn.

Exercise 88:   1 Nǐ háishi bié chōu le ba.   2 Wǒmen háishi míngtiān zuò ba.   3 Nǐ háishi zuò huǒchē qù ba.   4 Wǒmen háishi fā ge chuánzhēn gěi tāmen ba.

Exercise 89:   1 What's happened to his hand?   2 She's ill and can no longer come.   3 How come you haven't bought a ticket? Sorry, I forgot.   4 The lift is out of order. Let's walk up.

Exercise 90:   1 Qǐng wèn, zhè fùjìn yǒu yóujú ma? Yǒu, Xīnhuá Lù shang jiù yǒu yí ge.   2 Jì Ōuzhōu de hángkōngxìn duōshao qián? Guójì hángkōngxìn dōu shi liǎng kuài.   3 Qǐng wèn, zuì jìn de pàichūsuǒ zài nǎr? Dào hónglǜdēng wǎng yòu guǎi, pàichūsuǒ jiù zài dì-èr ge lùkǒur.   4 Nǐmen de diànhuà zěnme le? Wǒ yě bù zhīdao wèishénme, kěshi xiànzài zhǐ néng dǎjìnlái, bù néng dǎchūqù.   5 Chuánzhēnjī huài le ma? Méi you. Tíng diàn le.   6 Wǒmen zǒu něi tiáo lù qù? Háishi zǒu dà lù ba; wǎnshang xiǎo lù bù hǎo-zǒu.

Chapter 16

Exercise 91:   1 Wǒ něi ge dōu xiǎng mǎi.   2 Nǎr dōu yǒu Zhōngguó fànguǎnr.   3 Wǒ shénme shíhou dōu yǒu gōngfu. 4 Wǒ shéi dōu méi qu kàn.

Exercise 92:   1 huài   2 shǎo   3 bái   4 xiǎo   5 rè   6 shòu 7 wǎn   8 màn   9 cuò   10 jìn   11 guì   12 nán (kùnnán) 13 liángkuai   14 tǎoyàn

Exercise 93:   1 buwán   2 buqǐ   3 bujiàn   4 bují   5 dedào

Exercise 94:   1 Qǐng nǐ shuō màn (yi) diǎnr.   2 Qǐng nǐ mài piányi diǎnr.   3 Qǐng nǐ lái zǎo diǎnr.   4 Qǐng nǐ zuò hǎo diǎnr.

Exercise 95:   1 Xiāngjiāo zěnme mài? Liǎng kuài liù yì jīn, liǎng jīn wǔ kuài.   2 Shuǐguǒ dōu guì le ma? Shì a, píngguo xiànzài mài yí kuài èr yì jīn, bǐ qùnián guì le sān bèi.   3 Nǐ zuò huǒchē qù kǒngpà láibují le. Méi fázi, wǒ mǎibuqǐ fēijīpiào (or zuòbuqǐ fēijī).   4 Yàoshi wǒmen gǎnbushàng liù diǎn sìshiwǔ de huǒchē zěnme bàn? Bié zháojí, liù diǎn wǔshiwǔ hái yǒu yì bān.   5 Fēijī jiù yào qǐfēi le, qǐng kuài yi diǎnr. Nǐ shuō shénme? Qǐng nǐ shuō màn yi diǎnr.
6 Jīnnián xiàtiān nǐ qù nǎr? Nǎr piányi wǒ qù nǎr.

Chapter 17

Exercise 96:   1 He has already given me the money.
2 May I put my bag here?   3 Who has taken my camera?
4 Will you please take this upstairs?

Exercise 97:   1 What about the large size? Try it on and see.
2 Which is the best method? Let's all think about it and see.
3 I forget where I put it. I'll go and look for it.   4 When will the train arrive? Can you go and ask, please?

Exercise 98:   1 Tā lèi de zǒubudòng le.   2 Yǔ dà de wǒmen bù néng chūqu le.   3 Zhōngguó cài hǎo-chī de shéi dōu xiǎng chī.   4 Tā de xiāngzi dà de shí ge rén dōu bānbudòng.

Exercise 99:   1 Zuótiān yǒu diǎnr lěng.   2 Nàr de dōngxi yǒu diǎnr guì.   3 Gōngyuán wàitou yǒu diǎnr chǎo.
4 Tā àiren de yīfu yǒu diǎnr zāng.   5 Zài Lúndūn qí zìxíngchē yǒu diǎnr wēixiǎn.

Exercise 100:   1 wán   2 gānjìng   3 xià   4 hǎo

Exercise 101:   1 Qǐng nǐ bǎ zhèi fēng xìn gěi Wáng xiānsheng. Hǎo.   2 Fēijī shénme shíhou zài Xiānggǎng jiàngluò? Bù zhīdao. Wǒ qu wènwen kàn.   3 Tā jīntiān hěn máng ma? Hěn máng, máng de hái méi chī wǔfàn ne.
4 Nǐ zhǎodào tā le ma? Méi you, wǒ bǎ dìzhǐ nòngcuò le.

Exercise 102: 1 Please come tomorrow morning, the earlier the better. 2 The more I worry the less I can speak. 3 Why is it that the more he eats the skinnier he gets? 4 There are more and more people who study Chinese.

Exercise 103: 1 Tā Fǎyǔ shuō de duō(me) hǎo a! 2 Xué Zhōngwén duō(me) bù róngyi a! 3 Yàoshi wǒmen yǒu chuánzhēn duō(me) fāngbiàn a! 4 Kànjiàn hóngdēng bù tíng duō(me) wēixiǎn a!

Exercise 104: 1 Yìqiān wǔ(bǎi). 2 Liǎngwàn sìqiān liùbǎi qīshíbā. 3 Shíbāwàn liùqiān sānbǎi jiǔshiwǔ. 4 Liùyì qīqiān bābǎi sìshiwàn. 5 Shíyīyì wǔqiān sìbǎi èrshiliùwàn.

Exercise 105: 1 … wǒ fēi chī bù kě. 2 … fēi guānshang chuānghu bù kě. 3 … fēi gàosu tā bù kě. 4 … fēi gěi qián bù kě.

Exercise 106: 1 Nǐ xiǎng chī shénme? Suí nǐ biàn, nǐ diǎn shénme wǒ jiù chī shénme. 2 Nǐ xíguàn zhèr de tiānqi le ma? Xíguàn le, xiànzài wǒ juéde yuè rè yuè hǎo. 3 Zhèi ge gōngyuán duō piàoliang a! Kě bú shì ma! 4 Nǐ duì zhào xiàng yǒu xìngqu ma? Yì diǎnr yě méi you. 5 Nǐ mǎi de nèi fú Zhōngguó huàr jiàqian shi duōshao? Yíwàn bāqiān wǔ. 6 Nǐ wèishénme měi tiān dōu zài mángzhe liàn tàijíquán? Wǒ huí Yīngguó yǐqián fēi (bǎ tàijíquán) xuéhuì bù kě.

Chapter 19

Exercise 107: 1 The luggage has already been sent to your room. 2 The fax will be sent straight away. 3 This suitcase of mine was checked three times at the airport. 4 The delegation has been invited to go to the tenth floor. 5 The television was broken by his son.

Exercise 108: 1 zāng 2 è 3 wēixiǎn 4 zháojí 5 jìdé 6 jiàngluò 7 chūkǒu 8 huíguó 9 bú bì 10 rùjìng

Exercise 109: 1 sì fēn zhī yī 2 èrshiwǔ fēn zhī yī 3 bǎi fēn zhī shíqī 4 bǎi fēn zhī líng diǎn bā 5 bǎi fēn zhī jiǔshijiǔ diǎn jiǔ

Exercise 110: 1 Yì nián zěnme huì yǒu sānbǎi liùshiliù tiān ne? 2 Yīngguó rén zěnme huì bù hē xiàwǔ chá ne?

3 Zuò huǒchē zěnme huì bǐ zuò fēijī wēixiǎn ne?
4 Chī Zhōngguó cài zěnme huì róngyi pàng ne?

Exercise 111: 1 Wǒ cónglái méi qù-guo Zhōngguó. 2 Wǒ cónglái méi yòng Zhōngwén xiě-guo xìn. 3 Wǒ cónglái méi pèngjiàn-guo zhèi zhǒng shì. 4 Wǒ zǒngshi hěn xiǎoxīn, cónglái méi diū-guo dōngxi.

Exercise 112: 1 Nǐ de qiānzhèng děng-le duō jiǔ? Píngcháng chàbuduō yào liù ge yuè, xìngkuī wǒ rènshi Dàshǐguǎn de rén, yíxiàr jiù nádào le. 2 Nǐ jīntiān zěnme méi chuān xīzhuāng? Bié tí le, wǒ de yīfu quán bèi tōu le. 3 Jīnnián qìchē jìnkǒu zēngjiā le ma? Zēngjiā le, zēngjiā-le bǎi fēn zhī qī diǎn wǔ. 4 Lù shang rén tài duō, qǐng nǐ kāi màn diǎnr. Nín fàngxīn, wǒ kāi-chē cónglái méi chū-guo shì. 5 Bào shang shuō bǎi fēn zhī qīshi de nán xuésheng dōu chōu-yān. Zěnme huì yǒu zhème duō ne? 6 Nǐ wèishénme yào xué Zhōngwén? Yì fāngmiàn shi wǒ duì wàiyǔ yǒu xìngqu, yì fāngmiàn shi wǒ xiǎng zhēnzhèng liǎojiě Zhōngguó.

Mini-dictionary

In the following list, the numbers refer to the chapter in which the word first appears.

bú yàojǐn doesn't matter 10
bú zài le passed away 14
búdàn not only 12
búguò however 11
Búxiè Don't mention it! 1

cài cuisine 9
cái only then 14
càidān menu 9
cānjiā to take part in 11
cāntīng restaurant 7
céng floor 14
cèsuǒ toilet 5
chá tea 4
chá to check 17
chàbuduō almost 9
chàdiǎnr very nearly 19
cháhú tea pot 5
cháng often 8
cháng long 8
cháng to taste 9
chàng-gēr to sing 18
Chángchéng The Great Wall 10
chǎo noisy 4
chǎo to stir-fry 18
chāozhòng overweight 15
chē vehicle 6
chēcì train number 7
chéng wall 11
chēng to weigh 15
chéng to succeed/complete 16
Chénghuáng City God 5
chénglí inside the city 14
chī to eat 4
chī-sù de vegetarian 9
chī yào to take medicine 10
chóngxīn anew 19
chōu-yān to smoke 4
chù office 13
chū guó to go abroad 10
chū shì to have an accident 19
chuān to wear 8
chuānghu window 17
chuánzhēn fax 13
chuánzhēnjī fax machine 13
chūchāi away on business 12
chuī to blow 17
chūjìng to leave the country 18
chūkǒu export 16
chúle X yǐwài apart from 18

chūmén to go out
  of the door 17
chūntiān spring 16
chūzūqìchē taxi 6
chūzūqìchēzhàn taxi rank 6
cì occurrence 9
cóng from 6
cónglái always 19
cù vinegar 18
cuò mistake 12

dà big 6
dǎ to hit 9, 10
dǎ diànbào to send a
  telegram 13
dǎ diànhuà to make a
  phone call 10
dǎ tàijíquán to do taichi 9
dǎ zhēn to have an injection 10
dàbèixīnr T-shirt 8
dàhòutiān day after day
  after tomorrow 17
dài to bring with, carry 4
dài to wear (accessories) 8
dàibiǎo to represent 11
dàibiǎotuán delegation 13
dàifu a doctor 10
dàjiā everybody 1
dǎkāi to open 11
dàlù main road 6
dāng to serve as 12
dāngrán of course 11
Dānmài Denmark 2
dānrénfáng single room 4
dào to, to arrive 6
dǎo-chē to change buses 6
dǎomài to profiteer 13
dàoqī to expire 7
dàqiántiān day before day
  before yesterday 17
dàshǐ ambassador 15
dàshǐguǎn embassy 15
dǎsuan to plan to 7
dàxiǎo size 9
dàxué university 6
dāying to respond, agree to 17
de (marker) 2, 5, 7
de (marker) 12
Déguó Germany 2
děi must 6
děng to wait 8

kànjiàn to see 12
kǎo-yā Peking duck 7
kè 'quarter' 7
kě certainly 16
kè a lesson 19
Kě bú shi ma! Too right! 18
Kěkǒu Kělè Coca-Cola 4
kěndìng bound to be 15
kěnéng maybe 5
kèqi polite 6
kěshi but 3
késou to cough 17
kěxī what a pity 18
kěyǐ may; OK 4
kǒngpà I'm afraid 13
kōngqì air 9
kòngr free time 13
kōngtiáo air-conditioning 17
kǒuyīn accent 14
kū to weep 18
kuài dollar; yuan 5
kuài quick, soon 7, 11
kuài (measure) 11
kuàichē fast train 7
kuàizi chopsticks 18
kuàngquánshuǐ mineral
  water 4
kùnnán difficult 16

là peppery hot 18
lā pull 20
lái come, bring 6, 12, 18
láibují can't catch 16
láidejí will catch 16
làjiāo chilli 18
lán blue 8
lǎo old 2
lǎoshī teacher 9
lǎowài foreigner 18
làzi jīdīng chicken
  with chilli 18
le (particle) 4, 6, 7, 8, 10
le + a (particles) 15
lèi tired 11
lěng cold 8
lí separated from 14, 16
lǐ Chinese mile 16
liàn qìgōng to practise qigong 9
liǎng two 4
liàng (measure) 15
liángkuai cool 8

liánxi to practise 12
liánxùjù soap opera 18
liǎo to finish 17
liǎojiě to understand 19
líng zero 3
lǐngdǎo leadership 13
lǐtou inside 5
liù six 3
liúlì fluent 12
liúxia to leave behind 14
liúxuéshēng foreign student 6
liúxuéshēnglóu foreign
  students' building 6
lǐwù a gift 11
lóu building, floor 4
lóushang upstairs 8
lóuxia downstairs 8
lù road, route 6, 15
lǜ green 8
lǜdēng green light 15
lùkǒur intersection 15
Lúndūn London 2
lúnzi wheel 17
Luómǎ Rome 14
lǚxíng to travel 13
lǚxíng zhīpiào
  traveller's cheque 13
lǚyóu to go touring 11
lǚyóujú tourist bureau 12
lǚyóutuán tourist group 13

ma (particle) 2
mǎ horse 8
ma (particle) 16
máfan troublesome 13
mǎi to buy 5
mài to sell 5
mǎibuqǐ cannot afford 16
mǎideqǐ can afford 16
mǎimai trade 9
Mǎláixīyà Malaysia 2
mǎlù main road 15
màn slow 12
mǎn full 16
máng busy 7
Máng shénme? Busy
  doing what? 14
Màngǔ Bangkok 19
mángzhe busy at 18
máo 'dime'; 10 cents 5
mǎshang at once 6

méi not 4
měi each 10
méi fázi no way 13
méi guānxi not at all 1, 13
méi shìr not at all 1
méi xiǎngdào unexpectedly 12
Měiguó USA 2
Měiqiáo American
  expatriates 3
měiyuán American dollars 13
Měizhōu America 15
mén door 11
miàn noodles 9
mián'ǎo quilted jacket 9
miǎnfèi free of charge 17
miào temple 5
mǐfàn cooked rice 18
mílù to lose the way 15
míngnián next year 7, 9
míngpiàn namecard 2
míngtiān tomorrow 7
míngxìnpiànr postcard 15
míngzi name 2
míxìn superstition 16
Mòxīgē Mexico 2
mǔqin mother 3

ná that, in that case 2, 7
ná to take 12
náli? where?; 'polite
  response' 12
nàme so 8
nán south 5
nán difficult 16
nán cèsuǒ gents' toilet 19
nán de male 8
nánrén male person 8
nàr there 4
nǎr? where? 5
ne (particle) 5, 9, 13
ne + a (particles) 15
nèi that 5
něi? which? 3
nèiháng expert 18
néng be able 10
Ng Mmh 9
nǐ you 1
Nǐ hǎo How are you? 1
nián year 4
nǐmen you (plural) 2
nín you (polite) 1

niúnǎi milk 4
nòng to get, make 17
nóng dense 18
nǚ cèsuǒ ladies' toilet 19
nǚ de female 8
nǚ'ér daughter 12
nuǎnhuo warm 8
nǚrén female person 8
nǚshì Ms 19
nǚwáng the Queen 11

Òu! Oh! 7
Ōuzhōu Europe 15

pà to fear 4
pài to dispatch 13
pàichūsuǒ local police
  station 14
páijià quoted price 13
páir label, brand 17
páizi label, brand 17
pàng fat 8
pángbiānr beside 14
pàngshòu build, body size 9
pèngjiàn to bump into 12
péngyou friend 2
piànr tablet 10
piányi cheap 16
piào ticket 7
piàoliang beautiful 4
píjiǔ beer 4
píndào television channel 18
píng (measure) 4
píngcháng usually 9
píngguǒ apple 16
píngxìn surface mail 15
pīnyīn to spell sounds 19
Pǔtōnghuà Universal
  language 11

qī seven 3
qí to straddle 8
qián money 5
qiān to sign 16
qiǎn shallow, light 17
qiān thousand 18
qiánbāor wallet 19
qiāndìng to sign
  (a contract) 19
qiántiān day before
  yesterday 7

qiántou in front of 5
qiānzhèng visa 19
qiáo to live abroad 3
qiàtán to hold business talks 19
qìchē motor vehicle 6
qǐfēi to take off 16
qìgōng qigong 9
qǐng please; to invite 1, 7
qǐng wèn please may I ask 5
qīngcài green vegetables 18
qīngchu clear 9
qǐngtiě invitation card 13
qìngzhù to celebrate 19
qíshí actually 11
qiūtiān autumn 16
qù to go 5
qū district 14
quán all 16
qùnián last year 7

ràng to allow; by 17, 19
rè hot 4
rén person 2
Rénmínbì Renminbi 13, 20
rènshi to get to
  know, recognise 3
rénxíngdào pavement 15
rénxínghéngdào
  pedestrian crossing 15
rì day 7
Rìběn Japan 2
Rìběn huà Japanese
  language 11
róngyi easy 11
ròu meat 9
ròupiàn sliced pork 18
rùjìngkǎ immigration card 11
rùkǒu entrance 20

sān three 3
sànbù to stroll 18
sǎosao elder brother's wife 14
shàng to ascend, go to 6, 8, 10
shàng bān to go to work 7
shàng-xià up and down 14
shāngdiàn shop, store 6
Shànghǎi Shanghai 2
shàngtou on top of 5
shàngwǔ morning 7
shàngyī upper garments 17
shānshang up the hill 8

shānshuǐ landscape 18
shānxia foot of the hill 8
shǎo few, less 9
shéi who? 1
shéi de? whose? 3
shēn deep, dark 17
shēng to give birth to,
  be born 10, 14
shěng province 14
Shèngdàn kuàilè
  Happy Christmas 19
shēngrì kuàilè birthday
  happiness 19
shèngxia to remain over 19
shēngyì business 18
shénme? what?
  what kind of? 3
shēnqǐng to apply for 19
shēntǐ health, body 12
shēntǐ jiànkāng
  good health 19
Shēnzhèn Shenzhen 12
shì to be 2
shí ten 3
shì business, matter 4
shì municipality 14
shì to try 14
shi ... de (*construction*) 11, 19
shì-biǎo to take
  someone's temperature 17
shìchǎng market 5
shìde yes! 14
shīfu (*form of address*) 5
shíhou time 7
shíjiān time 7
shìshi kàn try it and see 17
shítou a stone 11
shíyóu petrol, oil 11
Shíyóubù Ministry
  for Petroleum 11
Shíyóubù bùzhǎng
  Minister for Petroleum 12
shízìlùkǒu crossroads 15
shòu thin, slim 8
shǒu hand 12
shōu to accept 18
shòu to suffer, receive 18
shòu huānyíng
  well received 18
shòu kǔ to suffer hardship 18
shòu lèi to put to much trouble 18

Picture Credits: Jacket (front cover): special photography David Murray
& Jules Selmes top left; ROBERT HARDING PICTURE LIBRARY: left (main
image); Gina Corrigan bottom right; G. & P. Corrigan top centre;
K. Gillham top right; HUTCHISON LIBRARY: centre above, bottom centre,
bottom centre above; Michael Macintyre top of spine; IMPACT PHOTOS:
Alain le Garsmeur centre right above and back cover; Michael Good
centre below and centre of spine; Alain Evrard centre right below